GERMAN AND POLE

National Conflict and Modern Myth

GERMAN AND POLE

National Conflict and Modern Myth

HARRY KENNETH ROSENTHAL

A Florida State University Book

University Presses of Florida

GAINESVILLE

Library of Congress Cataloging in Publication Data

Rosenthal, Harry Kenneth, 1941–
   German and Pole: national conflict and modern myth.

   "A Florida State University book."
   Bibliography: p.
   Includes index.
   1. Poland–Foreign opinion, German. I. Title.
DK4185.G3R67   301.15´43´9438   76–2402
ISBN 0–8130–0500–0

Printed in Florida, U. S. A.

CONTENTS

To My Parents

PREFACE

In a general sense this book can be seen as a continuation of Robert Franz Arnold's *Geschichte der deutschen Polenlitteratur von den Anfängen bis 1800* (Vienna, 1899). Specifically, what the author hopes to accomplish is to present a coherent argument concerning the development of the German myth of the Pole and to explore to what extent this myth made possible the Nazi slaughters in Poland during the Second World War.

Perhaps it would be helpful to discuss briefly what this book is not. It is not an attempt to endorse the German view that the Pole's defects have justified a Polish subservience to the German. Nor is it an attempt to endorse the cliché of the German left that, as Johannes Guttzeit claimed, the German's sense of guilt has resulted in his blaming the Pole for German misdeeds. Nor, unlike Jan Chodera's assertions, is it an attempt to perpetuate Polish stereotypes. The author cannot agree with Chodera that the spirit of German poetry resulted in the concentration camp or that the German has committed a 1000-year war of aggression against the Pole. Instead, rather than desiring to justify any of these clichés, the author wishes simply to trace the evolution of the German view of the Pole. Being able to understand that evolution and to answer the questions he has posed is the prize the author hopes to present to the reader.

During the course of this study, the author has explored not only the usual printed sources for research. He has researched archival material and has read all the writings he could obtain having to do with the German image of the Pole. Indeed, he hopes that his bibliography may be of interest, and particular use, to the specialist. More importantly, he hopes that the specialist can accept his assumption that the researcher can in some ways gain greater insights into mass perceptions by reading day-to-day journalism than by examining the literary works of genius.

The author particularly wishes to make explicit what may be only implicit in certain sections of the book. He wishes to establish that the German image of the Pole has constituted a myth or a traditional story of unknown authorship—ostensibly with a historical basis—that has served to explain some phenomena. In this case, the German myth fulfilled the psychological needs of those who believed in it, and it helped to render intellectually justifiable their political, social, and economic claims. The myth resulted also from specific material situations. Thus the author has sought to analyze both the psychological and material bases of the German image of the Pole. Coping with these twin tasks has enabled the author to reach whatever conclusions this book contains.

Since the author's approach to the style of the Notes and Bibliography is somewhat individual, it might be useful to include a word of explanation. While the form of the archival references will vary somewhat depending on the archive, this variation has been recorded in the German form which a researcher would need to use to order the files in each of the appropriate archives. English has been employed for the most part in describing newspaper and book citations, except that the geographical place names of publications have not been usually anglicized. The author has made every effort to provide complete information on all of the resource materials, but occasionally a first name or page number was not available at the time the research was done. However, the reader will find all of the pertinent information which the author himself used in ordering these items in various archives and libraries in Central Europe and North America where the research for this study was conducted.

The author recognizes that he owes thanks to the ACLS-SSRC for its support and to the various libraries and archives in Merseburg, Potsdam, Poznań, Leipzig, Berlin, Stuttgart, Koblenz, New York (Columbia University Library), and Urbana, Illinois (the University of Illinois Library). All were helpful in allowing him to use their materials. Without these aids, he could not have completed his task.

He would also like to express his appreciation to colleagues in his field for their valued observations: R. C. Raack, Ludwik Krzyzanowski, Witold Jakóbczyk, Lech Trzeciakowski, Mack Walker, Wolfgang Kohte, Arthur Smith, Jr., Zygmunt Gasiorowski, and Anna Cienciala. His thanks must be expressed also to his teachers to whom he owes much: Fritz Stern, Peter Brock, Henry Roberts, Joseph Rothschild, Joseph Bauke, and Werner Conze. Thanks must be offered to colleagues who assisted him not in the specifics of his search but in the greater issues of academic inquiry: David Abosch, Richard Burns, Seymour Chapin, Milton Ehre, JoAnn Linburn, Earl Phillips, Donald and Judith Reinken, and Edward Wynot. And, finally, the author must express his appreciation to his editor Elizabeth Turpin of Texas A&M University and to the staff of Florida State University Press.

H. K. R.
Los Angeles
March 1975

GERMAN AND POLE

National Conflict and Modern Myth

CHAPTER ONE
To 1894

The Roots of German–Polish Conflict

Although "myth" is a term that is anthropological rather than histori-cal, it can be useful in describing how the Germans evolved a particular stereotypical image of the Pole. First, a number of Prussian-German wri-ters forged into a cogent whole various negative assessments of the Polish people. Then after a period of Hakatist respect for the Poles, this image, although out of date, gained acceptance in Weimar Germany as being a valid description of the Polish people. The power of this myth and the elements within it that varied from period to period must be recognized and studied by the historian.

The historian must also recognize the function of this particular myth because the German image of the Polish people as embellished in the Weimar period provided an expedient method of explaining how a devel-oping country had managed to compete successfully in a confrontation with a developed country. Since the Germans could not appreciate the accomplishments of another society in a different and less powerful set-ting, they needed some way either of understanding or of denying the accomplishments of the Poles.

Any variations in this German view of the Pole were determined strictly by the political needs of an individual German using the image. If a Ger-man wished to compel the granting of government credits, he would see the Pole as powerful and virile. If he wished to stress the superior national character of Germany, he would view the Pole as weak and easily dis-placed. If he wished to unleash his resentments and keep the door open for territorial adjustments, he would accuse the Pole of being aggressive and cruel. If he sought an alliance with the Pole, he would reverse his views so

1

that the Pole would become praiseworthy. It is significantly easy to see that at no time did a substantial segment of German society advance an image of the Pole which would conflict with its own political interests.

Any serious analysis of the German-Polish relationship must determine the extent to which the German myth or stereotypical image of the Pole was valid. Obviously, the myth had some basis in fact since the Germans did live in a society which was more numerous, wealthier, and more powerful, and one which was industrialized earlier. While the Germans could boast of more achievements of a Great Power variety, the Poles could boast of surviving adversity and developing their society and economy under more difficult circumstances. What the Germans were never able to understand was that, although the Poles' accomplishments were of a *different kind*, they were nonetheless just as real as the German's traditional Great Power accomplishments. Perhaps it will be easier for present-day partitioned Germany to advance to this level of understanding.

The German-Polish story began very early, when various tribes met on the plains of Central Europe. Yet, where and when the Germans first met the Poles is a matter of speculation. When the Germans began to develop a stereotypical image of the Pole is even more uncertain. In ancient times, Indo-European tribes occupied the part of Europe that corresponds to the border areas of present-day Germany and Poland; but these tribes probably were not the direct ancestors of either the present-day Germans or the present-day Poles. Later—in the 6th century A.D.—when the Germanic tribes migrated to the west, Slavic tribes followed in their wake. Yet, even at this time, neither a German nor a Polish community had been formed; therefore, it would be unreasonable to assume that more than a thousand years ago the German had already met his eastern neighbor and had already developed a consistent attitude as to what sort of a person the Pole was.

Moreover, if Germanic tribesmen had formed an opinion of the Western Slavs between the 6th and 10th centuries, it could only have been that these Slavs were "heathens."[1] After all, at the beginning of recorded Polish history in the 10th century, the basic dichotomy in Europe was Christian-Pagan rather than Germanic-Slavic or German-Pole. And surely, on the open plains of East Central Europe where the heathens were predominant, one would not expect the Germanic peoples to have an image of Slavic heathens different from their image of Baltic heathens or Uralic heathens.

Also the identity "heathen" could easily change if the heathens could adopt (or submit to) Christianity. For conversion, the heathens needed merely a political authority to impose Christianity as their group's religion. Some heathens, such as the Magyars, who were neither Slavic nor Germanic, already possessed both a recognized leadership and a political leader. The Poles, on the other hand, first found their leadership only a little more than a millennium ago when the Piast dynasty summoned the Polish state into existence. Sometime before the decade of the 960s, the founder of that dynasty, a leader named Mieszko, began to extend his control of territories in the vicinity of the city of Poznań. By 962, he emerged as the leader of a full-grown state of medieval form. In 966 when Mieszko accepted Christianity, the Poles lost their heathen identity. At this point, the original Christian-heathen dichotomy in German-Polish relations vanished.

Mieszko himself has always been a figure of mystery to the historian. Who was he? How could a new state suddenly appear in 962? How was the state organized? Several German writers, speculating in the 20th century, have suggested similar answers. For example, Albert Brackmann has called Mieszko a "slavified Viking." Others, such as Franz Lüdtke, Friedrich Kopp, and Erich Reimers, have written of him as a nordic man or spoken of his Germanic blood and his Scandinavian name Dago.[2] Needless to say, Polish writers have disagreed with these German views.

But again there is no evidence that Germans of the 10th century—the Germans in the Holy Roman Empire of the German Nation led by Otto I—viewed Mieszko (or Dago) as anyone other than the leader of a state with which they had to reckon. There is no evidence that either Otto or any later German emperors viewed conflicts with Mieszko or later Polish kings any differently than conflicts with any other competitors for power. There is no evidence that a specific German hostility towards Poland developed at this time or that any later German hostility was caused by Mieszko, either in his person or his politics.

Nor is there evidence of any political or military *Drang nach Osten*, which is so often ascribed to the Germans. The German emperors at a fairly early date succumbed to the lure of the south. Italy with its splendid past (they were *Roman* emperors, after all), as the seat of the leadership of the Christian world, fascinated them and absorbed their expansionist attention. Italy, not East Central Europe, exhausted their planning and consumed their energies. In fact, later German writers were to chide these emperors for neglecting their eastern border areas.[3] In such circumstances, the logical conclusion is that later 20th-century talk of an actual conflict of national aspirations from the 10th to the 13th centuries must be viewed skeptically.[4]

The actual German movement to the east (or, as many German writers contended, the Germanic movement back to the east) partook of a quieter and much more prosaic character. On the one hand, German colonists, partly in answer to official invitations, settled on Polish territories between the 11th and 14th centuries. As has been insisted by German writers such as Jacob Caro, Werner Emmerich, and Dietrich Schäfer, the colonization was peaceful.[5] Schäfer, indeed, described this settling as more peaceful than the colonization of the United States of America or of the rest of the Americas or Australia or South Africa. On the other hand, the Teutonic

Knights, though formally invited by Polish leaders at the beginning of the 13th century, had a less pacific purpose. Launching a religious crusade, they planned either to Christianize the Baltic pagans called the "Prussians" or to annihilate them. Achieving the latter, these crusaders, mainly of Germanic origin, colonized their conquered territories, made Königsberg a major Baltic urban center, and assumed the name of the Prussians.

Regardless of how or why the Germans had come among the Poles, problems arose. The German colonists had brought with them energies. As invited colonists, they enjoyed specific legal rights that enabled them to go about their business in an orderly way. To the Polish sovereign they were assets to the community. But they alarmed the native Polish nobility and clergy, who feared not only an increase of royal authority based on an alliance between the Polish king and the German colonists but also an increase in foreign influence.[6] Furthermore, both the peasants and the townspeople—perhaps envious of the rights that their ruler had granted to the newcomers, perhaps envious of the Germans' higher standard of living, perhaps repelled by the colonists' usual disdain for the native population, perhaps irrationally fearful of anything new—participated in the reaction against the Germans, thus providing later German authors with evidence of the birth of a nationalistic Polish hatred of Germans.[7] Kurt Lück in 1943 even went so far as to assert that that national feeling, which the colonists had aroused, had made one nation of the many individuals who spoke Polish and had made synonymous from that time forward the Poles' patriotic fervor and their hatred of Germans.[8] Other German writers at various times have concurred with Lück's assertion.[9] From the opposing standpoint, the question can be raised about what was the Germans' view of the Poles and of the Polish community in which they had settled.

The integration of the Germans into the Polish community proved to be a major deterrent to the development by the colonists of a clear-cut, detached concept of the Pole.[10] The colonists could have come east expecting to find free land, or they could have been scornful of the natives. But, regardless of their opportunities and attitudes, they must have been aware of, and resented, the backlash of Polish opinion concerning their presence.[11] In the course of time, however, the Germans assimilated the language, mores, and religion of their Polish neighbors. In short, they became Poles before they could develop and send home a well-defined, stereotyped image of the Pole that whatever public opinion there was in the lands of the Holy Roman Empire could accept and make its own.

The Teutonic Knights also failed to develop or establish a stereotypical image of the Pole since these religious warriors, whatever may have been their effects on Polish sensibilities, conducted their activities far removed from the major geographic areas and major national issues of the German people.[12] The great issues of German life—ranging from the interactions of the emperor and the pope to the problems of social and economic change —were foreign to them. Moreover, what could these knights have reported? They could have said that they had defeated the Prussians; that they were developing these lands; that their ambitions conflicted with those of the Polish leadership which, through the arranged marriage in 1386 of Jadwiga of Poland to Jagiello of Lithuania, ultimately succeeded in forming the Polish-Lithuanian Commonwealth. Further, these knights could have reported that the Poles saw themselves as an outpost of Christianity against the heathens of the east.[13] In describing the Polish struggle to defeat them, the knights would have recorded their own defeat in 1410 at Tannenberg[14] and the agreement at Toruń in 1466 that the lands of the Teutonic Knights were to become a fief of the Polish crown. Regardless of any later development of a stereotypical image of the Pole by the Germans in these lands, the period through the 15th century failed to produce any significant image. And the Knights' defeat obviously failed to engender any German belief in Polish superiority.

During the 16th century, the Germans' respect for the Poles increased very little. And this was unfortunate for the Poles of both that period and later since the 16th century was the Polish "Golden Age," a time of flowering in literature and a period of Great Power achievements in politics. But the Germans of that time, living essentially within the Holy Roman Empire and absorbed in the impact of Luther, took little note of the outstanding Poles such as Jan Kochanowski or of a land of impressive dimensions.[15] The Germans kept their focus on their own affairs. Later, when the first substantial German interest in the Polish community was aroused, they were to find themselves concerned with a Poland that was far different from the successful literary and political entity of the 16th century.

One consequence of Luther's coming did play an important role in later German-Polish relations. The Teutonic Knights had by that time become an anachronism, a crusade to convert nonexistent heathens in a time of schism in the church. If, however, the knights were to remain an instrument of the church, they had to decide to which church they owed allegiance. In 1521 when the question arose as to whether they could still have a religious vocation, Albert of Hohenzollern, their leader at that time, answered in the negative. Becoming a Lutheran, he secularized the order. He also recognized the suzerainty of the Polish king. Thus, the coming of Luther ironically confronted a Polish Catholic king with a secular German state called "Prussia" after the defeated Baltic heathens. This new state, which was immediately adjacent to the king's land, was vitally concerned with events in East Central Europe. When the king of Poland later dealt with people as "Germans," these were the new Prussians.

The developments of the next century lent more significance to these events. On the one hand, Prussia, through inheritance, became attached to the state of Brandenburg in 1618, thus confronting the Polish king with a more formidable German neighbor. On the other hand, weakened by internal difficulties, the Polish-Lithuanian Commonwealth was inviting the attentions of predatory forces. Besides a Cossack rebellion in the Ukraine, the Commonwealth had to contend with invasions by Swedish, Turkish, and Russian armies. This combination of events not only critically disabled the once-mighty Polish-Lithuanian Commonwealth but also enabled Prussia to force the Polish state to recognize Prussian independence and compelled Poland to yield to advances by Russia on the border in the east.

Only the first of these developments, however, was completely reassuring to the Prussian leader, Frederick William, the Great Elector. Although he understood the dangers of a very strong Polish state and welcomed its reduction in strength,[16] he had no desire to become a client of Sweden. Consequently, he sought to establish good relations with an independent Poland and hoped to be able to preserve a balance of power in the area. Neither ideology nor stereotypes of the Polish people, but only the interests of his state determined Frederick William's attitude toward Poland. In his political testament, for the sake of Prussia, he called on his successor to be a good neighbor to Poland.[17]

Prussia lacked the power, however, to control the destiny of Poland. Despite Frederick William's advice to his successor to be a good neighbor, Poland gradually became exhausted. Although in 1683 Jan Sobieski had added to the annals of Polish martial daring by fighting the Turks at the gates of Vienna, the nobility of the Polish-Lithuanian Commonwealth, when they gathered to elect Sobieski's successor, found themselves choosing from among major contenders who were not Polish. Further, the foreign pressures so increased in intensity that Poland was hardly able to resist Russian power. The nobles ultimately were forced to "elect" the Russian candidate, Augustus of Saxony, who was a German. Under these circumstances, the Prussians, as well as other Germans, first began to take note of Poland, but as an exhausted Poland that was a mere caricature of the Poland of the 16th-century "Golden Age."

These Germans had begun to notice Poland primarily because the candidacy of Augustus of Saxony had resulted in a spate of pamphleteering within many of the German states; as a result, many literate Germans began to read about Poland for the first time. But they were reading pieces, as Robert Franz Arnold related, that were mocking the Poles,[18] because their first introduction was to a weakened Poland.

Once Augustus had succeeded in gaining the throne, Polish affairs worsened. Though Augustus had a title, he commanded very little Polish support. The Poles thus had a king, but their state lacked strong leadership and direction. Without these, the Poles were powerless to withstand the

Russian and Swedish conflict on Polish territory and to prevent the Hohenzollern from calling himself king in Prussia. Poland had been reduced to a mere passive object of the actions of others. The Poles helplessly watched Peter the Great of Russia secure a dominant position in their land and saw Prussia increase its power also.

However, German writers in the main dismissed Augustus's contribution to this decline and placed the blame instead on the Poles themselves. In 1711 a book entitled *Das verwirrte Pohlen* typically declared that "in this great, confused part of the world, unhappy Poland is obviously the most confused province."[19] The term "confused" had become the insulting adjective usually applied to Poland by German stylists in their attacks on Germany's eastern neighbor. The phrase "Polish freedom" was always employed in an ironical sense.[20] Although this point of view did not remain unchallenged, its impact was significant. Although in 1727 Pastor Samuel Friedrich Lauterbach published his own chronicles, a much-read collection of anecdotes and gossip that reveal a warm attachment to Lauterbach's adopted home,[21] it was questionable whether even such writing could successfully counterbalance the irony which was originating in Saxony and the continual decline of Polish political strength.

This decline in Polish state power, coupled with the increasing strength of Russia, Prussia, and Austria, culminated in the Polish partitions of 1772, 1793, and 1795.[22] What is not as well known are the consequences of these partitions on the way that Prussians and other Germans evaluated the Poles. This is true despite the fact that common sense would suggest that these partitions would force many Germans—obviously Prussians before all others—to take note of Poland. In other words, not only had a substantial Prussian interest in what happened in Poland finally been created, but the Germans in Saxony and the Habsburg lands were also viewing Polish events with interest.

One judgment was voiced by the Prussian king, Frederick the Great. Two decades before the first partition, he had already viewed Poland as an object of Prussian territorial ambitions. In 1752 Frederick had written that West Prussia should "not be conquered by weapons but consumed in peace in the manner of an artichoke, piece by piece." At that time, he thought that Poland's elective monarchy would create a confusion from which Prussia would benefit.[23] But twenty-one years later, in a letter to Voltaire, he denied that the partition had been his idea. He strongly maintained that partition had been the only way to avoid a general war.[24] Despite such protestations, it was obvious that Frederick had seen in Poland a helpless victim whose dismemberment he had continually desired.

This impression was confirmed in Frederick's conversation of January, 1785. Although recognizing Poland as "a remarkable land," he asserted that

"Poland is free and the Poles are slaves; the constitution is republican but there is a King at the top; the land is infinitely large and has almost no inhabitants; the Poles love war and have conducted famous wars for centuries and nevertheless they have no fortresses and instead of a regular army only the *levy en masse* of courageous but undisciplined men. . . . The Poles are brave and valiant but also—with a very few exceptions—unstable and frivolous. Only the women show an astonishing strength of character and are many times the true men."[25]

In short, Frederick was convinced that the Poles could not compete with the efficient Prussian state. He considered that the Poles, especially the Polish males, lacked the ability to transform their talents and advantages into achievements.

When Frederick looked at his newly won Polish territories, he could even conclude that the Poles lagged behind Canada in the matter of cultivation.[26] As a result, he believed, as his Potsdam letter of April 1, 1772, to Johann Friedrich von Domhardt announced, that any advance in the public and private order would require the addition of at least two or three Germans in each village.[27] He thereby implicitly contended that the higher civilization of the German people was required to rescue the Poles and to upgrade them from what he called "Polish slavery." The superior German civilization also was needed to repair the consequences of an alleged "Polish anarchy" that presumably resulted from the inborn characteristics of the Polish people.[28] And Frederick's officials concurred. For example, Eugen von Bergmann and Wilhelm Vallentin wrote that the Poles under these officials' supervision appeared to them to be wild barbarians taking refuge in brandy and living in a land which they had made desolate.[29]

The immediate consequence of these impressions, besides the establishment of government schools and the development of roads, was additional colonization in vacant areas of the new provinces.[30] Yet the 20th-century reader may find it difficult to realize that only the 18th-century economic and military needs for taxes and men motivated this colonization.[31] Frederick not only failed to forbid the settlement of those colonists from the sections of post-first partition Poland, but he even actively sought settlers from that area. To be sure, most of these colonists consisted of Germans, but Poles also came.[32] In fact, Frederick employed some of these Poles as teachers in his schools.[33]

Obviously, although Frederick was no nationalist of the 19th- or 20th-century variety, he did provide ready fuel for this nationalist view. He and his officials enunciated an entire complex of reasons why the Germans should despise the Polish people. Later, German nationalists would ask whether Germans could really believe in equal rights for the Poles when the Poles could be accused of failing to match the standard of cultivation of the Iroquois. Also they raised the question of whether Germans could really believe in equality with the Poles if the Poles were supposed to need German civilization to assure their passage from barbarism. Such judgments and interpretations were passed on from generation to generation through innocuous sources such as schoolbooks like Franz Lüdtke's 1915 *Preussische Kulturarbeit*. These statements were also spread in writing about Frederick the Great that the schoolboy and the hero-worshiper alike devoured. They became a part of what the average German who knew little else about the Poles took for granted as "conventional wisdom."

After Frederick's death, Frederick William II continued Frederick's partition policy in 1793 and completed the partitioning of Poland in 1795. As was typical of that time, Frederick's successors were motivated to measure power in terms of territory and population and to view favorably any acquisition, but the larger the better. They were so far removed from any primary influences of nationalism that they intentionally increased the proportion of ethnic Poles in their state to the point that by 1795 Prussia had become a multinational state.[34] The officials were simply unconcerned that their state had, after the partitions of the 1790s, incorporated so much Polish territory that it extended to the east of Warsaw.

In the cultural realm, this forced expansion of the Prussian state led many authors to assume critical positions.[35] Some, like Friedrich von der Trenck (1726–1794) wrote frank defenses of Prussia's actions.[36] Others, writing in the enlightened journals like the *Berlinischer Monatsschrift* (especially in a series of letters written in the summer of 1791), applauded the efforts of the Poles to revive their national life.[37] In Posen (Poznań), theatergoers could write their own reviews of the Polish theater.[38] In the wider life of Germany, the great Schiller was among the literary writers who described the Poles in a favorable light. In his "Demetrius," Schiller ascribed to the Polish people qualities of wisdom and courage which others had sought to deny.[39] Schiller in this way helped to counteract the negative assessments of the Poles which reflected the impressions of Prussian officials. Like Lauterbach, Schiller offered the literate Germans who were interested in Polish affairs an alternative to the simplistic cry of "confused Poland."

In short, these two opposing assessments of the qualities and abilities of the Polish people had been formulated by various German writers by the turn of the 19th century. The first, and widely disseminated, image was used to condemn the Pole unreservedly for his lack of power and for his weakness that had permitted foreign domination and partition. Mirroring this German response, all of the various supporting records—from the early Saxon writings to the decrees of Frederick the Great and the statements by officials such as *Kriminalrat* Baumann—revealed a dominant tone of contempt for Poles.[40] The second, and far less popular, image placed some value on specific achievements in, or aspects of, Polish life. This respect was evidenced, as indicated earlier, in the work of writers such as Lauterbach, Schiller, and I. S. Kaulfuss of the Posen *Gymnasium*.[41] There were, of course, some middle-of-the-road evaluations. An anonymous author in an 1808 publication, although agreeing that the Prussian government ought to respect the customs and traditions of the Polish people more than it had in the past, still considered that Prussian administration had benefited Polish life.[42] Such a judgment was fair and realistic. But the huge majority of Germans, not only in the Prussian state but in the west and south, still remained totally unconcerned with Polish affairs. At this point the age of Frederick the Great came to an end.

With the coming of the French Revolution in 1789, the old Europe of the enlightened despot found a worthy foe and an eventual conqueror. In Central and East Central Europe, anything seemed possible during the general upheaval. For example, Poland had disappeared from the map, but in 1807 a Grand Duchy of Warsaw appeared on that map. German states had disappeared to return enlarged or not at all. Austria had been defeated by Napoleon in 1805 but not destroyed. The Prussia of Frederick had been broken in 1806 at the battle of Jena, and there was the question of whether this proud state would disappear from the map. More importantly, the greatest tension centered around the question of supremacy. Would Napoleon of France or Alexander of Russia emerge victorious in their contest for domination of Europe?

These uncertainties obviously forced the Prussian leadership to ponder its policies anew. After Jena, these men and woman realized that their state had been preserved in the peace treaty of Tilsit (1807) only for reasons of Russian convenience. Their state had become a mere buffer between Alexander and Napoleon. They could even suspect that Napoleon's Polish creation, the Duchy of Warsaw, could enjoy the possibility of a much more glorious future—only if the French were to defeat the Russians decisively. Here, then, was a time of turmoil, a time of danger when new ideas would have to be explored and old ways questioned.

While the Prussian chief minister, Baron Freiherr von Stein, in a sense welcomed this situation, he did not necessarily also welcome French victories or French occupation of German soil. Rather, he had envisioned a new state which would command the freely offered loyalties of independent citizens. He wanted to see the Prussian citizens, of whatever group or origin, governing themselves in their own towns or villages and, eventually, participating with the royal authorities in the formulation of national policy. Basically he had a vision of loyal Polish men and women who would be fully satisfied to be Prussian citizens.[43] And the times permitted him to hope for the eventual acceptance of these dreams and plans. Indeed, he was fortunate enough to have an opportunity to implement some of them.

The Prussian defeat at Jena had set the stage for Stein because this debacle opened the way to his period in office. Although the years 1807-1808 proved to be too brief a period to translate most of his program into policy, Stein did manage to start the wheels of reform. And when the French demanded that vanquished Prussia find a new chief minister, Hardenberg did not completely disavow his predecessor's plans. Thus, even though Hardenberg failed to implement the plans in the way Stein had wished, at least he retained much of Stein's new Polish policy.

How then had Stein approached what was to become known as the "Polish question"? The minister's Nassau memorandum of June, 1807, provides an answer. First of all, Stein wrote a devastating critique of the Polish people. He began by accusing the Polish nobility of fickleness, frivolity, sensuality, and intemperance. He then dismissed the middle class as too few in number and the peasantry as lacking prosperity, freedom, and the rudiments of a civilized existence. He went on to praise the reform constitution of May 3, 1791, but he lamented the continued dominance of the nobility under its provisions. Finally, he considered that the partitions achieved through foreign force had ended the hopes raised by the constitution. Furthermore, he felt that fulfillment of these hopes was being denied by the exploitation of foreign bureaucrats even if these bureaucrats had brought with them the rule of law.[44]

Still, even though in his analysis Stein had assessed the negative aspects of the various classes of the Polish people, he protected the Poles' national reputation by explicitly rejecting the charge that these negative qualities had been Polish characteristics from time immemorial. Instead, he blamed the current situation on the intervention of foreigners and remarked that the Polish people had been rich in education, energy, and excellent men from the 14th to the 17th centuries.[45] He thereby implicitly rejected the assertion that the Poles' inferiority required the settlement of German colonists in Prussian Poland.

Stein's assessment led him to support a program which would respect the Polish people's pride in its identity and assure it of the state's support of its individuality.[46] And Stein was concerned enough to provide more than mere verbal support. Believing as he did in the inherent worth of the Polish people, he hoped that the Prussian state would encourage the community to develop its potentialities. Stein expected, therefore, to implement a certain degree of local Polish self-government. And when Prussia finally could act on these proposals and work out the Polish community's relative position within the Prussian state, Hardenberg acknowledged and responded positively to Stein's program.

But of course the government could only act on Stein's program if it had responsibility for Polish territories. That opportunity came only after the final defeat of Napoleon in 1815, which gave Alexander far-reaching influence in determining which Polish lands would be reassigned to Prussia. It made Alexander's Russia the leader in East Central Europe, and it made

Prussia, in its handling of the province of Posen (which it was to receive at the Congress of Vienna), both an imitator of Alexander and a modifier of Stein.

Ultimately, Hardenberg was able to harness together Russian power and Stein's plans only because of Alexander's liberalism. Alexander had accepted the proposition that his Polish territories should be granted a substantial recognition of their special non-Russian national identity. In support of this proposition, he even created within his domains a supposedly distinct Polish kingdom, permitting institutions that were, theoretically at least, independent. Alexander also styled himself a Polish king as well as a Russian tsar. Thus, Russia could honor her Polish citizens' national heritage. Hardenberg concurred, because he wished not only to assure a balance of Poles and Germans in order to reduce Polish desires for their own national state but also to keep the Polish community quiet and the emperor happy. Therefore, Hardenberg allowed the Poles a special Polish governor for the province of Posen (in addition to the *Oberpräsident*, the head of the Prussian bureaucracy in the province) and Polish-dominated institutions.[47]

There were obvious difficulties implicit in this situation. As long as its power could not parallel that of Russia, the Prussian government would have to change its policy if Russia changed hers. But Prussian officials had committed their state to a specific course of action, and the Polish community could justly accuse these officials of duplicity if they changed policy. Beyond that, however, changes of policy are common within governments, even without the influence of foreign pressure. Since the men who believed in supporting the nationalistic views of the Poles would not be in power forever, strife was certain to develop as the story of 19th-century Prussian policy toward the Polish community began to unfold.

The sequence of events began with a specific commitment by Frederick William III to the Polish nobles and clergy who held a preeminent place in the Posen of 1815. Frederick announced to these dominant members of the Polish community that they also had "a Fatherland" in Prussia, and he assured them that they would find their nationality and religion respected and their language used in governmental publications, the courts, and the schools. He stressed that their entry into all levels of bureaucracy within the province would be welcomed, that one of their nationality, Anton Radziwiłł, would be appointed governor of their province, and that even their flag would be proudly displayed at the town hall in the city of Posen.[48] In spite of these generous assurances, a number of unanswered questions still loomed large. Did the Prussian authorities view the Polish community as a semiautonomous equal or simply as an object of Prussian government action to which special privileges had been granted? The Polish community passionately asserted the necessity of the former. Was

Radziwiłł to be a governmental official who was obliged to follow the orders of that government which had appointed him or was he to be free to represent an independent authority? What was Radziwiłł's position vis-à-vis *Oberpräsident* Zerboni di Sposetti, the man at the top of the provincial bureaucracy? But of the most concern was the question of how lasting could be the conditions of Russian liberalism, Prussian government willingness to develop Stein's program, and cooperation by the Poles—all of which had made the settlement of 1815 possible.

Any rational man in 1815 would have wondered about the permanence of all these conditions, but he would have been especially interested in how long the Prussian government would be willing to work with the Polish community. As is obvious from the discussion up to this point, the Prussian bureaucrats, in the four decades of their work in territories that were once a part of the Polish state, had considered various strategies of economic development. They had had to ponder the role of the Polish community in the upgrading of Prussia's new provinces. Many of the Prussian bureaucrats had come to the conclusion that they could progress faster by ignoring the Polish and concentrating on the German settlements. The official Justus Gruner, for example, had opted for a gradual germanization of Prussia's Polish territories at a time (1807) when the very existence of Prussia was in doubt.[49]

After 1815 when Prussia's existence seemed more secure, others, following Gruner's lead, developed a mosaic of reasons why the Polish community should be considered merely an object of action—never an initiator. For example, Carl von Clausewitz, the brilliant military theorist, contributed the following to the mosaic.[50] Clausewitz first asserted that the Poles' geographical position, in effect, determined their policy. If the Polish community did succeed in creating a state with its center at Warsaw, it would immediately demand the Prussian province of Posen and later the Prussian province of West Prussia, since both of these areas had sizable Polish populations. Then, East Prussia, the former land of the Teutonic Knights, would once again become a virtual fief of the Polish crown. But, beyond these territorial aggressions, any independent action by the Polish community would also threaten Prussia in a second way. Just as geography predisposed the Poles toward a nationalistic desire for Prussian state territories, geography and elementary military strategy prompted a Polish-French alliance against Prussia and Austria. Therefore, at any time that France, the senior partner, chose to employ the Polish community, Germany would have to fight a two-front war against France and Poland. So the Polish community at best could be considered to be only a French puppet.[51]

Another military man, Carl von Grolman, made his own contribution. Obviously inspired by Frederick the Great, Grolman had proposed in his memorandum of 1816 the settling of German colonists on former Polish lands in Posen and West Prussia, the construction of German schools in these areas, and the buying of Polish estates offered for sale by their owners.[52] Later, he amplified his proposals to make the following assertions:

1. The province of Posen, because of its geographical position, located close to Berlin and forming the connecting link between Silesia in the south and Prussia in the north, belonged to Prussia and any idea of a separation would be considered high treason.

2. The members of the nobility and clergy who held sway in the Polish community had used their positions to educate the Polish young people to rebel against the Prussian state. Yet since the Polish nobility's economic situation was insecure, the Prussian state could take advantage of this condition by buying the Polish estates and thus liquidating a significant element of Polish leadership. Such an action would ultimately secure Prussian control of Posen.

3. The peasants within the Polish community were found to be the "most slovenly, inoffensive creatures under the sun." The Prussian state could be assured that this group would cause no difficulties.

4. German farmers were to be settled in groups. (Grolman thus rejected Frederick the Great's idea of two or three German families to a village.) These clusters would provide the state with a secure base in the east.

5. Prussia should dissolve the province of Posen and distribute its territory among the other, old-Prussian provinces.[53]

Grolman's proposals could not be put into effect, however, because the Prussian state never had enough money to buy out the estate holdings of the Polish nobility, and the Polish peasantry would not remain inactive indefinitely. But the impact of Grolman's proposals was unfortunate for the Polish community since such writings as his spread the stereotypical image of the incompetent Pole which had originated in the 18th century.

Yet the Prussian officials should have recognized the potentials of the Polish people. The actual Polish community which Prussia had the responsibility of governing possessed great energies, as the events of 1830 demonstrated. In that year, the French revolted, and they alarmed all of Europe as usual. Then the Belgians, seeking independence from the Dutch, followed the French example. The Russians, in turn, became so upset that diplomats expected the dispatch of tsarist armies to crush the Belgian rebels. However, in 1830 when the tsar mobilized the Polish troops of his

Congress Kingdom, he stirred a rebellion closer to home, a full-scale war which lasted into 1831. Moreover, his Polish troops had revolted, and some 2000 to 2500 Prussian Poles, mainly nobles, unobstructed by the local officials in Posen who were Polish, rushed to the aid of their compatriots, the Russian Poles. The Prussian Poles remained to fight the Russian troops despite Governor Radziwiłł's suspension, governmental demands that they return home, and the replacement by Germans of the local Polish officials of the Prussian bureaucracy in Posen.[54] To be sure, the Russian armies with their superior power emerged victorious, but the Polish troops proved beyond any doubt that they were capable of more than ruining estates and drinking brandy.

What the Prussian bureaucracy learned, however, was another story. While many within the Polish community under the leadership of Dr. Karol Marcinkowski turned their attention to the quiet work of economic development, the Prussian officials sent to the province of Posen Edward Flottwell, a man who would lend his name to the period from 1830 to 1841.[55] A protégé of Heinrich Theodor von Schön, the long-term *Oberpräsident* of West Prussia and then also East Prussia, Flottwell had had a successful career within the Prussian bureaucracy. In the process, he had obviously appropriated the ideas of Schön and the liberal bureaucrats who favored using state power for the improvement of society.[56] The state, they asserted, had an obligation to lead. Since they considered that the projects of the state must come first, they felt that those who defied the state were traitors.[57]

Flottwell's program, therefore, had a twofold thrust. On the one hand, he asserted the authority of the state in order to transform society: he moved to make the German language the official language of the province of Posen, increasing the resources devoted to the teaching of German and improving the province's transportation network. On the other, he sought to punish the state's enemies: he suspended local self-government, an action which meant the disappearance of the *Landräte* and of the patrimonial system of justice. In addition to replacing Polish justices of the peace by German officials, Flottwell sought, without much success, to convince the king to authorize a firm rebuke to the Polish rebels who had gone to Russian Poland to fight in 1830–1831.[58] The rebels received offers of limited amnesty without any political rights if they would return to Prussian territory; those who failed to return were assessed only reduced penalties, and in 1840 full political rights were restored to all. Despite this defeat, however, Flottwell's program had made the Poles of Posen fully aware that they were subjects of the king of Prussia, that they owed him their full obedience, and that they should therefore consider themselves Prussians first and foremost.

In his famous farewell memorandum of March 15, 1841, at the completion of his service in Posen, Flottwell summarized his program for the

benefit of his successors.[59] Like Gruner, Grolman, and Clausewitz, Flottwell's basic purpose had been to strengthen the ties binding Posen to
Prussia. He had assumed that German culture was superior to Polish culture although it was questionable whether he had ever actually sampled
Polish culture or could appreciate the literary works that Mickiewicz was
then producing. But the Prussian official was supposed to be able to employ his cultural advantage to transform the Polish segment in Posen into a
community with the same traditions, customs, and loyalties as any other
Prussian community. While he was an official in Posen, Flottwell had
increased educational opportunities, improved transportation, adminis-
tered impartial justice, and freed the peasant from the patrimonial system
of justice. This program, he contended, should be continued even if many
within the Polish community still clung to a dream of independence.

The question arose, of course, as to why so many within the Polish
community preferred to dream of a separate state and other fruits of
independence rather than to enjoy the program that Flottwell had provided. Flottwell countered this critical query by charging the Polish clergy
and nobility with the full responsibility for influencing the entire Polish
community in what he considered an absurd fashion. Of course, he had
failed to respect the Polish nobles who had left Posen to fight and die in
Russian Poland. He likewise failed to respect Dr. Karol Marcinkowski,
whose labors had resulted in the construction of the Posen hotel meeting
hall (called the "Bazar"), as well as in the organization of the Society for
the Promotion of Education. Instead, Flottwell focused his attention on
the priests and women within the Polish community. He considered that
some of the women, especially the wives of the nobles, were actually the
most powerful members of the Polish group because they educated their
families to dream of a restored Polish state. Ironically, Flottwell hoped to
reduce the influence of these women of the nobility by fostering the
development of a middle class. Yet when this class did develop, it likewise
proved to be nationalistic.

Flottwell's exaggerated concern for the influence of the wives of the
nobles deserves further comment. Frederick the Great had praised their
character. General Boyen later saw in them the most bitter opponent of
the partitioning powers. He attributed their bitterness to the imposition of
a foreign administration that had robbed these aristocratic women of their
previous influence in political matters.[60] Exhibiting this same respect for
Polish women—if from a contrasting place in German cultural life—Heinrich Heine, on a journey to Posen in 1822, spoke of the "true Polish
woman, a Vistula Aphrodite."[61] Eighty-five years later, the nationalist
Hugo Ganz reported that the eastern problem had a sexual basis, while on
December 8, 1909, the *Bromberger Tageblatt* reported that Frau Ottilie
Stein had asserted at a Hakatist meeting that Polish women filled Polish
men and even Polish children with their hatred of Germans.[62] In the

1930s a Nazi author saw a determined enemy in the Polish woman who, by her powers of attraction, made foreign men so forget themselves that they were moved to father healthy children for the benefit of the Polish community.[63] Could it be that, in the eyes of such a writer, the German girls and wives were so dull that the foreign women in Posen or West Prussia or Warsaw seemed magnificent in comparison? Or is it that many males from many backgrounds have let their imaginations roam when confronted by females outside their group? Or can the persistence of this sort of literary praise of the Polish woman be explained by admitting her influence within the Polish community, while conceding the typical male imagination and recognizing a lasting disinclination on the part of many Germans who observed the development of the German community to tender any respect for the Polish male? Whatever the explanation accepted, it must be acknowledged that many Germans have continually refused to concede that Polish males have made any achievements.

Flottwell's ideas pointed up other interesting aspects of the Prussian-Polish situation. First of all, the liberal Prussian bureaucrats refused to recognize that the Polish community possessed specific rights, including the right to a certain sphere of national autonomy. Second, on their part the Poles refused to respect the settlement of 1815. Third, Russian enthusiasm for Polish autonomy had waned by 1830. If Prussia were still to follow the Russian lead, Prussia would also have to treat the province of Posen as a political subdivision that was permitted to obey only the directives from the higher levels of the Prussian bureaucracy. Fourth, since the liberal Prussian bureaucrats saw the Polish community as culturally inferior, they tended to treat the Poles in Posen as second-class citizens who were entitled nevertheless to the guarantees of a state governed by law. They were inclined to underestimate Polish achievement, exaggerate Polish weaknesses, and spread their opinions among those with whom they came in contact. Since the bureaucrats enjoyed prestigious positions, they socialized with the professional and economic leaders of Prussian society. Therefore, the following image of the Pole was disseminated, particularly among the Protestants, liberals, and nationalists in Germany. As Manfred Laubert later related, many Germans came to accept this view of German-Polish relations:

"The struggle between the two is unavoidable; it has lasted close onto 30 years and will continue until one party has won. The stronger must triumph. Which is the stronger? Is it the Poles with a Catholicism taught by ignorant and fanatical priests, with a language which no one understands except the 700,000 Poles within a Prussian population of 13 million, without a literature, with a population without science, industry, and arts but with a sense of inconstancy and discord . . . ? "[64]

As a second consequence, since such German opinions as well as Polish images of the character of Prussian oppression increased local tensions, the German and Polish communities began to become increasingly isolated from one another and perhaps increasingly ignorant of each other.[65]

As was true of the German image of the Polish woman cited above, it should be recognized that not only were these views just described spread among those in the Prussian bureaucracy, but also they endured. For example, on October 7, 1901, a prominent Bromberg official supported the town's request for a university by using the argument that "culture determines the final victor in every struggle among peoples; the higher overcomes the lower."[66] He added that the Poles were incapable of creating their own culture. Of course, some German authors and journalists did note that the so-called higher culture was not vanquishing the lower or so-called nonexistent culture. These writers attributed this phenomenon, as did the *Posener Tageblatt*, to modern methods of minority-group organization.[67] Other observers simply mentioned the Polish community's good fortune in finding itself in a state not only governed by law but also committed to improving the conditions of all those residing within its borders. Still, during the decade of the 1830s and later, most of the bureaucratic, journalistic, and literary critics of the Polish community continued to reflect Flottwell's views.

As an aside, it should also be noted that the present-day observer is presumably less certain about what kind of evaluation should be placed on these negative assessments of the Polish community in Posen. The Prussian bureaucrats seemingly considered the Poles "culturally inferior" because Poland had been partitioned and the Poles enjoyed a lower standard of living than the Germans. All kinds of other complaints also flowed from this consideration of Poland's partition and the Polish people's lower per capita income in comparison with that of the German people. In the 20th century, although Poland is united while Germany is divided, the Germans in both East and West Germany still continue to enjoy a higher standard of living. However, some 20th-century critics deny the value of mere economic growth, and others even deny the value of the nation-state. Thus, for 20th-century analysts, Flottwell's words tend to raise more questions than they answer.

In the early 1830s, Flottwell's views were challenged by liberals in the south and west of Germany, where contact with flesh-and-blood Poles was lacking. In the state of Baden, for example, even though there was no Polish community, there was strong antipathy towards Russian and Prussian absolutism. Here, in the atmosphere of "the enemy of my enemy is my friend," the southwest liberals uttered loud cries of support for the gallant Poles, fighting Russian absolutism in a desperate battle against overwhelming odds. Despite the fact that the only Poles these liberals saw, and for a very limited period at that, were refugees retreating to Paris, the strong vocal support for these largely unknown Poles was continued.[68] Thus, motivated more by anti-Russian feeling than by a pro-Polish commitment,[69] poets expressed sentiments such as

"In Siberia, in Siberia, he hears no loving sound; he sees himself buried deeper as if already placed—while living—in the coffin . . . In Siberia, in Siberia, alas, you poor Polish troop, for you stones must cry, without tears is only the Tsar."[70]

Or,

"On the Day of Judgment, I will indeed need the trumpet. Then when God calls the dead to earth, when he wants to frighten them from their graves, he must first wake the trumpeters from their vault. That will be a day of joy . . . to sound against the Russians."[71]

Or,

"In the graves of noble Poles, buried in snow and frost, lies the last comfort of humanity."[72]

In a recent study, one historian has contended that enthusiasm among German liberals for Poland during this period had been based largely upon an illusion. These liberals of the southwest had believed that the entire Polish people had unified to demand Polish independence and that the Polish community had planned to introduce a constitutional monarchy based upon the French model.[73] Yet as Anneliese Gerecke has asserted, most of the Polish rebels in Prussia were nobles. The Warsaw rebels consisted of students of the School of Cadets, some adult nobles, and elements of the left. The Polish leadership in Warsaw did not suggest a later Poland which would be any more than the Poland of 1793. The Polish leaders were not French democrats. They had failed even to abolish serfdom. But the Baden liberals, failing to realize the real nature of the Polish leadership, had conjured up a huge mass of democrats on the Vistula instead of recognizing that the *ancien regime* actually maintained its hold on the Polish body politic.

And these same misconceptions continued to cloud the views of the Baden liberals just as the Flottwells remained prisoners of their own illusions. Then Frederick William III died in 1840 and was succeeded by Frederick William IV, a friend of the Radziwiłł and Raczyński families. The accession of a new ruler opened the door for a change in German-Polish relations. Frederick William IV proceeded to act on the "Polish question." Stating that the French government had made very good Frenchmen out of Alsatians only because it had permitted these Alsatians to remain German, he pledged that he would follow this example in dealing with the Polish rebels.[74] In 1840 he granted full amnesty to those Poles who had left Prussia to fight the Russians in the period 1830–1831. He appointed Prussian officials who were friendly to the Poles to bureaucratic positions in the province of Posen. He raised the salaries of the Prussian officials who studied Polish. He also published the public decrees in Polish as well as in German. He ordered that the children in predominantly Polish schools be taught in Polish. In 1842 he allowed the Prussian-Russian convention on the extradition of deserters and criminals to lapse while allowing Poles who had been living in Paris or England, Russian Poland, or Austrian Poland to flock to Posen. Against the advice of *Oberpräsident* Carl von Horn of Posen, Frederick agreed also to the succession of the Polish priest Leon Przyłuski to the position of Archbishop of Posen-Gnesen. Przyłuski was succeeding Archbishop Marcin Dunin, who had frequently come into conflict with Prussian officialdom. Of course, many bureaucrats like Carl von Horn still allowed Flottwell's views to govern their own actions in Polish affairs. Frederick William IV had also warned the Poles of Posen to view themselves as Polish-speaking Prussians rather than as Poles.

Meanwhile, during the early and middle part of the decade of the 1840s, the Polish community continued to organize itself in Posen. Throughout Europe the Polish people were attracting recognition for a nationalism that threatened to make a mockery of the cherished beliefs of Prussian bureaucrats.

In Posen the Polish leaders meeting at the Hotel Bazar expanded their work of economic development. They granted scholarships to needy students and began to set up local agricultural associations. They worked hard but quietly. Throughout Europe Polish poets and historians gained recognition for their cultural talents and for the Polish people. German translators published German editions of the works of notable Polish authors such as Adam Mickiewicz, Juliusz Słowacki, Zygmunt Krasinski, and Joachim Lelewel. It was thus possible for a Prussian, or any other German for that matter, to examine the quality of Polish literature.[75] But the Germans were more likely to read the words of the great German nationalist Ernst Moritz Arndt than the works of Mickiewicz or Lelewel. Arndt contended in 1843 that

"Poland's history is characterized from beginning to end by levity, frivolity, wildness, and disorder; the Pole remains forever a big, wild boy. . . . Why has God created such people as the Irish and Poles who remain forever minors?"[76]

Although Arndt theoretically favored an independent Poland as a buffer state between Prussia and Russia, he took a pessimistic view of the possibility that the Poles could ever achieve this sort of independence. Arndt stated bluntly that "one must let Poland by itself and out of itself make of itself what it can however it can."[77] The Poles would shortly try to do just that.

The 1840s proved to be one of the more interesting decades in European history. It began quietly and ended in an uproar. The first Polish activity in 1846 resulted in a conspiracy that the police speedily uncovered and the courts decisively condemned. Then in 1848 most of Europe once more followed the French example by plunging into revolution. Demands for constitutional governments, national states, and social justice resounded throughout the continent. German liberals and both the German and the Polish nationalists also were making these demands. The Germans and Poles shared a common hatred of the absolutism of the tsar. Therefore, in March German mobs in Berlin freed the imprisoned Polish conspirators. Many of these Germans had also hoped that the two peoples could cooperate as equals in an alliance. But if this were to be possible, a substantial segment of Germans, both inside and outside of Prussia, would have had to concede that the Polish community was more than merely the object of Prussian bureaucratic decrees.

At this point, it would be well to stop for a moment to investigate the identity of those who hoped for a German-Polish alliance against the Russian tsar. On the Polish side, it should be clear that the Poles who may have entertained such hopes were living on Prussian state territory. The Poles in Russian Poland would have had no opportunity to express their opinions, even if they had developed any. Living under the rule of Tsar Nicholas's police and the military, they would not be challenging their Russian masters until 1863. In 1848 the Russian Empire was an oasis of enforced stability. The Poles in Austrian Galicia had problems of their own to occupy their attention. The peasant masses in Galicia had been used in 1846 by the Austrian authorities to crush a Polish plot. Since the Polish community had suffered severe losses, it was still attempting in 1848 to recover. On the Prussian side, affairs were a bit more complicated. The mob in Berlin consisted of Germans who knew little about the Poles and saw in the Polish political prisoners merely a romantic symbol of resistance to oppression. Ignorance of the Polish community had produced a similar romantic image of the Pole in the south and west of Germany. On the other hand, the Germans in the province of Posen constituted 40 percent of the total population and occupied most of the positions in the local Prussian bureaucracy. Therefore, they had a real and active interest in the doings of the Polish community.

When politicians or writers outside of Posen talked of creating an independent Poland which would include Prussian territories, the local men and women reacted to their own firsthand interests. On March 20, 1848, for example, some of the Germans in the districts of Culm, Thorn, Strasburg, Lobäu, and Graudenz declared that they considered a separation of their province from Germany "to be completely impossible . . . we declare here and before the entire world that we are German through and through."[78] On March 23 a delegation from Meseritz repeated this message to Frederick William IV, and other groups took similar action.[79] A *Verein zur Wahrung deutscher Interessen* was founded.[80] On March 30 a German committee in West Prussia declared that it wanted justice for Germans as well as for Poles; it further contended that West Prussia was "won for civilization from the night of barbarity through German blood. . . . Accordingly, Prussia is the property of the Germans."[81] On April 5 a Danzig resolution reiterated that "we are Prussians, we are Germans and always want to be so and remain so."[82] By April 7 the *Regierungspräsident* of Bromberg reported that these Germans were not merely talking. They had begun to arm themselves.[83] They considered themselves Germans and Prussians, and they intended to remain so.

The Prussian officer corps reacted to this conflict within the framework of its societal responsibilities. Its first concern was to insure the continuity of public order and to uphold the authority of the Prussian state.[84] On March 31, 1848, the commander of the first army gave a succinct statement embodying the army's value system: "It is not our intention to do battle with the Polish nationality, but it is our intention to step in without consideration with weapons in hand wherever the legal order is violently disturbed."[85] On April 11 General von Colomb added the following statement criticizing the actions of the Poles in Posen:

"The Poles may not consider themselves thereby in any way justified in shattering the legal order in the province of Posen. . . . moderation and indulgence also have their borders and, if a land is to be guarded against plundering and murder, against total anarchy, if the good citizen is not to appeal in vain for the protection of law, then ruinous bands at various points in the province must be dispersed."[86]

Another characteristic reaction was that of Frederick William IV, who hoped to satisfy his Polish friends, his Prussian responsibilities, and his German sentiments by commissioning the creation of a plan that would satisfy all three. He proposed as his miracle man General Wilhelm von Willisen, to whom he gave the task of dividing Posen in such a way that he would satisfy both the native Poles and the Germans. On April 5 Willisen came to Posen, and on April 14 Frederick divided the province into German and Polish sections. But also on April 14 the Germans declared that their areas would be incorporated into a Polish state only over their dead bodies.[87] On April 16 a declaration issued in Bromberg demanded not only that the petitioners' district remain in Prussia but also that Willisen be removed from his post and stand trial for contributing to disturbances which had resulted in the flowing of innocent (which, to them, meant "German") blood.[88] On April 18 some 3000 Germans in the city of Posen petitioned the Prussian government to keep their city in Prussia. Their pleas were seconded by other groups.[89] Obviously, Frederick William had not succeeded in pleasing all the factions.

But if Frederick William was the victim of conflicting goals, his officials knew exactly what they were seeking. Indeed, one interesting index of bureaucratic sentiment was the government's promotion of Arndt's *Polenlärm und Polenbegeisterung.* The bureaucracy actually suggested that local officials purchase and distribute copies of Arndt's work.[90] In promoting Arndt's work, Prussian officialdom also sanctioned the view that the Slavic family of nations, to which the Poles belonged, had never founded anything which endured. It spread the belief that world history had demonstrated the Polish people to be less worthy than the German people. These officials emphasized that the Germans who championed the Polish cause had neither a political, a spiritual, nor a moral justification to sacrifice the children of their own blood in order to please the Polish community.[91] Ultimately the pressure of these views forced Frederick William to withdraw his offer to partition Posen. All Posen thus remained Prussian.

For future reference, it should be noted here that one of the more obscure sources of pressure on the Prussian Frederick William had been a nobleman named Otto von Bismarck who, although he did not yet enjoy any measure of public stature, had attempted to influence public opinion with his letter to a Magdeburg newspaper on April 20, 1848.[92] In this letter, Bismarck started with a premise promoted by Clausewitz. That is, Bismarck believed that the Posen Polish community could have no goal other than complete independence. Bismarck then argued, like Clausewitz, that this core Polish kingdom would lust for East Prussia, Silesia, and Pomerania as well as West Prussia. He concluded with the far-from-original observation that the German and Polish peoples were fated to be sworn enemies.

In the west of Germany, where German liberals and nationalists had attempted to create a German national state, Bismarck's conclusion appeared to be supported by the flow of events. First, the liberals, with their romantic image of the Pole predominated. Then, when the Germans of Posen made their interests known, pro-Polish sentiments decreased drastically. At this point, most German politicians and editors began to perceive a definite split between German and Polish interests. In fact, only one newspaper, the *Deutsche Reform*, an organ of the extreme left, continued to champion the Polish cause vigorously.[93] Of course, the German National Assembly on June 1 did declare that it recognized the rights of non-Germans in religion, education, and internal administration, and these guarantees did find their way into the draft constitution of March 28, 1849.[94] But there is a difference between being the object of minority guarantees and being an independent agent able to arrange for the future. From a practical standpoint, these guarantees eventually proved to be meaningless since the draft constitution was not accepted in 1849 by either the king of Prussia or the other German rulers.

In Cologne another solution to the Polish question was attempted. The men involved were Karl Marx and Friedrich Engels who, in the *Neue Rheinische Zeitung*, savagely condemned the National Assembly's failure to act "honorably" in the Posen question and ironically commented that the Assembly even wanted the Polish community to thank it for the partitioning of Polish lands.[95] They then called the Poles a "necessary" people. They saw that the Poles were necessary to the German people because the partitions of Poland had made Germany dependent upon Russia, and they recognized that only an independent and democratic Poland could prepare the way for a democratic Germany.[96] Marx and Engels then concluded by demanding both the creation of a viable Polish state and a war with Russia.[97]

While these articles by Marx and Engels formed the basis for the development among German Marxists of a lasting and positive evaluation of the Pole which amounted to a Marxist stereotype, even Friedrich Engels could not totally escape Arndt's influence. In his letter to Marx on May 23, 1851, he wrote of the Poles:

"The more I think about this business, the clearer it is to me that the Poles are *une nation foutue*, an instrument which is needed only until Russia herself is swept into an agrarian revolution. From that moment on, Poland has absolutely no further *raison d'être*. The Poles have never done anything in history except engage in brave, rowdy stupidity."[98]

Perhaps these sentiments merely reveal how many Germans by 1851 had accepted automatically a negative picture of the Pole. To these Germans, the image of the Pole was an antagonistic one, complete with all sorts of negative overtones. Perhaps these sentiments reveal how few Germans, excluding certain Marxists, could envision a stable German-Polish relationship.[99]

In any event, most of the Prussian bureaucrats apparently could not, and after 1848 they had lost any remaining traces of sympathy for the Polish cause. No new Flottwells had appeared. Although the Prussian ministers considered pursuing Grolman's plan of abolishing the province of Posen, they decided against it.[100] Because the Prussian officials did not know what to do, they did little of substance. Instead, the various officers and officials took up their pens. For example, Major von Voigts, in his account of the events in Posen in 1848, emphasized the cruelty which the Polish rebels allegedly displayed.[101] Instead *Oberpräsident* Noah in his

Die staatsrechtliche Stellung der Polen in Preussen and the historian Heinrich Wuttke in his *Polen und Deutsche* championed the German cause.[102] But only their pens could be active. To put it in the words of a senior Prussian official, Eugen von Puttkammer, "to reconcile it [the Polish movement] is impossible; to exterminate it inhuman."[103]

This relative inactivity thus accurately reflected the impasse. In the realm of action, a stalemate had been reached between the Prussian government and the Polish community. Each side was aware that it could not force the other to bend to its will. The Poles in Posen and West Prussia could not physically compel the Prussian government to grant them independence, while the Prussians could not subdue the Polish community to the point of betraying its dream of independence. On the other hand, there was no stalemate in the development of the Prussian image of the Pole. The stereotype of the Pole as an incompetent and thoroughly corrupted malcontent deepened its hold on most of those few Germans in the Prussian state service who thought at all about him or the dilemmas posed by the existence of a Prussian Polish community. The Germans, though not all of them, thus lacked any respect for the Polish people or for the community's struggle to preserve its own identity, either by revolution or through community organization.

A notable example of this lack of respect for Polish achievements occurs in Heinrich von Treitschke's writings. In 1862 this famous historian described an eternal hostility between German and Pole as well as the Pole's lack of loyalty and political incapacity.[104] Later, he expanded upon these themes and wrote also of the Pole's mistreatment of foreign peoples, of the Polish noble's incompetence, and of the benefits of a German administration.[105] In short, Treitschke the historian came to the aid of Treitschke the politician by supplying the latter with material for his political campaign. Speaking in Heidelberg in 1873, he even added that the little man in Posen "doesn't thank the German government but he knows very well why he should thank it."[106] In praising the Germans for knowing how to get things done, this nationalist had found himself in agreement with the old Prussian king, Frederick the Great.

A more modern denunciation of the Poles, as distinct from the "traditional" Prussian one, came from E. Kattner in 1862. Kattner proclaimed that "the Poles represent in alarming clearness the medieval powers of nobility, clergy, and serfdom and their consequences—economic, spiritual, and moral decay."[107] Kattner also saw Poland as a feudal state in which the nobles' whims dictated state policy. Even though being a feudal state was Poland's historical task, it was, at the same time, the reason for her historical decline.[108] Of course, his analysis included some allegations of a more traditional nature. For instance, he alleged that the Pole's personality structure was rigid, that he lacked any sense of loyalty, that he hated the

Germans, and that he was unstable.[109] Kattner even added the usual paragraph on the corrupting influence of the Polish woman who, as always, was making German lads forget their parents, fatherland, and religion.[110]

These attacks continued from many sources. In materials to be found in state archives, government documents recorded typical denunciations by Prussian officials of 1860 or 1881 criticizing Polish activities and the Poles themselves for their lack of Prussian feeling and their abundance of "subversive" Polish emotion.[111] In one of the novels of the time, Gustav Freytag contrasted German order with Polish disorder.[112] In the works of history, Adolf Beer and Jacob Caro asserted, respectively, that the Pole lacked the ability to sustain a state and that the Pole owed his advance to a state of culture to the German.[113] Leopold von Ranke, from his viewpoint, placed the history of the Polish people outside the scope of the history of European civilization, which he called Romance-Germanic civilization.[114]

How can this mosaic of anti-Polish views be explained? At least partially, it can be attributed to an obvious German reaction to the events of 1848. Beyond that, it may be supposed that the 18th-century negative assessment of the Pole was still current because the conditions of that time remained. The Prussian officials still ruled over one part of the partitioned Polish nation and state. Moreover, after 1848 the Prussian aristocracy did not trust the Polish aristocracy to help it to maintain the status quo in Central Europe. Furthermore, the newly aroused desire for a German nation-state obviously made nationalistic Germans question the advisability of permitting a Polish community in Prussia. Finally, in their celebrations when Germany was united in 1871, the enthusiastic Germans could only feel a great superiority over the still-partitioned Polish nation.

Yet the Polish community had shown great strength. It had demonstrated its loyalty to its political dream along with its determination to work toward its goals. Moreover, evidence of this determination was readily available. The activities of the Polish archbishop forced the Prussian government to stoop to demand the removal of the Archbishop Przyłuski from the Posen-Gnesen archbishopric.[115] It had previously imprisoned his predecessor, Dunin, and would imprison his successor, Mieczysław Ledóchowski. Thus, at the level of reality, the Polish community proved to be a tenacious foe. At the level of doctrine, the typical, post-1848 Prussian officials found it necessary to deny the Polish community's obvious qualities. And the image of the Pole which they projected continued to be more powerful than the historical actuality.

This was especially true in the last thirty years of the 19th century as more and more Germans rejoiced in the power of their state in contrast with the limitations of the crippled Polish community. Yet in the eastern provinces, as large numbers of Germans began to emigrate, Poles came to take their places. In the city of Posen, these Poles actively participated in the life of the area. They constructed a theater. They organized numerous cooperative societies which financed Polish industrial and commercial development. In the city, they founded banks. In the country, they expanded their agrarian organizations. They displayed such an amazing vitality that most Prussian officials, and even the man in the street, should have been aware of their diligence and success. In fact, the Poles created the very model of a minority developing its own economy and society despite its very junior status within a hostile state.

In this context, Bismarck's Polish policy, much discussed but not all new, could be criticized on the order of "too little, too late." What Bismarck did, in effect, was to accept the different, but all negative, ideas of Frederick the Great, Clausewitz, Grolman, and Flottwell and, at this late date in German-Polish relations, to finance their implementation to a moderate extent. Since, for instance, Bismarck had accepted both their belief in the superiority of the German culture over the Polish and their faith in the ability of the "higher" culture to defeat the "lower," he decreed that training in the German language should become the main object of the school curriculum. The German language replaced Polish in all except religious classes.[116] Bismarck accepted Grolman's and Flottwell's belief in the threat posed by the priests. And after the Archbishop of Posen-Gnesen had been arrested, he convinced the pope of the need to replace this Polish clergyman with a German. Since Bismarck also accepted the belief in the threat posed by the nobles, he agreed in 1886 to the creation of a colonization commission with a fund of 100 million marks to purchase Polish estates and settle German colonists.[117]

Despite these concerted efforts, Bismarck's program proved to be an utter failure. For example, some Polish students mastered German so well that they had an advantage in business over German competitors. Bilingual, they could seek out both German and Polish customers while the German was restricted to his own language group. Other students learned only to repeat German phrases but never learned the German language. For instance, *Germania*, a German Catholic newspaper, reported in 1890 that a student, asked to write "Fuchs, du hast die Gans gestohlen, gieb sie wieder her, sonst dich der Jäger holen, mit dem Schliessgewehr," replied with "Fuks tu hast die Ganc gestollen, giebski wieder her, samst du Jaeger hollen, miske flieke wehr."[118] Obviously, such students would never know if German culture were superior to their Polish backgrounds. Also, in schools where the students of German nationality were in the minority, these German students who were assumed by Bismarck to belong to the "higher" culture tended instead to assimilate to the Polish norm and thus to become Polish in language and customs.[119] In church affairs, the presence of a German archbishop in Posen from 1886 to 1890 failed to damage the Polish community's sense of identity, while Bismarck's interference in church affairs aroused the Catholic Center party enough that they cried "to Germanize is to make Protestant." In the land question, the colonization commission's purchases raised the price of land but failed to dampen the Poles' ambitions to own their own land.[120] In short, Bismarck's program not only failed—it backfired.

Even though these specific results illustrate Bismarck's lack of skill in domestic politics, they only partially convey his most fundamental error. In the final analysis, he had failed because he had accepted totally not only Grolman's and Flottwell's policies but also programs which were based on a lack of understanding of the achievements of the Polish people both in Posen and throughout Europe.[121]

Flottwell, for instance, believed that the Polish community was incapable of creating a culture, and Bismarck fully accepted this allegation. But considering that segment of culture which is called literature, a journalistic or literary observer in either 1870 or 1970 would have to conclude that Bismarck had simply not troubled himself to examine the vitality of Polish culture. And he could have. During the period from the 1870s to the 1890s, there appeared a number of translations of the works of Krasicki, Mickiewicz, Słowacki, Krasinski, Sienkiewicz, Orzeszkowa, and others.[122] German historical societies which were founded to investigate the history of Posen and other eastern provinces published their studies in German.[123] Thus, the Polish achievements which had been made on many fronts were no secret, and even though this information was available to Bismarck, he never appeared to question the supposed superiority of German culture.

Bismarck apparently had accepted also without question the "traditional" description of a Polish society dominated by aggressive nobles and clergy.[124] He had done so in his capacities as German chancellor and Prussian minister-president, not only at a time in the 1870s and 1880s when the description was still accurate, but also later, when cooperatives were flourishing, Polish banks were expanding, and Polish peasants were organizing.[125] So he attacked the old feudal powers within the Polish community by purchasing Polish estates; but at the same time, he alienated the new urban and agricultural forces by his attacks on the Polish language and the Catholic religion. Thus, even though Bismarck ironically made a real contribution towards uniting the "masses" behind the national cause, he failed to recognize it because he never understood the effects and consequences of his actions.

Perhaps he failed to recognize the negative elements of what he was doing because he had inherited and accepted Grolman's stereotypical image of the Polish peasant. To the end of his life, Bismarck subscribed to the myth that the Polish peasant was a passive fellow who served bravely when called to arms, who took little interest in political or national affairs, and who guzzled brandy.[126] And he even thought that the peasant could possibly be termed pro-Prussian because he was supposed to fear a return to the chaos of the 18th century. Since Bismarck assumed that the Posen Polish peasant also felt a gratitude for the beneficial rule of Prussian law,[127] he thought he could ignore the peasantry and concentrate his energies on a supposedly incompetent and treacherous elite of nobles and clergy. Yet, the peasant was organizing. What was wrong with Bismarck's policy was that he acted on the basis of a myth. He based his entire program on the stereotype of the Pole which had originated in the 1770s and 1830s but was no longer valid. Psychologically, he failed because he could not surrender that picture of the Pole which suited his needs. And so he acted on the basis of an illusion.[128] To summarize with brutal directness: Bismarck failed because he continued to employ in the last third of the 19th century the obsolete perspectives and programs of the 1770s and 1830s.

Paradoxically, Bismarck's successor fell into the same trap. The Iron Chancellor's successor was General Georg Leo von Caprivi, who, despite being credited with a friendlier policy towards the Poles, apparently maintained the same fundamental perspectives as Bismarck. Like his predecessor, Caprivi mostly ignored the peasantry and paid surprisingly little attention to the growing Polish middle class as potential negotiating partners who could influence the later course of Prussian-Polish relations.[129] Instead, he believed it sufficient to concern himself with the nobles and clergy, whom he fundamentally distrusted.[130] Most importantly, he could not bring himself to treat the Polish nobles and clergymen as groups worthy of genuine respect and as the bearers of legitimate political aspirations. More often, it was Caprivi's policy to accept Polish overtures and Polish votes in the *Reichstag* in exchange for minimal concessions on the part of the Prussian state. For example, he placed a Polish archbishop in Posen-Gnesen, permitted private instruction in Polish in Posen schools, and granted Polish organizations the right to audit their own books. Perhaps he felt that, since Bismarck in almost three decades of power had failed to make the province of Posen significantly more German than it had been in 1862, the Prussian state had little to lose by a minimal relaxation of Bismarck's schemes to germanize the Polish community.[131] In any event, Caprivi failed to blaze any significantly new trails. The Caprivi era was very important nevertheless. It displayed on its demise in 1894 the visible bankruptcy of Prussian officialdom. Bismarck's policy had failed. Repression had not destroyed the Polish national movement. Even Caprivi's attempts at limited compromise had not achieved any satisfactory balance or agreement between the Prussian state and the Polish nationality.[132]

What options remained? An even better financed repression, a greater willingness to compromise? The Caprivi period, in effect, publicly revealed the dilemma which von Puttkammer's memorandum had privately expressed four decades before. Could a policy which insisted on making self-conscious Poles into self-conscious Prussians lead anywhere but to an impasse? On the other hand, could the Prussian government have any other goal? Could this dilemma, now made public, be confined any longer to the corridors of the ministries? Or for the first time since 1848, would a politically aware public living mainly in the eastern provinces become actively concerned? When many of these Germans did become involved, an era drew to a close.

At this point, it might be beneficial to review briefly what kind of Polish community actually existed when the German public first considered the "Polish question." First, the Poles had organized themselves and developed their lands. Politically, the *Koło Polskie* had united all Polish deputies from the provinces of Posen and West Prussia into one parliamentary faction. Economically, agricultural associations and commercial cooperatives had contributed to community development by producing a growing national wealth. Culturally, the Marcinkowski society had educated Polish students while Sienkiewicz and others had excited their sense of national pride. Moreover, the Prussian-Polish masses had been roused to national consciousness and to a greater effort toward community solidarity and self-defense by Bismarck's clumsy policies. Thus, as opposed to Grolman's legacy of an 18th- and early 19th-century negative stereotype of the lazy, incompetent, drunken Pole, the real Prussian Pole was emerging as a man of substantial accomplishments. And the individual's accomplishments were reflected in the substantial development of the Polish community as a whole. Therefore, in its search for an effective response to the "Polish question," and to the existence of a vigorous, successful Polish community within Prussia, the German public would be confronted with a strange dichotomy: on the one hand, the Pole was supposed to be lazy, incompetent, and drunken; on the other, he was characterized as a threatening competitor for national power and position.[133] And in this setting, a new era began.

Notes

1. Erich Maschke, *Das Erwachen des Nationalbewusstseins im deutsch-slavischen Grenzraum* (Leipzig, 1933), p.7.
2. Albert Brackmann, *Die Wikinger und die Anfänge Polens* (Berlin, 1942), p.18; Erich Maschke, *Die treibenden Kräfte in der Entwicklung Polens* (Berlin, 1939), p.2; Franz Lüdtke, *Ein Jahrtausend Krieg zwischen Deutschland und Polen* (Stuttgart, 1941), p.11; Friedrich Kopp, *Deutschland—Europas Bollwerk im Osten* (München, 1939), p.23; and Erich Reimers, *Der Kampf um den deutschen Osten* (Leipzig, 1939), p.78.
3. One example is found in Lüdtke, p.35.

4. Paul Kirn, in *Politische Geschichte der deutschen Grenzen* (Mannheim, 1958; Leipzig, 1934), denied that a national antithesis determined German and Polish policy at this time (pp.52, 53). Lüdtke, on the other hand, asserted that the medieval Polish king, Boleslaw Chobry, introduced the principle of aggression into Polish life (p.20). He also stated that Bolesław acted out of his own desires only (p.48). In *Kleine Geschichte Polens* (Gütersloh, 1963), Helmut Carl saw a direct connection between Bolesław's policy and the policy of Gomulka. However, Jobst Gumpert viewed Bolesław's policy as a personal, not a national, policy in his work, *Polen-Deutschland* (München, 1966), p.35.

5. Jacob Caro, *Geschichte Polens* (Gotha, 1863), II, 194; Werner Emmerich, *Der deutsche Osten* (Leipzig, 1935), p.36; Dietrich Schäfer, *Osteuropa und wir Deutschen* (Berlin, 1924), p.183.

6. Among others, see Erich Schmidt, *Geschichte des Deutschtums im Lande Posen unter polnischer Herrschaft* (Bromberg, 1904), p.138.

7. Among others, see Gumpert, p.37; and Caro, II, 556.

8. Kurt Lück, *Der Lebenskampf im deutsch-polnischen Grenzraum* (Berlin, 1943), p.26.

9. Johannes Altkemper, *Deutschtum und Polentum in politisch-konfessioneller Bedeutung* (Leipzig, 1910), pp.4–6; and Hermann Schreiber, *Land im Osten* (Düsseldorf-Wien, 1961), p.233.

10. Among others discussing the issue are Christian Petzet, *Die preussischen Ostmarken* (München, 1898), p.10; and Arthur Rhode, *Die evangelischen Deutschen in Russisch-Polen* (Lissa, 1906), p.8.

11. Adolf Warschauer, *Geschichte der Provinz Posen in polnischer Zeit* (Posen, 1914), p.123.

12. Max Lehmann records in *Historische Aufsätze und Reden* (Leipzig, 1911) that he saw Polish hatred of Germans more as a reaction against the Teutonic Knights than as a reaction against the average German (p.85).

13. In *Die Ostgrenze Polens* (Köln-Graz, 1955), Gotthold Rhode concluded that the Poles did see themselves as an outpost of Christianity pp.292–293.

14. In *Geschichte Polens* (Darmstadt, 1966), Gotthold Rhode asserted that the battle of Tannenberg first became a symbol of national pride in the 19th century (p.129).

15. Robert Franz Arnold, *Geschichte der deutschen Polenlitteratur von den Anfängen bis 1800* (Osnabrück, 1966), pp.7–8.

16. Hermann Gollub, *Der Grosse Kurfurst und Polen von 1660 bis 1668* (Berlin, 1914), pp.123–124.

17. Lehmann, p.86.

18. Arnold, p.30.

19. *Das verwirrte Pohlen* (Frankfurt and Leipzig, 1711), *Vorbericht*. [This volume is to be found at the University of Illinois Research Library.] Also see Arnold, pp.32–33.

20. Arnold, pp.32–33.

21. Samuel Friedrich Lauterbach, *Pohlnische Chronicke, oder Historische Nachricht von dem Leben und Thaten aller Hertzoge und Könige in Pohlen* (Frankfurt and Leipzig, 1727). [This volume is to be found at the University of Illinois Research Library.] Also see Adolf Warschauer, *Die deutsche Geschichtsschreibung in der Provinz Posen* (Posen, 1910), p.11.

22. In the first partition, Prussia was given West Prussia minus the cities of Danzig and Thorn. The second partition added the territory between Prussia in the north and Silesia in the south. From the third partition, Prussia received Warsaw.

23. Gustav Berthold Volz, *Die Werke Friedrichs des Grossen* (Berlin, 1913), VII, 161.

24. *Friedrich der Grosse* (Leipzig, 1886), II, 204.

25. Ibid., p.384.

26. Heinrich Berger, *Friedrich der Grosse als Kolonisator* (Giessen, 1896), p.54; and Manfred Laubert, *Die preussische Polenpolitik von 1772–1914* (Cracow, 1944), p.9.

27. Berger, p.69; Laubert, p.12; and Franz Lüdtke, *Preussische Kulturarbeit im Osten* (Leipzig and Berlin, 1915), pp.13–14.

28. Lüdtke, *Preussische Kulturarbeit*, p.16; and Laubert, p.7.

29. Eugen von Bergmann, *Zur Geschichte der Entwickelung deutscher, polnischer und jüdischer Bevölkerung in der Provinz Posen seit 1824* (Tübingen, 1883), p.12; and Wilhelm Vallentin, *Westpreussen seit den ersten Jahrzehnten dieses Jahrhunderts* (Tübingen, 1893), p.25.

30. Laubert, p.12. In *Der ostdeutsche Volksboden* (Breslau, 1926, editor Wilhelm Volz) Laubert remarked that the scattered German colonists soon assimilated into the Polish population and thus failed to serve as teachers of a higher civilization (p.332).

31. Manfred Laubert, *Das Heimatrecht der Deutschen in Westpolen* (Bromberg, 1924), p.4; and Otto Hoetzch, *Osteuropa und Deutscher Osten* (Berlin, 1934), p.308. Berger, though, saw Friedrich as a pioneer of the German people since he did spread German culture (p.4).

32. Gotthold Rhode, *Das Siedlungswerk Friedrichs d. Gr. und die Deutschen aus Polen* (Posen, 1939), pp.24–34; Max Beheim-Schwarzbach, *Hohenzollernsche Colonisationen* (Leipzig, 1874), p.427; and Berger, pp.24–25, 65.

33. Lehmann, p.88.

34. The *Historia Polski* (II, Part 1, p.362) records that 40 percent of the Prussian population in 1795 consisted of Poles.

35. Warschauer, *Geschichtsschreibung*, p.23.

36. Arnold, pp.74–75.

37. Ibid., p.119.

38. Moritz Jaffé, *Die Stadt Posen unter preussischer Herrschaft* (Leipzig, 1909), p.82.

39 "Demetrius," an unfinished tragedy, was first published in 1815.

40. Warschauer, *Geschichtsschreibung*, pp.33–34. The title of Baumann's work was *Darstellungen nach dem Leben. Aus einer Skizze der Sitten und des Nationalcharakters der ehemaligen Pohlen.*

41. Ibid. The title of Kaulfuss' work was *Ueber den Geist der polnischen Sprache und Literatur.*
42. Ibid., p.49. The title was *Ueber Preussens Verwaltung seiner ehemaligen polnischen Provinzen. Ein Versuch zur Darstellung der Gründe, die ihren Abfall vom Mutterlande veranlassten.*
43. Hoetzsch, pp.311–312; Lehmann, p.98; Georg Baron Manteuffel-Szoege, *Geschichte des polnischen Volkes* (Berlin, 1950), pp.23–24.
44. Erich Botzenhart, ed., *Freiherr vom Stein* (Berlin, 1931–1937), II, 228–229.
45. Ibid., p.229.
46. Ibid., pp.230–231.
47. Hoetzsch, p.312.
48. The Poles wanted still more. See Hoetzsch, p.318; and Laubert, *Polenpolitik*, p.33.
49. Hoetzsch, pp. 312–313; Manfred Laubert, *Der Flottwelsche Güterbetriebsfonds in der Provinz Posen* (Breslau, 1929), p.5.
50. Carl von Clausewitz,, *Politische Schriften und Briefe* (München, 1922), pp.224–225.
51. Ibid., p.225; Clausewitz contended that the land between the Vistula and the Oder—with the exceptions of the cities of Posen and Danzig—was unfavorable for the erection of a defensive line; he foresaw a retreat to the Oder in the event of war.
52. Manfred Laubert, *Carl v. Grolman als Sekundant des Oberpräsident Flottwell im Kampf um die Posener Mischehenfrage* (Posen, 1943), p.1.
53. Emil von Conrady, *Carl von Grolman* (Berlin, 1896), III, 274–294.
54. Laubert, *Polenpolitik*, p.63; Manfred Laubert, *Die Behandlung der Posener Teilnehmer am Warschauer Novemberaufstand vom 1830/1* (Marburg, 1954), p.188; Manfred Laubert, *Eduard Flottwell* (Berlin, 1919), p.32.
55. Hermann Kötschke, *Die deutsche Polenfreundschaft* (Berlin, 1921), p.22; Kötschke calls Flottwell the first Hakatist.
56. Laubert, *Flottwell*, pp.18–19; Hoetzsch, p.325.
57. In *Polenpolitik*, Laubert reminds us that liberalism and anti-Polish measures coexisted (p.42).
58. Laubert, *Flottwell*, p.29.
59. Edward Flottwell, *Denkschrift, die Verwaltung der Provinz Posen von Dezember 1830 bis zum Beginn des Jahres 1841 betreffend* (Berlin, 1897); Laubert, *Polenpolitik*, p.61, Alexander Wäber, *Preussen und Polen* (Munchen, 1907), pp.277–279; Heinrich Geffcken, *Preussen, Deutschland und die Polen* (Berlin, 1906), pp. 159–168; Geheimes Preussisches Staatsarchiv, Rep. 30, Nr. 696, Nr. 4, Königlich Preussische Regierung zu Bromberg, Akten betreffend: Agitationen des Polenthums. [Allgemeine Vorgänge—out of place, but still here.]
60. Friedrich Nippold, ed., *Erinnerungen aus dem Leben des General-Feldmarschalls Hermann von Boyen* (Leipzig, 1889–1890), I, 98.
61. *Heinrich Heine's sämmtliche Werke* (Hamburg, 1876), XIII, 154.

62. Hugo Ganz, *Die preussische Polenpolitik* (Frankfurt am Main, 1907), p.31. See also *Bromberger Tageblatt*, No. 287, December 8, 1909, [found at Geheimes Preussisches Staatsarchiv, Rep. 30, Nr. 685, Königlich Preussische Regierung zu Bromberg, Acta betreffend: die Stärkung und Förderung des Deutschtums in der Provinz Posen].

63. Hans Joachim Beyer, *Das Schicksal der Polen* (Leipzig and Berlin, 1942), p.158.

64. Laubert, *Polenpolitik*, p.75.

65. Manfred Laubert, *Skizzen zur Posener Stadtsgeschichte vor 100 Jahren* (Posen, 1940), p.97.

66. Denkschrift über die Errichtung einer Universität zu Bromberg. Geheimes Preussisches Staatsarchiv, Rep. 30, Nr. 679, Königlich Preussische Regierung zu Bromberg, Akten betreffend: die Förderung des Deutschtums in den Ostmarken.

67. See *Posener Tageblatt*, No. 569, December 5, 1905, [found at Geheimes Preussisches Staatsarchiv, Rep. 30B, Nr. 685, Königlich Preussische Regierung zu Bromberg, Akten betreffend: die Stärkung und Förderung des Deutschtums in der Provinz Posen].

68. Anneliese Gerecke, *Das deutsche Echo auf die polnische Erhebung von 1830* (Wiesbaden, 1964), p.138.

69. Wolfgang Hallgarten, *Studien über die deutsche Polenfreundschaft in der Periode der Märzrevolution* (München and Berlin, 1982), p.13.

70. Karl Aspern, *Geschichte der Polen* (Regensburg, 1916), pp.118–119; Ernst Ortlepp was the author.

71. Ibid., pp. 105–106; Georg Herwegh was the author.

72. Hallgarten, p.21. Nikolaus Lenaus was the author.

73. Gerecke, p.137.

74. Manfred Laubert, *Die Verwaltung der Provinz Posen 1815–47* (Breslau, 1923), p.130.

75. Walther Recke and Albert Malte Wagner, *Bücherkunde zur Geschichte und Literatur des Königreichs Polen* (Warsaw and Leipzig, 1918), pp.170–175. Joachim Lelewel's *Geschichte Polens* appeared in 1846 in Leipzig.

76. Ernst Moritz Arndt, *Versuch in vergleichender Völkergeschichte* (Leipzig, 1843), p.316.

77. Ibid., p.327.

78. Geheimes Preussisches Staatsarchiv, Rep. A181, Nr. 2314, Königlich Preussische Regierung zu Marienwerder, Acta betreffend: die im Jahre 1848 ausgebrochenen Unruhen der polnischen Bevölkerung des hiesigen Regierungs-Bezirks.

79. Wolfgang Kohte, *Deutsche Bewegung und Preussische Politik im Posener Lande 1848–49* (Posen, 1931), p.26.

80. Walter Bleck, *Die politischen Parteien und die Posener Frage in den Jahren 1848/49* (Posen, 1914), p.11.

81. Geheimes Preussisches Staatsarchiv, Rep. A181, Nr. 2314, Königlich Preussische Regierung zu Marienwerder, Acta betreffend: die im Jahre 1848 ausgebrochenen Unruhen der polnischen Bevölkerung des hiesigen Regierungs-Bezirks.

82. Ibid.
83. Ibid.
84. Geheimes Preussisches Staatsarchiv, Rep. 6B, Nr. 500, Landratsamt Meseritz, Acta betreffend; die im Jahre 1848 in der Provinz Posen ausgebrochenen Kriegerischen Unruhen. Oberpräsident Posen to Landräthe of March 21, 1848.
85. Geheimes Preussisches Staatsarchiv, Rep. A181, Nr. 2314, Königlich Preussische Regierung zu Marienwerder, Acta betreffend: die im Jahre 1848 ausgebrochenen Unruhen der polnischen Bevölkerung des hiesigen Regierungs-Bezirks.
86. Geheimes Preussisches Staatsarchiv, Rep. 6B, Nr. 500, Landratsamt Meseritz, Acta betreffend: die im Jahre 1848 in der Provinz Posen ausgebrochenen Kriegerischen Unruhen.
87. Geheimes Preussisches Staatsarchiv, Rep. A181, Nr. 1456, Königlich Preussische Regierung zu Marienwerder, Acta betreffend: die im Jahren 1848 ausgebrochenen Unruhen der polnischen Bevölkerung des hiesigen Regierungs–Bezirks. Landrath von Zychlinski of April 14, 1848.
88. Ibid. Central-Bürgerausschuss für den Netzdistrikt zur Wahrung preussischer Interessen im Grossherzogthum Posen.
89. Geffcken, p.77; Kohte, p.168.
90. Geheimes Preussisches Staatsarchiv, Rep. 6B, Nr. 500, Landratsamt Meseritz, Acta betreffend: die im Jahre 1848 in der Provinz Posen ausgebrochenen Kriegerischen Unruhen. Beckersche Geheime Ober-Hofbuchdruckerei to Landraths-Amt of April 30, 1848.
91. Ernst Moritz Arndt, *Polenlärm und Polenbegeisterung* (Berlin, 1848), pp.2–3.
92. Wolfgang Windelband and Werner Frauendienst, eds., *Bismarck, Die gesammelten Werke* (Berlin, 1933), XIV, 105–106.
93. Bleck, p.64.
94. Geheimes Preussisches Staatsarchiv, Rep. A181, Nr. 1458, Königlich Preussische Regierung zu Marienwerder, Acta betreffend; die im Jahre 1848 ausgebrochenen Unruhen der polnischen Bevölkerung des hiesigen Regierungs-Bezirks. Laubert, *Polenpolitik*, p.101.
95. *Marx-Engels-Lenin-Stalin. Zur deutschen Geschichte* (Berlin, 1954), II, Part 1, 261.
96. Ibid, pp.274–275.
97. Ibid., pp.276–277.
98. D. Rjazanov (David Borisovich Gol'dendach), ed., *Karl Marx, Friedrich Engels Briefwechsel* (Berlin, 1929), III, Part 1, 206.
99. Wilhelm Liebknecht was especially interested in the Polish question. In 1868 he published a series of articles on this topic.
100. Siegfried Baske, *Praxis und Prinzipien der preussischen Polenpolitik von 1849–1871* (Hamburg, 1960), pp.37–38.
101. C. von Voigts, *Aktenmässige Darstellung der polnischen Insurrektion im Jahre 1848* (Posen, 1848), pp.4–5.
102. Kohte, pp.206, 130.
103. Baske, p.105; Laubert, *Polenpolitik*, p.108 (Eugen von Puttkammer to Manteuffel of September 24, 1851).

104. Heinrich von Treitschke, *Das deutsche Ordensland Preussen* (Leipzig, 1916), p.15; the original had appeared a half century before. For more on Treitschke and his allies, see Gerd S. Biedermann's *Polen im Urteil der nationalpreussischen Historiographie des 19. Jahrhunderts* (Erlangen, 1967).

105. Heinrich von Treitschke, *Deutsche Geschichte im Neunzehnten Jahrhundert* (Leipzig, 1879–1894), I, 65–66, 112–113, 143–144, 257.

106. Heinrich von Treitschke, *Zehn Jahre deutscher Kämpfe* (Berlin, 1879), p.441; delivered in Heidelberg on December 10, 1873.

107. E. Kattner, *Deutsche Abrechnung mit den Polen* (Bromberg, 1862), p.6.

108. Ibid., p.99.

109. Ibid., pp.18, 40, 43, 46.

110. Ibid., p.25.

111. Geheimes Preussisches Staatsarchiv, Rep. 30, Nr. 693, Königlich Preussische Regierung zu Bromberg, Acta betreffend: die erneuerten Bestrebungen für die polnische Nationalität. Two examples are Polizei-Directorium (Posen), of December 19, 1860; and Landrath des Kreises Czarnikau, of November 24, 1881.

112. Gustav Freytag, *Soll und Haben* (Leipzig, 1866), II, 26–27.

113. Adolf Beer, *Die erste Theilung Polens* (Wien, 1873), p.33; Caro, III, 13.

114. Leopold von Ranke, *Geschichten der romanischen und germanischen Völker von 1494 bis 1514* (Leipzig, 1885), "Zur Einleitung."

115. Baske, pp.197–199: Przyłuski died in 1865 before he could be sent to Rome.

116. Ibid., p.241; Laubert, *Polenpolitik* p.126; *Handbuch der Politik* (Berlin and Leipzig, 1912–1913), II, 627; Ludwig Bernhard contributed the article.

117. The commission itself was directly subordinate to the Staatsministerium (the Prussian council of ministers) and consisted of the Oberpräsident of Posen and of West Prussia, members nominated by the king for three-year terms, and commissioners appointed by the Prussian minister-president, the minister of agriculture, the minister of the interior, and the finance minister. The commission rarely assembled because 78 administrative assistants attended to the everyday business of arranging the details of purchasing the estates, dividing them into medium-sized plots, settling Germans on these plots, and providing for necessary social services.

118. *Germania*, No. 80, April 9, 1890.

119. Hans Delbrück, *Die Polenfrage* (Berlin, 1894), p.20.

120. They also stirred an ironic backlash. The minister of agriculture on July 3, 1891, raised the question of empowering the commission to purchase German estates. The Germans had asked why bankrupt Poles should find a government buyer when bankrupt Germans found their possessions at auction (DZA Merseburg, A.b. die Staatsministeriale Sitzungs-Protokolle [Rep. 90a, Abt. B, Tit. 111, 2b, Nr. 6, Band 106], July 3, 1891).

121. Otto Fürst von Bismarck, *Gedanken und Erinnerungen* (New York and Stuttgart, 1922), II, 149–150; *Stenographische Berichte über die Verhandlungen des Landtages*, Haus der Abgeordneten (1886), 1 (January 28, 1886), 164–175.
122. Recke and Wagner, pp.154, 171–175, 185–186, 188.
123. Warschauer, *Geschichtsschreibung*, pp.100–108.
124. *Stenographische Berichte über die Verhandlungen des Landtages*, Haus der Abgeordneten (1872), 2 (February 9, 1872), 701; *Stenographische Berichte über die Verhandlungen des Reichstages,* 1, Lp. 6, S. I (December 3, 1884), p.157.
125. Willy Andreas, ed., *Bismarck Gespräche* (Bremen, 1965), II, 48–49. On January 12, 1873, Bismarck remarked that he had been struck by the progress which the Poles had made in Posen and Silesia.
126. *Stenographische Berichte über die Verhandlungen des Landtages*, Haus der Abgeordneten (1886), 1 (August 23, 1866), 80.
127. Horst Kohl, ed., *Die politischen Reden des Fürsten Bismarck* (Stuttgart, 1892–1905), III, 199.
128. Bismarck, like Clausewitz, saw in Poland only a French puppet; see *Stenographische Berichte über die Verhandlungen des Landtages*, Haus der Abgeordneten (1886), 1 (January 28, 1886), 170. In the reopening of the "Polish question," he could only see difficulties for Prussia; see Bismarck, pp.352, 358. In fact, one of the few things he did that Frederick the Great had not done was to expel 30,000 to 35,000 Polish laborers in 1885. For more on Bismarck and the Poles, see Józef Feldman, *Bismarck a Polska* (Warsaw, 1966); and also see his *Problem polsko-niemiecki w dziejach* (Katowice, 1946).
129. Harry Kenneth Rosenthal, "The Problem of Caprivi's Polish Policy," *European Studies Review*, 2, No. 3 (July, 1972), 255–264.
130. Harry Kenneth Rosenthal, "The Election of Archbishop Stablewski," *Slavic Review*, 28, No. 2 (June, 1969), 265–275.
131. For instance, Caprivi publicly refused to consider abolishing the colonization commission; see *Stenographische Berichte über die Verhandlungen des Landtages*, Haus der Abgeordneten (1891), 4, (May 2, 1891), 2105–2107.
132. It is probable that the Poles would have longed for a national state of their own no matter what the Germans had done.
133. On Polish accomplishments, see Kazimierz Zimmerman, *Ks. Patron Wawrzyniak* (Cracow, 1911); Witold Jakóbczyk, *Patron Jackowski* (Poznań, 1930), Alfred Kucner, "Polityka 'Koła Polskiego' w Berlinie w 'erze' kanclerza Capriviego" (Nauka i Sztuka, 6 (October-November-December, 1947), 42–76; Lech Trzeciakowski, *Walka o polskość miast poznańskiego na przełomie XIX i XX wieku* (Poznań, 1964); Ludwig Bernhard, *Die Polenfrage* (Leipzig and München, 1920).

CHAPTER TWO
1894–1921

From Regional
To National Conflict

In the three decades following the Caprivi era, the approach to, and treatment of, the "Polish question" in Germany underwent a radical transformation. At first, the discussions of the Polish community's strength and the character of the Poles took place mainly in the eastern provinces of Germany with the greater part of the discussion concerned with the former. After the end of the First World War, the Germans viewed the reemergence of Poland not as a reason for increased respect for the Polish people but as a basis for a generalized German denunciation of the Pole.

In the development of the Germans' concepts of the Polish community and the Poles, the timing of significant departures was thus quite unfavorable for Poles. The Germans had ignored the Poles in their century of greatness, not becoming involved with Polish affairs until Poland was collapsing. Then in the postwar period 1918–1921, the average Germans became more aware of the Poles than ever before but at a time when their viewpoint was distorted by defeat. The Germans directed their anger and their bitterness at the Polish community, thus setting the stage throughout Germany for the later myth of the Pole in the Weimar period.

In 1894 this process began with the founding of the *Verein zur Förderung des Deutschtums in den Ostmarken* (The Association for the Strengthening of the German Nationality in the Eastern Marches). For the second time in their history—1848 had been the first—German landowners and townspeople in the eastern provinces had attempted to set the course of Prussian governmental policy.[1] And incidentally, as a result of their efforts, the number of German writings on the Poles increased substantially, thus enabling the researcher of today to gain a clearer concept of how these Germans viewed the Poles.

To understand these German men and women who were popularly called "Hakatists" after the last names of the founders of their society— Hansemann, Kennemann, and Tiedemann—is to understand a contradiction. These people were proud of the power of their industrial German Reich while, at the same time, they were struggling fervently to maintain a superior position for their own German community in the agrarian east. Indeed, the Hakatists openly complained to the world that their position was threatened and that they were forced to defend it. But they saw themselves working only "for the German, not against the Pole."[2] They thus worked continuously for the German community (or, more properly, themselves), regardless of whether or not they received governmental assistance.

The emergence of the Hakatist organization was, in fact, directly connected with an antigovernment demonstration, a pilgrimage to the old chancellor and latter-day critic of the government Otto von Bismarck. First, Hansemann, Kennemann, and Tiedemann organized a journey to Varzin.[3] Then, a week after Bismarck had spoken, these leaders publicly appealed to all German citizens to meet with them in order to organize a new society to fight for the old Bismarckian policies.[4] Even though this action would mean opposing the Caprivi government, it could easily be accomplished. On the day before their call to organize, the Emperor Wilhelm II had sharply criticized his Polish subjects for not being unconditionally Prussian.[5] This royal rebuke, signaling the approaching end of Caprivi's power, made it difficult for his government even to attempt to answer its critics.[6]

Besides, what could Caprivi's government say? In the second half of the 19th century, various groups of men and women had attempted to form mass organizations similar to the *Verein zur Förderung des Deutschtums in den Ostmarken*, but their attempts had been doomed to failure because the bankruptcy of government policy had not then been visible.[7] Even though various organizations had cried out that "the Germanization of our eastern territories is more important than the uncertain friendship of Poles who in their heart of hearts are hostile to Germans,"[8] the politically aware had assumed that the government knew what it was doing. When that confidence had vanished, the Tiedemanns wanted to create an organization to advance their interest independently of the workings of Prussian or Reich policy.

The new is born out of the old, and any new creation will contain a mixture of both the constant and the unique, regardless of whether the creation is material or ideological. In this case, the constant was Bismarck's speech to the Posen pilgrims:

"The struggle is not with the entire Polish people but with the Polish nobility and its followers. . . . I believe that many of you have Polish-speaking workers and servants and thus have come to know that the danger does not emanate from the lower classes ("very true," shouted the Poseners). . . . The masses of the lower classes are satisfied with Prussian administration which is not always perfect but treats them better than that to which they had been accustomed in the times of the Nobles' Republic. . . . Take a look at your neighbors in Upper Silesia; have not both nationalities lived there for centuries in peace, although there are confessional differences there? What is it that is missing in Silesia? . . . I am sorry to say it is the Polish nobility. . . . Earlier, the Poles were a passive power but today, supported by other European powers, they would be an active enemy and as long as they did not have Danzig, Thorn, and West Prussia . . . they would constantly be the ally of our enemy."[9]

Another fundamental contribution to the emergence of the Hakatist movement was based on Tiedemann's attitudes, stemming possibly from his somewhat prosaic past.[10] First of all, in 1881 he came into possession of an estate which, in his estimation, had been very nearly ruined by the former Polish manager. Then, in 1889 when he purchased a neighboring parcel of land, he considered its poor condition to be additional evidence of alleged Polish inability to sustain a viable economy. Could it be, one wonders, that the run-down estates which Tiedemann had observed merely confirmed in his mind all the old legendary stories of Polish inefficiency? Like the Prussian bureaucrats of the 1770s, he had experienced conditions which seemed to confirm all the allegations of Polish inefficiency. And like the Prussian bureaucrats of the 1770s, his experiences seemed to lead him to conclude that the Germans had the right to treat the Poles as objects to be manipulated.

Another characteristic of the Hakatist movement was the absence of racism. The *Ostmarkenverein* accepted for membership Germans of Slavic origin—a Wilmowski, a Hünerasky, a Kownatzki.[11] Since the notion of "blood" remained foreign to this group, this view prevented any easy identification of the Hakatists with the later Nazis. The Hakatists even wished to make Germans out of Poles, and since the later Nazis searched the backgrounds of Germans to make certain that a history of only "German" ancestors was present, it is easy to perceive a basic difference between the viewpoints of the Hakatists and the Nazis.

The Hakatists' basic formulations also contained much else that was traditional. They believed, for instance, that the partitions of Poland had been caused by Polish "maladministration," that the Polish people had no special rights in Prussia, and that the Germans, having brought economic prosperity and culture to the eastern provinces, had a right to these territories.[12] Therefore, the Hakatists advocated that the Prussian government exert itself to the fullest in the securing of the German position. They recommended doing this partly by the purchase of Polish lands throughout the eastern provinces.[13] But there was something new in their vehement insistence that the threat posed by the vigorous and successful activities of the Polish community had been underestimated for too long.

This vehemence of the Hakatists, backed by the viability of their thriving voluntary association, interjected a fresh awareness into German assessments of the Poles. Rather than merely repeating previous negative charges against the Poles, the Hakatists attempted to profile the actual dimensions of the challenge posed by the actions of the Polish community. With the formation of the *Ostmarkenverein*, there was, for the first time in forty-five years, a sizable group of Germans looking at the Polish issue with true passion.[14] In a sense, the Hakatists had ironically paid the Poles their greatest compliment. After all, the Hakatists had contended that their organization was defensive in nature because it had to protect the Germans in the east from the Polish threat. Moreover, unlike Bismarck, they were well aware that the Polish problem was more than the challenge of a few nobles and clergy. They had recognized the viability and extreme success of Polish institutions such as the Marcinowski society, the agricultural associations, and the commercial cooperatives. As a token of their respect for these achievements they had demanded uninhibited and immediate emergency measures to defend the German community in the eastern provinces.

One example reveals both their perception of the threat posed by the successes of the Polish community and of the need for energetic counter-measures. The Hakatists had actually opposed the Poles at the prosaic level of insuring the presence and prosperity of a German, not a Polish, veterinarian in this town; a German, not a Polish, doctor in another town; a German, not a Polish, pharmacist in a third town. They were convinced that insuring the permanence of the German community required the presence of German professionals. Yet for decades the Marcinkowski society had provided scholarships for Polish students who became Polish professionals. There were Polish doctors or veterinarians or pharmacists in these same towns. In fact, the Germans in these towns had to rely on the services of these Poles since the Hakatists were usually unsuccessful in their efforts to import German professionals from the central and western parts of Germany. In 1904 the *Ostdeutsche Rundschau* (Bromberg) even demanded that the Prussian government finance German competition in professional activities because "the Poles for the longest time possess in the gigantic fund of the Marcinkowski society such a national treasury."[15]

Actually, at the turn of the 20th century publicists in the east could only disagree as to the extent of the Polish threat of dominating the eastern provinces through a superior communal organization. Wilhelm von Massow, writing about organized Polish boycotts of German merchants, bleakly concluded that "we find taking place not only a pushing back [of the German] but also an economic detachment of the Pole from the Germans."[16] In the following words he summarized his fears that the German position, relative to the Poles, would decline: "The danger—of becoming a Polish land that despite the fact of its belonging politically to Prussia nevertheless appears in its population fully detached from the organism of the state—threatens our entire East and the consequences thereof are obvious."[17] With these words, Massow revealed how great a distance he had moved away from those German writers who had recognized only the political consequences of Polish females. In the two decades following the end of the Caprivi era, many German writers such as Massow had acknowledged not only Polish development but also, in the context of contemporary events, the inappropriate nature of the basic conceptions of a Flottwell.

The recognition of the new era of Polish competition was so widespread, in fact, that it led to the following debate. Waldemar Mitscherlich, a prolific writer on economic and social topics, led an opposition to the pessimistic pronouncements. Regarding the boycotts, he unequivocally asserted that "no Polish economy exists within the Prussian state" and that "the practicality of an economic boycott all the way down the line of economic life is a utopia."[18] He also claimed in 1911 that in the period since 1815 more progress had been made by the German community in the east than by the Polish community.[19]

Mitscherlich also reported the opposition of a "complete row of politicians" who attempted to discredit his conclusions.[20] It could be assumed that this opposition involved a certain amount of crass personal interest. After all, the Hakatists could not demand a national defense fund for the eastern provinces if they needed none. It follows that the Hakatists paradoxically had the greatest stake in the credibility of the Polish threat. While others could deny the ability and ridicule attempts of the Polish community to achieve anything lasting, the Hakatists could not. Moreover, they had evidence to support their contentions. This proof was strong enough to convince even the sharper critics of the Poles that the Prussian Polish community was capable of substantial achievement. Moritz Jaffé, for example, had devoted much of his life to studying the history of the city of Posen, and although he took a frankly negative attitude towards his Polish neighbors, his words of 1909 speak for themselves: "They [the Poles] have become sober, thrifty, and diligent."[21] Of course, since he lacked any trace of pro-Polish sentiment, he quickly added that the Prussian Poles lacked many qualities necessary for success in business—speedy comprehension, daring, tenacity. But even so, he found that he had to acknowledge Polish development, even if he believed that the Prussian government deserved the credit for the Posen peasants' climb from "barbarism" to the level of determined, diligent, self-sufficient men.[22]

Despite a complete lack of sympathy for the Polish community, Hugo Ganz, whose 1907 book has been mentioned already, also recorded the accomplishments of the Prussian Poles. For example, he quoted an official to the effect that "earlier one was able to recognize even at a great distance which village or house was Polish and which was German. This has completely changed. The Poles have become diligent, thrifty, and sober."[23] Like Jaffé, however, since Ganz still wanted to play the old Prussian game of belittling the Poles, he quoted a German to the effect that the assimilation of Germans into the Polish community could be traced to the attraction which "the Polish woman exercises on the German."[24] Even though this certainly was primitive reporting for one who knew of the Prussian Polish accomplishments, the coexistence of these two ways of thinking in one book epitomized the problem. Many Germans in the east wanted to accept the old negative clichés about the Poles of a bygone era as current descriptions, but they also recognized the quantity and quality of the successes achieved by the Polish community of the present.

On the other hand, other Germans had totally conceded the advances made by the Poles. Moreover, they were able to draw somewhat uncomfortable conclusions from this evidence. In 1898, Christian Petzt had stated that "an underestimation of the opponent's strength would take a severe revenge on us."[25] In 1900 a Leipzig lawyer communicated the following to the *Kujawischer Boten*: "moreover, it would be a completely vain exertion to [attempt to] germanize the Poles. What the Prussian government has not attained in one hundred years will not be achieved now when the national consciousness of the Pole has grown so mightily."[26] In 1901 the *Landrat* of Bromberg rejected the old belief that the Polish nobles and clergy were responsible for "difficulties" in Polish areas. Noting that the number of estate owners in his district had greatly declined, he concluded that the influence of the noble also must be declining. Furthermore, he reported that the Polish intellectuals had assumed a considerable role in the Polish national movement.[27]

Both the Hakatists and those whom their evidence had convinced became enthusiastic and vocal sources of propaganda, uniquely dedicated to treating Polish organizations as a serious threat. They found it necessary to treat the Prussian Poles cautiously, with the respect due a formidable adversary. In this regard, they stood, ironically, as Prussian opponents of Frederick the Great, Arndt, and Bismarck. And in a sense, they tended to rehabilitate the Poles in German eyes, by producing a new, virile, image for them. At the very least, they created in Prussian society an organization which was compelled to publicize Polish achievements in order to rouse the Prussian government and the German nation sufficiently that they would finance and put into operation Hakatist goals and programs. Therefore, at their peak just before the First World War, the Hakatists had nearly 55,000 members trying to counteract the negative German attitudes toward the Poles of an earlier period. The Hakatists were trying to rally the German nation to a "defense of the German" by stressing the might of the Poles.[28] Paradoxically, however, the later emergence of an independent Poland not only would prove the validity of the Hakatists' views but would cause them—and their audiences—to reverse themselves and deny the Poles' basic worth in an attempt to make the Polish successes seem illegitimate.

In 1894 the government which the Hakatists tried to involve in a campaign of self-defense initially was hostile. But after Caprivi's resignation, the Hakatist influence grew until, four years after their founding, Caprivi's successor in the Prussian government issued an edict. This mandate stated that it was the task of the government to strengthen the German and Prussian consciousness of the population in the east. Further, the Prussian officials, therefore, in addition to their regular tasks, would be ordered to work during their off-duty hours to strengthen German consciousness.[29] This Prussian government, which earlier had forbidden private Polish instruction in Prussian schools, also placed another 100 million marks at the disposal of the colonization commission and also forbade public meetings conducted in Polish. With this decree, the government intended to pave the way for its officials to join the Hakatists.

Some Prussian officials did develop close working relationships with the men of the *Ostmarkenverein*. For example, they informed the Hakatists of professional-level job openings in their communities and requested Hakatist assistance in filling these vacancies with qualified Germans.[30] They then considered candidates who were armed with Hakatist recommendations.[31] These same officials also looked to the *Ostmarkenverein* for subsidies for their professionals who already resided in the eastern provinces. Moreover, they might even hope that the Hakatists could on occasion arrange for such things as the purchase of a drugstore by Germans.[32]

The writings of other officials revealed the impact of Hakatist concepts on at least parts of the Prussian bureaucracy. For instance, in 1901 the *Erster Bürgermeister* of Bromberg wrote:

"As long as the language of a great nation lives, it lives and it naturally desires to have its own political life. This is valid in the fullest extent for the Poles with their 600-year past of a Polish kingdom. Their fight for their own nationality is natural. It is also worthy of praise."[33]

In fact, the *Erster Bürgermeister* respected the Prussian Poles so much that he reached the following blunt conclusion: "Having considered the Slavic movement and its present position, one can not conceal that the prospect for Germans in the eastern provinces is gloomy."[34] Then in true Hakatist fashion he argued for the establishment of a German university in Bromberg because of the vitality of the Prussian Poles. He insisted that the Poles, no matter how worthy a foe, must be defeated by the Germans.

Although the Hakatists had influenced Prussian officials into removing the "Polish question" from the list of officialdom's private concerns to a more public position, they could not control the Prussian government or Reich policy. They could secure local working relationships with bureaucrats and even influence the Prussian government now and then, but they never stirred considerable segments within either the Prussian or the German body politic. The apathy of the German man-in-the-street was their greatest enemy, one which they could not overcome. It was simply a case that German citizens in both Prussia and Germany were confronted with problems of greater importance. Even though the Prussian *Landtag* at times would heed advocates of a "hard" line and vote monies for this or that scheme, Prussia would never consider doing anything, as Puttkammer stated it, "inhuman" or "impossible." Also, not all of the politically aware Germans in the eastern provinces agreed with the Hakatists. In 1911 a petition of Claus von Heydebreck pointed out that "wide circles of our province . . . do not approve of the agitation—which is stirring people up—of the *Ostmarkenverein.*"[35]

Beyond this, there were structural reasons in the larger life of the German empire that explained the governmental inconsistency and inaction at both state and local levels. The German Reich had come into existence with an emperor who was the Prussian king; a chancellor who was the Prussian minister-president; an army which was basically the Prussian army and whose officers came from agrarian, aristocratic circles; a *Reichstag* elected by universal suffrage; a Prussian *Landtag* elected by the propertied classes; and a bureaucracy that, like the army officer corps, came from aristocratic circles. In order for basic, workable policies to be established, all of these elements had to be convinced or neutralized.

In examining the list, one might do well to start with the two personalities, the emperor and the chancellor. Who became emperor and what kind of person he was basically was the result of chance operating within the royal family. Therefore, over the course of several reigns and even at different stages of one reign, as the careers of Frederick William III and Frederick William IV had demonstrated, one could expect these men to hold different opinions and for royal policy to change. A similar process took place with the chancellors because, even though they were in fundamental agreement on governmental policy, each of them had his own emphases. Some paid little attention to the "Polish question" while others devoted many hours to its solution. All this made for a somewhat zigzag course of inconsistent government policy complicated by periodic inaction.

The social composition of the institutions produced a similar result. The army, bureaucracy, and *Landtag* were all dominated by a landed property class which could ill afford an "uninhibited" activity against the Polish community because such a campaign would entail expropriations of landed property, obviously an unwelcome precedent. Further, these expropriations could undermine the entire concept of the inviolability of property. The aristocratic class also needed Polish labor for their estates.[36] Moreover, the leaders of the army, the bureaucracy, and the Prussian *Landtag* sometimes had to negotiate agreements with the German *Reichstag*, which contained many Catholic deputies who refused to approve actions detrimental to the interests of their fellow Catholics, the Poles. All of these factors help explain why an "uninhibited" policy toward the Poles could not be sustained for long and why the Hakatist hopes for intervention to assist the German community in the east were so rudely disappointed.

Instead, government policy changed basically whenever the person of the chief minister changed. While relatively inactive under the administration of Hohenlohe, the government returned to the vigorous anti-Polish policies of Flottwell and Bismarck when led by Bülow, who believed that "in the struggles of nations, a nation is hammer or anvil, victor or vanquished,"[37] Bülow increased the capital of the colonization commission to 625 million marks, forbade the construction of homes for Poles in the eastern provinces, and refused to agree to a Polish successor to the deceased Archbishop Stablewski. Bülow watched unmoved as Prussian war veterans who were Polish were purged from membership in German veteran groups, and he rigorously eliminated religious instruction in Polish from the schools of Posen.[38] He did all of this, to use the Hakatist phrase, to defend the Germans.[39] Of course, he achieved little beyond a school strike by Polish children and a decline in construction which deprived German construction workers of jobs.[40] Bülow's successors had much less of an interest in Polish affairs and thus were relatively inactive. Finally, in 1914 the war cabinet expressed some pro-Polish sentiment by approving a Pole, Dr. Edward Likowski, to succeed Stablewski as the archbishop of Posen-Gnesen.

Despite the uncertain movements of a succession of Prussian governments, the years after 1894, as the activities of the Hakatists signified, represented a new era of public participation in the problems of German-Polish relations. In that period, German writers, journalists, politicians, as well as Hakatists and simple citizens, actively criticized government policy and unabashedly suggested policies of their own. But not all of the suggestions and criticisms were pleasing to the Hakatists. For instance, the renowned publicist Hans Delbrück looked forward to a reconciliation with the Poles despite his refusal to consider a Polish secession from Prussia.[41] The *Ostdeutsche Korrespondenz* questioned the ability of the Prussian educational system to germanize Polish students.[42] Later on, in the Nazi era, a German historian by the name of Wilhelm Münstermann attacked even the basic concept of using the school as a germanizing agent because of the supposed dangers of blood-mixing.[43] Many nationalists deplored the failure of the Prussian government to buy the property of Polish landowners so that German colonists could replace the Poles.[44] Colonization gave rise to yet another controversy—protestantization. Freiherr von Schorlemer had first voiced the slogan "Germanization is Protestantization." The Catholic Center party became convinced of its applicability,[45] and the party remained convinced of the basic truth of the slogan, even though some German Catholics in the east who had felt obliged to separate themselves from the Polish majority had formed their own Catholic societies.[46] Paradoxically, however, some German Protestants supported the Center in its opposition of colonization because they felt that German Catholics too readily fell victim to assimilation within the Polish community.[47] And so the discussion continued at political meetings and in the press, in books and in pamphlets, at clubs and in the corridors of government. The "Polish question" had been moved into the public realm. A second hallmark of the new era also moved to the forefront. A good many of the participants in the public debates of the post-1894 period were impressed by the substantial Polish development in the area of community organization and in the obvious success of the Polish community vis-à-vis the German majority. Of course, even though many Germans were irritated by, or concerned about, the extent of Polish successes, very few between 1894 and 1914 simply dismissed the Poles as human raw material which could endanger the Germans only insofar as it was female. Also there was little of that 18th-century disrespect for the Poles. There were few to claim that the dispatch of two or three German families to each Polish village would ultimately germanize the east. Most contributors to this debate realized that the Germans were in a vicious struggle which they might very well lose—which was, of course, the basic Hakatist premise. Before 1894 these writers, journalists, and politicians had not viewed the Poles as a serious threat, and after 1918 they would no longer be willing to credit the Poles with that much ability. Only in the period between 1894 and 1914, during the age of the *Ostmarkenverein*, did the Germans realistically respect the Poles for their actual accomplishments. To a great extent, then, the writing of this period was "realistic" in describing Polish activity.

Of course, ideas do not simply vanish because a "period" has changed. That the ideas of Arndt, for example, still appealed to German nationalists can be seen in the following conservative statement written in 1907:

"At this point we would also like to bring to your attention that there is nothing more dissimilar in the world than people. Therefore, if nations like the Germans, the Italians, the French, the Anglo-Saxons and others are justified to aspire to national-states, it does not follow that Poles, Czechs or Magyars possess the same right."[48]

Meanwhile, other writers not only refused to admit any Polish capacity for achievement but also sought to discredit or deny the actual Polish successes in order to maintain the image of the utterly incompetent Pole. For example, in 1905 the *Posener Tageblatt* wrote that "certainly these successes have only been made possible by the endless, laborious cultural work of the Prussian government and by the mixture of German blood with the Polish."[49] In 1907 Hugo Ganz reported that "a leading political personality" had claimed that "only through us have they learnt to work and to form a middle class."[50] Other publications, like the *Kujawischer Boten*, discovered new defects in Polish activities. For example, this newspaper alleged that "the Polish press perceives as its most important task unflaggingly to fill the reader day after day with hatred against all that is German."[51]

In order to buttress still further the German claim to the eastern provinces, German publicists reinforced old sentiments with fresh assertions. The Germans in the east, for example, sincerely believed that they had been the first to settle there, and in 1904 Erich Schmidt popularized this assertion. Schmidt's book, although not the first to discuss the dates of respective settlements in the east, nevertheless seemed to confirm the validity of this assertion and was often cited as proof that the so-called "indo-germanic" people had originally settled the areas forming the eastern provinces.[52]

Since 1848 there had been a great deal of discussion in the German community about the Poles as traitors. But why had the Poles been labeled traitors? A newsletter issued on the 200th anniversary of Sobieski's daring military feats at Vienna provides some background for this question:

"Also the Polish part of the population can not know and will not know a greater pride than to be members of the mighty Prussian state and German *Reich,* contemporaries and subjects of our most glorious hero-Emperor and witnesses of his wisdom and justice; a King, whose glory and lustre outshines by far all memories of an irretrievably vanished past."[53]

But the Poles did not follow this pattern. As the *Erster Bürgermeister* of Bromberg, Altkemper, and Massow had reported, the Polish community, instead of renouncing its national identity, cherished it and continually attempted to strengthen it.[54] Thus when the Poles refused to act in their role as German citizens, they were denounced as traitors.

The Prussian bureaucrat could easily find evidence of treason in even the humblest of endeavors. For example, if a Pole had organized a lending library, this would be called treason because, in the words of a Bromberg policeman, the goal of organizing the library would have been to awaken "in the Pole . . . a feeling of a special [Polish] national position" within Prussia.[55] Moreover, if a young Pole traveled on vacation to Russian or Austrian Poland, this was also considered treason because, in the words of Tiedemann, such a trip would weaken those feelings of loyalty to Germany which his schooling had inspired.[56] Also, if a mother with sixteen children or the director of a small hotel "agitated for the Polish cause" or even had "great influence on the women," this activity could be classed as treason.[57]

Interested German writers searched the past for evidence to buttress still further their allegations about the continual and varied acts of treason ascribed to the Poles. And they easily found the reinforcement that they wanted. For example, Heinrich Geffcken called the Polish support of their compatriots in 1830 "the spoiled fruits" of a reconciliation policy.[58] He accused the Poles of having once more betrayed their Prussian benefactors and thus of having committed treason against the state. In 1903 the *Kujawischer Boten* first surveyed Polish demands for independence and then scoffed at any hopes that the Poles would ever reconcile themselves to their assigned role as loyal and submissive subjects of the Prussian king.[59] In 1911 the *Posener Tageblatt* wrote that "history has irrefutably proven many times that each period of such a policy of flexibility has had as a result a flame-up of the Polish national movement, indeed, direct uprisings."[60] The stock interpretation, therefore, was that when the Poles refused to act within the limits of their role as German citizens, they committed treason.

In a serious allegation, but this time against the Germans, the German nationalists charged that the German community in the east was handicapped by serious weaknesses in its state of national consciousness. A Bromberg official testified in 1901 that "every Posener knows how extraordinarily weak has been the development of a feeling of having a home here and how many Germans believe themselves still to be living in enemy territory in a Posen which has been a Prussian province for over 100 years."[61] And in 1905 the *Posener Tageblatt* which also criticized flaws in German nationalism, wrote that "what puts us in a disadvantageous position vis-à-vis the Poles is the lack of a national consciousness on the part of wide German circles and the lack of a feeling of being deeply rooted in native soil."[62] In 1910 Cardinal von Widdern chided the Germans in the eastern provinces for lacking confidence in their own strength.[63] A Prussian government official in 1913 added that, despite experiencing Polish boycotts and other such tactics, these Germans had failed to develop a corresponding "buy German" attitude.[64] Also in 1913 the Bromberg *Regierungspräsident* made an unfavorable comparison between the deep disunity within the German community in the eastern provinces and the united structure of the Polish community.[65] In 1914 the Hakatists simply declared that there were too many Germans who lacked a national discipline.[66]

An official who worked for the colonization commission revealed some of the flaws in the German national consciousness: "but among our German landed proprietors are quite a number who make a sheer business of our national cause and place a pistol to our breast with the demand: buy me out immediately or otherwise the Pole, who has already offered me so much, gets it."[67] The *Posener Tageblatt* described more of the problem: "German men from the best social circles do not shrink before God and the world to prostitute the word of their king."[68] The *Posener Tageblatt* was aroused because these men had sold their estates to the Poles.

However, taking these instances alone fails to support the allegation that the Germans in the east lacked an adequate sense of national consciousness. And obviously, a few instances of selling estates to Poles or the buying of Polish goods cannot be used to tarnish the reputation of an entire community. Still, there were some elements of truth in what these journalists and officials had written. The Poles did seem to be far more dedicated to their national cause than the Germans to theirs. The Poles actively supported Polish community activities and organizations. At the very least, the Poles did not cry constantly that they were not receiving sufficient governmental aid. The German community, on the other hand, while accepting the necessity of Prussian control in the eastern provinces, was quite apathetic when asked to organize in its own defense. This apathy nourished the deep-seated belief by German nationalists that neither the German citizens, including those in the east, nor the Prussian state government was doing enough to assure German dominance in the eastern provinces.

Even so, there were few German publicists who were willing to deny that the German community, no matter how weak its national consciousness, deserved supremacy in the east. In other words, they contended that the flawed German was to be preferred to the incapable Pole. And since, to the publicists, the Pole could only be understood as a peasant or an uncultured fellow who staged an occasional and vicious outburst, rule by the Polish community could only be termed a triumph of "lack of culture" over "culture." What alternatives remained to permit rule by the remnants of the Polish nobility would be to sanction the return of feudalism. So the journalists and officials took the position that the Germans had to rule and that the German, whatever his failings, was urban, rational, middle class, modern. Certainly, they concluded, a modern man should deserve a position of authority over a peasant.

That so few writers dared to object to this conclusion confirmed the attractiveness of this assertion to the German public mind. In fact, before the First World War there was only one outstanding example of the minority view that the Poles deserved to rule themselves. Hermann Wendel, who published in 1908 the most favorable history of the Poles written prior to the birth of the German Democratic republic, began his presentation by defying the so-called "conventional wisdom" of the usual German interpretation of Polish history. That is, he denied that there were defects in the character of the Pole which supposedly had retarded Poland's social development or that these had been responsible for the collapse of Poland in the 17th century and her disappearance from the map in the 18th century. His words rang loud and clear:

"Separated by its geographical position from the land and water routes used by world commerce . . . [and] devastated . . . by external as well as internal enemies, ravaged by dynastic struggles, in a most exposed post on border guard duty for the Occident against the East, open on the flank to attacks by the Prussians, Pomeranians, and Mongolians—how in the world should this land have brought forth blooming cities and a strong middle class. . . ."[69]

To Wendel, therefore, the geographical situation of the Poles and not their character flaws had determined that the Polish state would decline.

Whereas Arndt and Treitschke had held that a study of Polish history revealed an absence of Polish achievement and personal abilities, Wendel redressed this historical interpretation, which bordered on myth, by parading forth a series of Polish achievements beginning with 1683: "It is not an accident," he declared, "that . . . the partitioning of Poland was first seriously considered when the Turkish danger had lost its terror for Europe."[70] Continuing his narrative of Polish history, Wendel next advanced to the 1790s and considered Polish triumphs in the era of the French Revolution:

"They [the Poles] crippled through their heroic resistance the intrigues of the feudal powers allied against France and thus perhaps preserved the city of the revolution from the devastation of fire and sword which the notorious manifesto of the Duke of Braunschweig threatened."[71]

Wendel thus obviously denied the charge that Polish history was devoid of Polish achievements. Moreover, he could only question the motives of those who appeared deliberately to overlook, ignore, or misinterpret the facts he presented.

Moving forward in time sequence, Wendel next reviewed the allegation that the Poles had acted as traitors during the Napoleonic period. In answering this criticism, he quoted Frederick William III's lament of 1798: "it has almost become a proverb among them [Prussian officials] that the normal Pole should only be handled with a whip."[72] Frederick speculated further that it was "no wonder and no real reason for indignation, that the Prussian Pole, flayed until he bled, raised the flag of rebellion, exalting, and shouted with joy for Napoleon as a liberator."[73]

Proudly displaying his political colors as a Social Democrat writing to others in his party, Wendel concluded his study by warning that "as against the military policy, the naval policy, and the colonial policy, the working class leads the fight against the Polish policy and also for reasons of culture, world peace, and the real national interest."[74] Yet Wendel's historical discussion was more than a rehashing of the Social Democratic tradition, because he believed that "the reactionary influence of Russia on Europe today may no longer be broken by means of a Polish buffer state. . . . The rebirth of Poland is only possible through the social revolution."[75] He thus supported the independence and studied the history of Poland not because of its alleged relation to anti-Russian intrigue but because he thought that Poland should be independent and because he valued Polish history. In doing so, he was part of a very small minority because the majority of German historians and journalists writing between 1894 and 1914 refused to view Polish history in its own terms.

The coming of the First World War altered the context within which the debate over a realistic evaluation of the Poles was being waged. Many Germans were curious to see how the Prussian Polish community would react to this war. The Poles, for their part, served when called and caused few problems on the home front. Posen, West Prussia, and Silesia were quiet, and the Poles did not, as some officials had feared they might, act as Russian agents.[76] During the war, there were a few incidents. For example, on April 9, 1917, officials found forty copies of a proclamation which appealed to the Poles for support of their Slavic big brother.[77] But such incidents were obviously insignificant. The Polish areas were generally passive.

As far as the German authorities were concerned, they were anxious to maintain domestic tranquility during this time of foreign upheaval.[78] As a result, they approved the promotion of Likowski to the position of archbishop of Posen-Gnesen. They talked also of restoring an independent

Poland to the map and did finally proclaim an independent Poland on November 5, 1916—but with indefinite frontiers.

Even though the Hakatists were out of favor by this time, they were able to remain active because they had never restricted themselves to being agents of the government. They issued reports on the situation in Prussian Poland as the public debate continued to rage.

For example, the Hakatist report from August 1 to October 31, 1914, concluded:

1. Those Poles who were liable for military service had willingly answered the call to arms. Many of these Polish soldiers fought loyally and courageously.
2. In Posen the civilian Polish population had shown not the slightest trace of enthusiasm for the war.
3. This passivity within the Polish community would have to be taken into account when the war was over and political decisions were to be made.[79]

Later, the Hakatists complained that none of the Polish newspapers ever spoke of "our troops"; instead, the papers used the phrase "the German troops."[80] Also, the Polish newspapers were criticized for never employing the phrases "for the Fatherland" or "on the field of honor."

The question then arose as to what concessions the German and Prussian governments should grant the Polish community. As far as borders of an independent Poland were concerned, the Hakatists contended that the price in men and treasury which the Central Powers had paid to free Russian Poland justified their considering their own interests when it came time to redraw the map of Central Europe and to rearrange it to include on it a restored Polish state.[81] As might have been expected, the Hakatist position commanded much support. Within a week of the 1916 proclamation of an independent Poland, the *Westpreussische Volksblatt* had warned that German security interests must determine the limits of Germany's eastern frontier, while the *Danziger Neuesten Nachrichten* repeated Clausewitz's arguments and warned of the dangers of a Polish irredenta.[82] There was also considerable agreement among German nationalists concerning the need to incorporate border territories into the new German security frontier.[83] Certainly no nationalistic Germans argued for the surrender of Prussian lands.[84] Max Weber had epitomized the feelings of many concerned observers when he wrote in the *Frankfurter Zeitung* that a solution absolutely satisfactory to both the Germans and the Poles was impossible.[85] And the average Germans likely would have added, "so the German interest must prevail."

In domestic affairs the *Ostmarkenverein* demanded that no changes in any of the laws regulating the Poles be considered until after the war had come to an end, while the Posen teachers' society protested against making any changes in school regulations during a world war just to please the Poles.[86] Among the Germans who were less blindly nationalistic, Baron Karl von Puttkammer was arguing that "a people [the Poles] must be governed with love," while Max Weber was pointing out that no one could hope to gain Polish support for the struggle against Russia unless the laws of Prussia were modified.[87] But most German officials agreed that a world war was not the proper setting for changes in domestic legislation. There were relatively few attempts even to change any aspect of the German-Polish relationship within Prussia. In fact, the organization of the German Polish society and the writings of Georg Cleinow constituted the boldest efforts to alter the existing relationship.

Founded in 1917, the German-Polish society was a discussion group which included among its members Hans Delbrück and Wilhelm Feldman. The group also attracted to its sessions such intellectual luminaries as Max Weber and Friedrich Naumann.[88] At the society's meetings, these men discussed the various issues concerning the Germans and the Poles, issues such as the possible emergence of an independent Polish state. On this particular question, Weber and Naumann agreed that the Poles should have their own state but also argued that the Poles should not seek to include Prussian territory. They also wanted any new Poland to leave military affairs in the hands of the German general staff. Bluntly stated, they wanted the Poles to continue to serve as cannon fodder for the Prussian war machine. Finally, the group wanted Poland to respect Ukrainian rights or, in other words, to acquiesce to the creation of a puppet Ukrainian state with borders which would include lands already claimed by Poland.[89] However, the talks collapsed when the Poles objected strenuously, thus demonstrating how difficult it would be to redraw boundaries in East Central Europe.

The contributions of Georg Cleinow were more significant, for he was a man who both made and recorded the history of the eastern provinces. In Cleinow's life history and in his changes in historical interpretation, the reader can discover many of the experiences and motivations of the post-1918 German "expert" on the east. Born in 1873, Cleinow had managed to make a variety of contributions before his death in 1936 just three years before Hitler's rape of Poland. During his varied career, he had edited a journal concerned with eastern affairs. He had served in the government during the First World War and had led two German groups in opposition to the incorporation of Prussian territory in the new Poland. He had formulated a plan in 1919 for the creation of new German states out of Silesia and South Posen and out of East Prussia, West Prussia, and the Netze district.[90] He had directed the seminar on the east in the *Hochschule für Politik* in Berlin. He had published a variety of works, including a bitter book on the German government's alleged betrayal of the east.

In addition to writing many volumes on Russia, he had portrayed historically the Polish community in his impressive *Die Zukunft Polens*, which was published in 1908 and 1914.

In his *Die Zukunft Polens*, published when the idea of an independent Poland seemed absurd, Cleinow exhibited little other than real admiration for Polish achievements within the Russian empire. In 1908 Cleinow wrote that "a completely independent Polish economic territory with its own organization was able to arise and [it] is united with the Russian economic territory almost solely through trading capital."[91] Given this economic situation, Cleinow had perceived two possible roads of development. He concluded that if Polish industry and Russian capital continued to work together, there would be a chance for a reconciliation between the two Slavic nations. But, if the Russian Congress Kingdom Polish industrialists could raise their own capital, they would achieve what some German writers had always feared would happen in Prussia—a Polish economic and social autonomy within an alien empire.[92] Certainly, any observer would have felt obliged to respect such an achievement, and Cleinow was prepared to do so.

Cleinow's *Die Polenfrage vor der Entscheidung*, a 16-page pamphlet, was just as unusual in expressing unabashed respect for Polish achievements. Cleinow presented his formulation in 1918 at a time when German armies had encountered no serious challenge on the eastern front: "The modern contents . . . of the Polish question is accordingly the struggle over the future possession of the provinces East Prussia, West Prussia, Posen, and Silesia."[93] This statement was remarkably pessimistic for a time when most Germans thought the outstanding question in the east was how far toward the east Germany's borders should extend. Cleinow, however, not only probably anticipated a later German defeat but also recognized in the Poles—Prussian, Russian, or Austrian—an extremely capable foe who had tenaciously added advance to advance. He evidently perceived that the Poles were much more serious adversaries than anyone outside the Hakatist camp could ever imagine.

Cleinow respected the Poles and their achievements even more than would the average Hakatists. Just as obviously, he was obliged by the pressure of current events to review the Polish situation and to discard what had become a myth by this time—the belief that flaws in the character of the Pole precluded Polish achievements at any given time or place.

How did Cleinow explain his reasons? "What the Poles have accomplished diplomatically in the last four years is worthy of admiration," he wrote in *Die Polenfrage*, referring here to the resurrection of the "Polish question" as a subject of international politics.[94] Unlike most of his contemporaries, Cleinow realized that the "Polish question" had vanished from the diplomatic conference table during the 19th century because

Polish demands for an autonomous Polish state were impractical. To restore this question to a place of prominence on diplomacy's crowded agenda represented a triumph of no mean proportions. After all, Roman Dmowski had been working in France and Britain to develop both governmental and popular interest in the Polish cause while Ignacy Paderewski had been doing similar promotional work in the United States. And both Dmowski and Paderewski finally were able to gain adherents with sufficient power and influence in these countries to win diplomatic support for Poland, a nation that possessed no state and could raise only a relatively small military force.

Cleinow took note of another, equally significant achievement on the part of the Poles—the uniting of an entire nation behind a political demand. Cleinow had recognized that he was studying an independence movement which commanded broad support among the masses, the support of the middle class, and the support of Piłsudski and his socialists. Ordinarily these three groups would have marched to different tunes. The latter two usually tended to produce weighty manifestos which not only failed to interest the workers and peasants and artisans but also exacerbated their relations with one another. On the other hand, the workers, peasants, and artisans themselves usually cared little for programs. Their chief concern was to try to sense what would add to their well-being. But in the Polish-inhabited territories, whether in the Prussian, Austrian, or Russian areas, all classes of Poles rallied to support the simple cause of independence.

In displaying the greatest respect for Polish economic, diplomatic, and political accomplishments, Cleinow had been able to paint a formidable picture of a community of people who were economically very capable, diplomatically worthy of admiration, and politically united in at least their main goal. He had strongly implied that Germany, threatened by a mighty force, stood on the defensive despite a military success which had thrust German armies deep into Imperial Russia. And Cleinow, far from underestimating the Polish threat, had respectfully traced a clear outline of this German enemy. In fact, one could say that Cleinow added the picture of the Pole as "super foe" to the German collection of basically less favorable images.

For only a fleeting moment, the images of the 1770s and 1830s were forgotten. As in these periods, a new situation was demanding a new image. At the time that Cleinow was writing, the image of a "super foe" could be used to rally Germans to the defense of the Reich. Like the earlier images, this concept of a "super foe" was based on fact, but unlike the earlier images, this one would be forgotten the moment that the situation which had called for its creation had passed into history.

Then the First World War came to an end after consuming millions of people both physically and spiritually. It had caused economic chaos when paper assets lost their value and physical holdings were destroyed. It had caused social dislocation as elites perished and masses demanded concessions as rewards for their suffering. It had resulted in the destruction of four mighty empires—the Romanov, the Habsburg, the Hohenzollern, and the Ottoman. And it had sowed additional seeds of dissension by throwing open the question of borders in vast sections of Europe and the Middle East.

In such a setting, few doubted that an independent Poland—for the first time since 1795 or perhaps even since 1697—would emerge. The Poles, after all, had a very strong claim to independence. First of all, the Central Powers had honored Polish demands by proclaiming an independent Poland in 1916. Secondly, President Wilson of the United States, whose armies and treasury had fought only in the last year of the war and thus were strongest at the end, had demanded independence for Poland. This demand strongly reflected Paderewski's success as a propagandist. Lastly, when the allies of the United States had recognized the right of the Poles to regain their freedom as an independent state, they finally rewarded Dmowski's efforts. It only remained to be decided where the boundaries of this new-old state would be drawn and what would be the relationship between the resurrected Poland and the crushed Germany.

In this situation, at least some Prussian officials had recognized that the times demanded new methods and new approaches. Some also appreciated the fact that the Poles, however they might have been labeled after 1848, were (for the moment at least) equals of the Germans. In one indication of this belated change of attitude, the *Danziger Allgemeine Zeitung* reported in December, 1918, that the government probably would speedily declare null and void all laws which placed the Prussian Poles in a legal status inferior to that of the Prussian Germans.[95] Additional evidence of the shift was provided by the official Helmut von Gerlach, who refused aid to the German minority in the East, which is not what the Prussian government had done in 1848 when it attempted to prevent the establishment of Polish control in its communities. Other officials also were aware that the Poles had the upper hand and must now be appeased. As one official made plain after a round of discussions in Berlin in July, 1919, the Prussian government had no choice but to accept the advent of superiority over formerly Prussian areas and to work for a smooth transition from German to Polish control:

"If we by our actions permit the reproach that we sabotaged the existing bureaucracy during our departure, it would most probably be to the greatest disadvantage of Prussia and Germany as well as the numerous remaining Germans in this abandoned territory and of those Germans who wish to depart."[96]

The political leadership also was obliged to accept the new situation. Having inherited a country which had just lost a world war, the new leaders had no choice but to acquiesce, however much they might have wished to do otherwise. So they bowed to the demands of the victors and signed the victors' peace treaty at Versailles. Under the terms of this treaty, the government was compelled to recognize the independence of Poland; and to recognize Polish boundaries which, in the end included much of Posen, West Prussia, and Upper Silesia; and to recognize the city of Danzig as a "free city" which would not be under either German or Polish state control. The Prussian government was required also to accept a Polish pledge to insure free transit between East Prussia and the rest of Germany, a Polish pledge of supplies of Upper Silesian coal for fifteen years, and Polish assurances that Germans in the new Poland would be protected. Whether the Germans would acquiesce to such a treaty, though, was another question. This was a quarter of a century after the question of German-Polish relations had passed beyond the corridors of Prussian state ministries.

One immediate German answer naturally could be expected to come in the reactions of those Germans living in the eastern provinces. As had been the case in 1848, their response to the proposal of Polish control was "no." During the interval 1918–1919, some had organized and fought the Poles in Posen, although not too successfully. In the Danzig area, many had organized and signed petitions. At least 100,000 Germans had agreed that "Westpreussen muss deutsch bleiben! Westpreussen darf nicht polnisch werden! "[97] These German men and women also had contributed at least 15,700 marks to the cause. Thousands more in Danzig registered their disapproval by signing an *Ostmarkenverein* petition.[98] For its part, the *Vereinigte deutsche Volksräte für Posen und Westpreussen* stated that any transfer of Prussian territory to the Pole would produce an eternal German-Polish national hatred, with all of its unhappy consequences.[99] And after the Prussian state territories had been transferred to the new Polish state, the German refusal to accept Polish control continued. Representatives of the area's various German political parties—National People's party, German Democratic party, German People's party, Social Democratic party, and Center party—advanced a German claim to the new Polish lands. These groups even demanded that postwar Germany retain the provinces of Posen and West Prussia, even if only in token fashion, on its maps. They also unsuccessfully urged that the government further institutionalize the German claim by calling the remnants of the provinces by the names of the provinces and thus remind the younger generation of what had been lost.[100]

As the bitter response of the Posen and West Prussian Germans grew stronger, it was matched by the bitterness of the Upper Silesian Germans as the events in that province followed their bloody course. The specific issue which was igniting passions involved the control over Upper Silesia. While the allies considered this question in their ministries, the local Germans and Poles struggled to settle it with their own forces. In August, 1919, violence flared, with the Germans relying on government troops and the Poles using the strike. As soon as the forces of the sixth German Army put an end to the upheaval, the civilians took over again. One of the things they did was to grant amnesty.

But in some ways the basic tensions of the situation were only intensified by the amnesty. The bitterness on the German side was reflected in the following comments which paraphrase the German view of how the amnesty actually operated: the Upper Silesians who go out after 9 p.m. to plot against the Germans remain unpunished while any Germans who merely show themselves on the street at that time are punished. The Upper Silesians who commit a crime for a political reason remain unpunished while the Germans who protect themselves from crimes are punished. The soldiers who desert to the Poles remain unpunished while the soldiers who defend the Germans are punished. In short, the Upper Silesian German community and the German soldiers in the province believed that all actions beneficial to the Poles were ignored while any actions favorable to the Germans were punished.[101]

This bitterness grew even more intense as a second revolt shattered the Upper Silesian calm in August, 1920. But following the plebiscite of March 20, 1921, the Germans, both in Upper Silesia and throughout the Reich, thought that Upper Silesia would remain within Germany. The contest drew slightly more than 700,000 votes for Germany and a little more than 475,000 votes for Poland. Despite this clear victory by the Germans, the Poles raised objections. In May a third Polish outburst embroiled the province in new controversy. Finally, the League of Nations divided the province between Germany and Poland. And the German Upper Silesians bitterly charged that the division of the province violated the results of the plebiscite, constituting a betrayal of the German community there.

The Germans in the center and west of Germany had also been touched by the bitterness, engendered by this struggle for control in Upper Silesia. Besides the influence of the returning soldiers who talked of their betrayal by the League of Nations' decision, approximately 800,000 Germans left the now-Polish eastern provinces between 1918 and 1923. Coming west, they voiced bitter resentment over lost homes and disrupted lives.[102] They complained of their betrayal in the signing of the Treaty of Versailles and of subsequent Polish actions which made remaining in their homes impossible.[103] They reported how the German officials and the landless Germans had left the east, thus depriving the landed German and the German industrial and commercial middle class of customers and markets for their products.[104] They spread their criticisms of Polish actions and of the Polish character to a broad spectrum of the population. In the end, they and the resentment dominant in the defeated Germany would make persons of Polish nationality a problem, one that the average Germans in Berlin or Leipzig, Bonn or Heidelberg, Hamburg or Kiel could no longer leave to the Prussian government for appropriate action.

Any observer who wishes to understand the subsequent German reaction to the Polish issue must realize how intense was the resentment dominant in the defeated areas, and any student of history must also recognize that the Germans were living in a strange political and military setting. The German armies had been undefeated at least formally when the First World War ended. Despite this fact, Germany, which was as strong after four years of conflict as the combined hostile European powers, was reduced by the disarmament clauses of the Treaty of Versailles to a position of slight power. This powerful and proud nation then stood virtually powerless against the pygmies of Europe and obviously strongly resented them all. But it most bitterly resented the Polish pygmy that drove 800,000 of its German countrymen from their homes in Posen, West Prussia, and Upper Silesia.

Poland's restoration to a place among nations thus presented a bitter challenge to Germany. The very existence of Poland, like the disarmament and reparations clauses of the Treaty of Versailles, epitomized what most Germans regarded as an unfair conclusion to a war they would not acknowledge they had lost. To change these conditions would be to wipe out the consequences of defeat, but to rationalize these conditions would be to deny that defeat had occurred. To achieve the latter, logical explanations were constructed.

Few Germans had thought at all about the Poles in 1890, but by 1921 Germans throughout the Reich were acutely aware of their existence. In 1890 most of the Germans who had thought at all about the Poles had tried to overlook the successful Polish efforts at community organization by concentrating on the past negative assessments of the Poles. By 1921 most Germans were desperately trying to reject the overwhelming contemporary Polish success by returning to the earlier negative images of the Poles. The Germans rationalized their way to the conclusion that these negative qualities had secured the Poles a victory which was therefore illegitimate. In the midst of all the furor, the Hakatist respect for the Poles over the previous two decades was completely forgotten. Those Germans in the eastern provinces who had known of the Hakatist views purposely forgot that they had been warned earlier about Polish capabilities. Partially because of previous ignorance about the Poles by the general population in most of the other provinces in Germany, a strong sense of shock and a revulsion against acknowledging Polish capabilities thus became the prevailing attitudes in the Germany of 1921.

Notes

1. This was the situation which the Germans had to face: the Pole in 1890 constituted a hefty majority of 60 to 65 percent in the Regierungsbezirk of Posen, a bare majority of 50 percent in the Regierungsbezirk of Bromberg, and sizable majority in the Regierungsbezirk of Marienwerder and the Regierungsbezirk of Danzig. They numbered approximately 3,000,000 in all of Prussia.

2. DZA Merseburg, A.b. den "Verein zur Förderung des Deutschthums in den Ostmarken" (Rep. 77, Tit. 1083, Nr. 10, Band 1); statutes of the Verein; Geheimes Preussisches Staatsarchiv, Rep. 30, Nr. 679, Königlich Preussische Regierung zu Bromberg, Acta betreffend: die Förderung des Deutschtums in den Ostmarken. Tiedemann's letter of November 8, 1894, to the Regierungs-Präsident of Bromberg.

3. DZA Potsdam, A.b. die Polen (Nr. 666, Band 10); *Ostrowoer Zeitung*, No. 64, June 2, 1894.

4. DZA Merseburg, A.b. den "Verein zur Förderung des Deutschthums in den Ostmarken" (Rep 77, Tit. 1083, Nr. 10, Band 1). Regierungs-Präsident of Posen's letter of September 23, 1894, to Eulenburg.

5. *Kölnische Zeitung*, No. 177, September 24, 1894.

6. The Staatsministerium recognized its predicament. DZA Merseburg, A.b. die Staatsministerial Sitzungs-Protokolle (Rep. 90a, Abt. B, Tit. 111, 2b, Nr. 6, Band 115), September 25, 1894; and DZA Merseburg, A.b. die Polenbewegung in der Provinz Westpreussen (Rep. 77, Tit. 870, Nr. 47, Adh. A, Band 1).

7. Adam Galos, Felix-Heinrich Gentzen, and Witold Jakóbczyk, *Die Hakatisten* (Berlin, 1966), pp.25–27.

8. *Kundgebungen, Beschlüsse und Forderungen des Alldeutschen Verbandes 1890–1902* (München, 1902), p.5; and Lotte Kaminski, *Die Auseinandersetzung um die polnische Frage zur Zeit der Reichskanzlerschaft des Fürsten zu Hohenlohe-Schillingsfürst* (Hamburg, 1938), p.21.

9. *Hamburger Nachrichten*, No. 220, September 18, 1894; Horst Kohl, ed., *Die politischen Reden des Fürsten Bismarck* (Stuttgart, 1892–1905), XIII, 267–280.

10. Franz Wagner, *Heinrich von Tiedemann zu seinem 70. Geburtstage* (Posen, 1913), p.5.

11. DZA Merseburg, A.b. den "Verein zur Förderung des Deutschthums in den Ostmarken" (Rep. 77, Tit. 1083, Nr. 10, Band 1); statutes of the Verein; Geheimes Preussisches Staatsarchiv, Rep. 30, Nr. 679, Königlich Preussische Regierung zu Bromberg, Acta betreffend: die Förderung des Deutschtums in den Ostmarken. Tiedemann's letter of November 8, 1894, to the Regierungs-Präsident of Bromberg. [Kownatzki, by the way, left the Verein in 1895.]

12. Franz Wagner and Fritz Vosberg, *Polenspiegel* (Berlin, 1908), vi–xvi.

13. Geheimes Preussisches Staatsarchiv, Rep. 30, Nr. 686, Königlich Preussische Regierung zu Bromberg, Acta betreffend: Die deutsche Sorge. Memorandum of January 8, 1907, sent by the Deutscher Osmarkenverein to Bülow.

14. The organization officially became known as the "Deutscher Ostmarkenverein" in May, 1899.

15. Special edition of the *Ostdeutsche Rundschau*, No. 57, 1904 [found at the Geheimes Preussisches Staatsarchiv, Rep. 30, Nr. 679, Königlich Preussische Regierung zu Bromberg, Acta betreffend: die Förderung des Deutschtums in den Ostmarken].

16. Wilhelm von Massow, *Die Polennot im deutschen Osten* (Berlin, 1907), p.55

17. Ibid.

18. Waldemar Mitscherlich, "Die polnische Boykottbewegung in der Ostmark und ihre Aussichten," in *Jahrbuch für Gesetzgebung, Verwaltung und Volkswirtschaft im Deutschen Reich*, 35, No. 3, 1911, pp.59, 64.

19. Ibid., p.83.

20. Waldemar Mitscherlich, *Die Ausbreitung der Polen in Preussen* (Leipzig, 1913), *Vorbemerkung*.

21. Moritz Jaffé, *Die Stadt Posen unter preussischer Herrschaft* (Leipzig, 1909), p.315; in *Geschichte des polnischen Volkes* (Berlin, 1950) Georg Baron Manteuffel-Szoege agreed (p.186).

22. Jaffé, p.320.

23. Hugo Ganz, *Die preussische Polenpolitik* (Frankfurt am Main, 1907), pp.16–17.

24. Ibid., p.31.

25. Christian Petzet, *Die preussischen Ostmarken* (München, 1898), p.19. Thirty-eight years later, in *Die Posener Polen von 1815–1914* (Schneidemühl, 1936), Richard Perdelwitz agreed: "Die Vergangenheit hat gezeigt, dass es falsch war, die Polen zu unterschätzen und zu glauben, sie durch wirtschaftliche oder kulturelle Zugeständnisse zu loyalen preussischen Untertanen machen zu können" (p.122).

26. *Kujawischer Boten*, No. 67, March 21, 1900 [found at Geheimes Preussisches Staatsarchiv, Rep. 30, Nr. 685, Königlich Preussische Regierung zu Bromberg, Acta betreffend: die Stärkung und Förderung des Deutschtums in der Provinz Posen]. In *Geschichte des Deutschtums im Lande Posen unter polnischer Herrschaft* (Bromberg, 1904), Erich Schmidt added: "Die Polen sind in Europa das jenige Volk, das zuerst-schon im Mittelalter-ein volles Bewusstsein seiner nationalen Eigenart in sich ausgebildet und es als sein Pflicht erkannt hat, diese Eigenart gegen fremde Einflüsse zu schützen" (p.280).

27. Geheimes Preussisches Staatsarchiv, Rep. 30, Nr. 701, Königlich Preussische Regierung zu Bromberg, Acta betreffend: Betheiligung des katholischen Klerus an der nationalpolnischen Bewegung. Landrat Bromberg to Oberpräsident Posen of May 21, 1901.

28. See Galos, Gentzen, and Jakóbczyk for various membership statistics pp.18, 24, 57, 145, 194.
29. Geheimes Preussisches Staatsarchiv, Rep. 30, Nr. 679, Königlich Preussische Regierung zu Bromberg, Acta betreffend: die Förderung des Deutschtums in den Ostmarken. Proclamation of April 12, 1898 [copies may be found in Königlich Preussischen Polizei-Direktion zu Danzig Rep. A209, Nr. 120, and Magistrat zu Dirschau Rep. A308, Nr. 447].
30. Geheimes Preussisches Staatsarchiv, Rep. 6B, Nr. 77, Landrats-Amts Meseritzer Kreises, Acta betreffend: die staatliche Unterstützung deutscher Aertze Apotheker, Rechtsanwälte. Letters of Deutscher Ostmarkenverein to Landrat Meseritz of July 28, 1904; July 21, 1905; and January 4, 1906; and Landrat Meseritz to Deutscher Ostmarkenverein of March 17, 1904. Deutscher Ostmarkenverein to Landrat Meseritz of December 7, 1906, mentions a similar request.
31. Ibid. Letters from veterinarians to the Landrat Meseritz of July 21, 1904, August 16, 1904, and September 3, 1904. Geheimes Preussisches Staatsarchiv, Rep. 6B, Nr. 81, Landraths-Amts Meseritzer Kreises, Acta betreffend: Förderung des Deutschtums in der Provinz Posen. Dr. Julius Herz's letter of August 25, 1901, to Landrat Meseritz.
32. Geheimes Preussisches Staatsarchiv, Rep. 6B, Nr. 77, Landrats-Amts Meseritzer Kreises, Acta betreffend: die staatliche Unterstützung deutscher Aertze, Apotheker, Rechtsanwälte. Letters of Deutscher Ostmarkenverein to Landrat Meseritz of July 25, 1906; May 1, 1907; February 27, 1908; and September 29, 1908. Geheimes Preussisches Staatsarchiv, Rep. 6B, Nr. 75, Landrats-Amts Meseritzer Kreises, Acta betreffend: Förderung des Deutschtums. Deutscher Ostmarken-verein to Landrat Meseritz of July 3, 1906.
33. Geheimes Preussisches Staatsarchiv, Rep. 30, Nr. 679, Königlich Preussische Regierung zu Bromberg, Acta betreffend: die Förderung des Deutschtums in den Ostmarken. Memorandum of October 7, 1901.
34. Ibid.
35. Geheimes Preussisches Staatsarchiv, Rep. 30, Nr. 685, Königlich Preussische Regierung zu Bromberg, Acta betreffend: die Stärkung und Förderung des Deutschtums in der Provinz Posen. Petition of July, 1911.
36. Max Weber, *Gesammelte Politische Schriften* (München, 1921), pp.7–30 ("Der Nationalstaat und die Volkswirtschaftspolitik"), and p.95 (*Frankfurter Zeitung*, February 25, 1917).
37. Fürst von Bülow, *Deutsche Politik* (Berlin, 1917), p.255; Walter Günzel, *Die nationale Arbeit der polnischen Presse in Westpreussen und Posen zur Zeit der Kanzlerschaft Bülows 1900–1909* (Leipzig, 1933), p.18.
38. Günzel, pp.11–15; Johannes Altkemper, *Deutschtum und Polentum in politisch-konfessioneller Bedeutung* (Leipzig, 1910), p.97.
39. Bülow, p.269.

40. Geheimes Preussisches Staatsarchiv, Rep. 30, Nr. 688, Königlich Regierung zu Bromberg, Acta betreffend: Förderung des Deutschtums, Königlicher Landrat des Kreises Filelne to Regierungs-Präsident zu Bromberg of February 14, 1910.

41. Hans Delbrück, *Die Polenfrage* (Berlin, 1894), pp.43–44.

42. *Ostdeutsche Korrespondenz*, No. 27, April 3, 1908 [found at Geheimes Preussisches Staatsarchiv, Rep. 30, Nr. 685, Königlich Preussische Regierung zu Bromberg, Acta betreffend: die Stärkung und Förderung des Deutschtums in der Provinz Posen].

43. Wilhelm Münstermann, *Die preussisch-deutsche Polenpolitik der Caprivizeit und die deutsche öffentliche Meinung* (Münster, 1936), p.62.

44. *Posener Tageblatt*, No. 567, December 3, 1905 [found at Geheimes Preussisches Staatsarchiv, Rep. 30, Nr. 685, Königlich Preussisches Regierung zu Bromberg, Acta betreffend: die Stärkung und Förderung des Deutschtums in der Provinz Posen].

45. *Germania*, No. 115, May 22, 1912.

46. Societies of German Catholics were reported by the following sources: *Posener Tageblatt*, No. 445, September 23, 1902; *Ostdeutsche Rundschau* No. 132, June 9, 1903; *Geselligen*, No. 150, June 30, 1903; *Bromberger Tageblatt*, No. 241, October 14, 1903; report of Landrat Schubin to Regierungs-Präsident Bromberg of January 28, 1904. Geheimes Preussisches Staatsarchiv, Rep. 30, Nr. 694, Königlich Preussische Regierung zu Bromberg, Acta betreffend: Agitation des Polenthums. Also the report of Landrat Meseritz to Regierungs-Präsident Bromberg of January 17, 1908. Geheimes Preussisches Staatsarchiv, Rep. 6B, Nr. 91, Landrats-Amts Meseritz, Acta betreffend: deutsche Katholikenvereine. Also see Galos, Gentzen, and Jakóbczyk, p.177.

47. *Vossische Zeitung*, No. 600, December 23, 1906 [found at Geheimes Preussisches Staatsarchiv, Rep. 30, Nr. 686, Königlich Preussische Regierung zu Bromberg, Acta betreffend: die deutsche Sorge].

48. Ernst Hasse, Deutsche Politik (München, 1907), I, Part 1, 122.

49. *Posener Tageblatt*, No. 569, December 5, 1905 [found at Geheimes Preussisches Staatsarchiv, Rep. 30, Nr. 685, Königlich Preussische Regierung zu Bromberg, Acta betreffend: die Stärkung und Förderung des Deutschtums in der Provinz Posen].

50. Ganz, p.13.

51. *Kujawischer Boten*, No. 37, February 13, 1904 [found at Geheimes Preussisches Staatsarchiv Rep. 30, Nr. 696, Königlich Preussische Regierung zu Bromberg, Acta betreffend: Agitationen des Polenthums. Allgemeine Vorgänge].

52. Schmidt, p.10.

53. Geheimes Preussisches Staatsarchiv, Rep. 30, Nr. 693, Regierungs-Präsidial-Registratur zu Bromberg. Acta betreffend: die erneuerten Bestrebungen für die polnische Nationalität. Special issue of the *Wongrowitzer Kreisblatt*, No. 35, September 5, 1883.

54. Geheimes Preussisches Staatsarchiv, Rep. 30, Nr. 679, Königlich

Preussische Regierung zu Bromberg, Acta betreffend: die Förderung des Deutschtums in den Ostmarken. Memorandum of October 7, 1901; see Altkemper, pp.246–247; and Massow, p.60.

55. Geheimes Preussisches Staatsarchiv, Rep. 30, Nr. 696, Königlich Preussische Regierung zu Bromberg, Acta betreffend: Agitationen des Polenthums. Allgemeine Vorgänge. Polizei-Präsident to Regierungs-Präsident of February 5, 1902.

56. Ibid., von Tiedemann's letter of July 21, 1909, sent to the Minister des Innern.

57. Ibid., Städtliche Polizei-Verwaltung (Bromberg) to Regierungs-Präsident of April 17, 1913, and October 25, 1913.

58. Heinrich Geffcken, *Preussen, Deutschland und die Polen* (Berlin, 1906), p.45.

59. *Kujawischer Boten*, No. 304, December 30, 1903 [found at Geheimes Preussisches Staatsarchiv, Rep. 30, Nr. 696, Königlich Preussische Regierung zu Bromberg, Acta betreffend: Agitationen des Polenthums. Allgemeine Vorgänge].

60. *Posener Tageblatt*, No. 405, August 30, 1911 [found at Geheimes Preussisches Staatsarchiv, Rep. 30, Nr. 685, Königlich Preussische Regierung zu Bromberg, Acta betreffend: die Stärkung und Förderung des Deutschtums in der Provinz Posen].

61. Geheimes Preussisches Staatsarchiv, Rep. 30, Nr. 679, Königlich Preussische Regierung zu Bromberg, Acta betreffend: die Förderung des Deutschtums in den Ostmarken. Memorandum of October 7, 1901, on the possibility of a university in Bromberg.

62. Posener Tageblatt, No. 569, December 5, 1905 [found at Geheimes Preussisches Staatsarchiv, Rep. 30, Nr. 685, Königlich Preussische Regierung zu Bromberg, Acta betreffend: die Stärkung und Förderung des Deutschtums in der Provinz Posen].

63. Cardinal von Widdern, *Polnische Eroberungszuge im heutigen Deutschland und deutsche Abwehr* (Lissa, 1913), p.110.

64. Geheimes Preussisches Staatsarchiv, Rep. 30, Nr. 688, Königlich Preussische Regierung zu Bromberg, Acta betreffend: Förderung des Deutschtums. Regierungsrat Schilling in his report of April 7, 1913.

65. Ibid., letter of April 9, 1913, to Oberpräsident.

66. Geheimes Preussisches Staatsarchiv, Rep. 6B, Nr. 76, Landrats-Amts Meseritzer Kreises, Acta betreffend: die staatliche Unterstützung deutscher Aertze, Apotheker, Rechtsanwälte. Deutscher Ostmarkenverein to Landrat Meseritz of March 25, 1914.

67. Ganz, p.17.

68. *Posener Tageblatt*, No. 485, October 15, 1905 [found at Geheimes Preussisches Staatsarchiv, Rep. 30, Nr. 865, Königlich Preussische Regierung zu Bromberg, Acta betreffend: die Stärkung und Förderung des Deutschtums in der Provinz Posen].

69. Hermann Wendel, *Die preussische Polenpolitik in ihren Ursachen und Wirkungen* (Berlin, 1908), p.6.

70. Ibid., p.15.

71. Ibid., p.21.

72. Ibid., pp.25–26.
73. Ibid.
74. Ibid., p.84.
75. Ibid., p.83.
76. Geheimes Preussisches Staatsarchiv, Rep. 30, Nr. 696, Königlich Preussische Regierung zu Bromberg, Acta betreffend: Agitationen des Polenthums. Allgemeine Vorgänge, Ober-Präsident Posen to Regierungs-Präsident Bromberg of November 26, 1914.
77. Ibid., Ober-Präsident Posen to Regierungs-Präsident Bromberg of April 9, 1917.
78. Ibid., Minister des Innern to Regierungs-Präsident Bromberg of February 9, 1917.
79. Geheimes Preussisches Staatsarchiv, Rep. A207, Nr. 601, Landratsamt Thorn, Acta betreffend: die polnische Bewegung im Kreise Thorn.
80. Ibid., report of November 1, 1914, to February 28, 1915.
81. Ludwig Raschdau, *Der Weg in die Weltkrise* (Berlin, 1934), pp.112–113; article of September 9, 1915.
82. *Westpreussischer Volksblatt*, No. 261, November 11, 1916; *Danziger Neuesten Nachrichten*, No. 265, November 10, 1916 [found at Geheimes Preussisches Staatsarchiv, Rep. A209, Nr. 1, Polizei-Präsidium zu Danzig, Acta betreffend: Neuorientierung in der Polenpolitik].
83. Galos, Gentzen, and Jakóbczyk, p.275; Fritz T. Epstein, "Friedrich Meinecke in seinem Verhältnis zum europaischen Osten," in *Jahrbuch für die Geschichte Mittel- und Ostdeutschlands* 3 (1954), 139–141. Also see Imanuel Geiss, *Der polnische Grenzstreifen 1914–1918* (Lübeck and Hamburg, 1960).
84. Erich Matthias, *Die deutsche Sozialdemokratie und der Osten 1914–1945* (Tübingen, 1954), pp.8, 17.
85. Weber, p.94, *Frankfurter Zeitung*, February 25, 1917.
86. *Westpreussische Volksblatt*, No. 252, October 31, 1917; *Danziger Neuesten Nachrichten*, No. 117, May 21, 1917 [found at Geheimes Preussisches Staatsarchiv, Rep. A209, Nr. 1, Polizei-Präsidium zu Danzig, Acta betreffend; Neuorientierung in der Polenpolitik].
87. Baron Karl von Puttkamer, *Die Misserfolge in der Polenpolitik* (Berlin, 1913), p.4; Weber, p.98 (*Frankfurter Zeitung*, February 25, 1917).
88. *Westpreussische Volksblatt* No. 249, October 27, 1917 [found at Geheimes Preussisches Staatsarchiv, Rep. A209, Nr. 1, Polizei-Präsidium zu Danzig, Acta betreffend: Neuorientierung in der Polenpolitik]. Also see Henry Cord Meyer, *Mitteleuropa in German Thought and Action 1815–1945* (The Hague, 1955), p.270.
89. Meyer, p.261.
90. Geheimes Preussisches Staatsarchiv, Rep. 30, Nr. 754, Königlich Preussische Regierung zu Bromberg, Acta betreffend: Neugestaltung der polnischen Verhältnisse. Cleinow's plan was mentioned in a report of the Regierungspräsident Bromberg of June 17, 1919.

91. Georg Cleinow, *Die Zukunft Polens* (Leipzig, 1908), I, 288–289.
92. Ibid.
93. Georg Cleinow, *Die Polenfrage vor der Entscheidung* (Berlin, 1918), p.3.
94. Ibid., p.5.
95. *Danziger Allgemeine Zeitung*, No. 282, December 2, 1918 [found at Geheimes Preussisches Staatsarchiv, Rep. A209, Nr. 1, Polizei-Präsidium zu Danzig, Acta betreffend: Neuorientierung in der Polenpolitik].
96. Geheimes Preussisches Staatsarchiv, Rep. 30, Nr. 753, Band 4, Königlich Preussische Regierung zu Bromberg, Acta betreffend: Der polnische Aufstand und die Ueberleitung an Polen. Regierungspräsident zu Bromberg von Bülow's summary of July 12, 1919, of discussions in Berlin.
97. Geheimes Preussisches Staatsarchiv, Rep. A419, Nr. 1–6, Deutscher Volksrat für Westpreussen und Posen, Werbelisten.
98. Ibid., Nr. 7.
99. Geheimes Preussisches Staatsarchiv, Rep. 30, Nr. 754, Königlich Preussische Regierung zu Bromberg, Acta betreffend: Neugestaltung der polnischen Verhältnisse. Memorandum of the Ministerium des Innern of June 10, 1919.
100. Geheimes Preussisches Staatsarchiv, Rep. 30, Nr. 753, Königlich Preussische Regierung zu Bromberg, Acta betreffend: Der polnische Aufstand und die Ueberleitung an Polen. Joint declaration of June 23, 1920.
101. Bundesarchiv Koblenz, R43/I/117, Reichskanzlei: auswärtige Angelegenheiten. Chef des Generalstabes (Breslau) to Reichswehrgruppenkommando I (Berlin) of November 11, 1919.
102. Jobst Gumpert, *Polen-Deutschland* (München, 1966), p.164; Erich Keyser, *Geschichte des deutschen Weichsellandes* (Leipzig, 1940), pp.172–174; Gotthold Rhode, *Völker auf dem Wege* (Kiel, 1952), p.10.
103. Geheimes Preussisches Staatsarchiv, Rep. 6B, Nr. 186, Landratsamt Meseritz, Acta betreffend: Polen-Aufstand. Petition of West Prussians to Staatsministerium of November, 1921.
104. Ibid.

CHAPTER THREE
1921–1943

The German Myth
of the Pole

The average German's sense of shock over the loss of formerly German provinces to the new Polish state was profound, but it was compounded further by ignorance. Germans had previously heard little and cared less about the Polish community within Prussia. They generally knew very little about such successful Polish community achievements as the agricultural cooperatives, the industrial cooperatives, and the scholarship societies.[1] Then a Polish state sprang to life, and the Germans suddenly feared the power of Poland. They feared that Poland would seize the remaining German eastern provinces by force[2] or that Poland would launch a "preventive war" against Germany.[3] There was also fear that Poland and Lithuania would dominate East Prussia, which was separated by a strip of Polish territory from the rest of Germany.[4] Furthermore, the Germans in the eastern and the other provinces sought an explanation for this new and unpleasant situation. The writers of the day obliged them by elaborating a "Weimar" image of the Pole. They attempted to explain away Germany's defeat and to negate the consequences of that defeat.

In one example, a very hard-working historian, Manfred Laubert, in 1923 wrote in a completely unexceptional manner that "one can not conceive of a European reconstruction and a lasting peace without the territorial restoration of Germany."[5] This sentence was nothing less than a summons to arms. In another book, Laubert and his collaborator termed the battle of Tannenberg (1410) between the Poles and their allies and the Germans a contest between nonculture (the Poles) and culture (the Germans).[6] Laubert thus asserted the superiority of the Germans through the ages and concluded that neither Polish independence nor the Polish control of any former Prussian state territory could be justified on a historical basis.

For that part of the German public that wanted poems and songs rather than historical writing, Franz Lüdtke provided both. In a work that contined his usual combination of nostalgia for the past and a determination to overcome current challenges, he exclaimed:

"Comrade, give me your hands, we want to stand firmly together! If one also destroys us, our spirit will not blow away. Where the Vistula roars and on the beach of the Warthe, we'll be called sons of the holy Eastern Provinces. Proudly we think of the homeland to which we remain eternally close; one day indeed the hour comes and then we are there once again! Where the Vistula roars and on the beach of the Warthe, we weave anew a holy brotherly bond."[7]

Lüdtke essentially repeated Laubert's message in verse, asserting the German right to the formerly German eastern provinces.

The programs of the German political parties in the 1920s conveyed this same message, by the way, as did the various governing coalitions of the Weimar republic. The parties considered as essential a complete or partial restoration of Germany's eastern frontiers. On May 12, 1919, all the parties in parliament had protested the frontiers that were established by the Versailles Treaty, and none of the parties subsequently changed position.[8] Naturally, since the *Reichstag* members belonging to these parties held the vote to confirm or deny the tenure in office of a chancellor and his cabinet, these government officials simply refused to recognize the permanence of the new Polish-German boundary, or even the permanence of Poland. A German government could conduct a trade war with Poland at the same time that it recognized the inviolate nature of its western frontier. The German government would continue to work for Poland's collapse because that policy corresponded to the wishes of the German people who were now anxious to have the German writers and politicians explain away Germany's defeat and to bastardize its consequences.

The army, or at least its noted commander, General Hans von Seeckt, maintained the same opinions as the German people. Seeckt perhaps best summarized the German bitterness of the Weimar period when he demanded that Poland vanish from the map and, in a memorandum, went so far as to predict that it would.[9] In his statement, Seeckt placed great emphasis on the so-called Prussian colonization mission and denounced the reemergence of Poland as the first great defeat for the advance of civilization. He even foretold a communist and then a yellow wave repeating the Polish assault upon the German shield of western civilization.[10]

Despite this atmosphere of emotional and psychological hostility, there were some realistic and objective writers. Ludwig Bernhard, to whom students of German-Polish relations will always be indebted because of his massive *Die Polenfrage*, kept the Hakatist respect for the Poles visible in the 1920s. For example, Bernhard in 1920 wrote that "the organization for struggle of the Poles under Prussian domination is and remains the model *in world history* [italics added] of how a national minority can assert its independent existence and can fortify itself against a far superior state power."[11] Elsewhere Bernhard added that "for the longest time the Prussian Poles possessed in their mighty system of organizations a state within the Prussian state, their own community."[12]

German journalistic interest in and scholarly accounts of the Poles increased dramatically at this time. While most of these writings reflected and reinforced popular prejudices, some of them were objective in their scholarship. In fact, there was a tremendous expansion in the serious study of Poland and the eastern provinces during this period. Albert Brackmann, for example, who became general director of the Prussian state archives in 1929, promoted serious research and studies. His colleagues trained such men as Gotthold Rhode, and the combined achievements of this group laid the foundation for sound, objective West German scholarship after the emotional and psychological resentments generated by the First World War had run their course.

There were areas of coexistence in the realm of everyday material relations not only between the German and Polish communities within Germany but also between Germany and Poland. For instance, German-Polish trade on the international plane assumed some importance.[13] In Prussia some Polish children received religious instruction in Polish,[14] and the Prussian state paid the salaries of some Polish teachers. In November, 1932, a nationalistic German politician could even make the following complaint:

"My last campaign trip also led me into the southern part of the border area. I am shocked at the nature and extent of the Polish agitation which often takes place under the cloak of the confession. Unfortunately, the officials and teachers are not completely free of elements which are well-disposed to the Poles and work for the Polish cause."[15]

On the other hand, it should be noted that the Polish group leaders were dissatisfied. They complained that their community in Prussia had no special treaty providing them with minority protection and that there were too few schools for the scattered Polish families.

But despite these aspects of the German-Polish situation, the bitterness of the Weimar period resulted not only in almost a collective ignoring of the previous Hakatists' respect for Polish communal achievements but also an almost total denunciation of the Poles. Why? Because the Poles were expected to pay the penalty for Germany's defeat in the First World War. In a sense, the bitterness of Weimar had led the German political public opinion to seize upon the old assessments made by Ernst Moritz Arndt as an accurate description of the fundamental and enduring character of Polish nature. Arndt's negative views, which had never been totally absent from German thought, were accepted and elaborated upon during the Weimar period. This was true despite the fact that his assessments were obsolete. After all, in spite of Arndt's pessimism, the Poles had reestablished their state within the European state system.

Since this Weimar elaboration of the 19th-century negative views of the Poles culminated in non-Nazi writings composed after Hitler came to power, it is useful to include in the present discussion the non-Nazi writings which appeared in the period 1933–1945. Indeed, it was only after 1933 that Kurt Lück fully summarized the Weimar image of the Pole.

Lück had led a life which was impressive in its intensity. Born in 1900 and destined to die on the eastern front in 1942, Lück could count among his many accomplishments the publication of encyclopedic volumes, the founding of a German society of university professors in Poland, many years of leadership of a 75,000-man German society *Kredit Luzk*, and military service not only in the struggle of 1918–1919 but also through his final participation in World War II. After his death and the end of the war, historians of the East German state, the German Democratic Republic, accused him of having been the head of a spy ring in Poland.[16] Thus, in death as in life, Lück was a man whose work had generated controversy.

During his lifetime, Lück's published volumes established him as the man who had most painstakingly sketched the dominant interwar German image of the Pole. That image, which was based on 18th- and 19th-century historical facts, sought to resolve both the Poles' victory in reestablishing their state and their concomitant unworthiness to maintain it. But that image was a myth, the substance of which can be seen in Lück's comments:

"In the innermost reaches of the Pole—so far as it has not been transformed by a Prussian education—we find an overwhelming obscurity of thought, whim, feeling, happiness, and enjoyment, in that of the German the ability to proceed according to plan, thoroughness, will, usefulness, work; in the first licentiousness (looked upon by him as "freedom"), a lack of breeding and perseverance, superficiality, an inclination to parliamentarianism, in the second a subordination of the individual to the welfare of the whole, breeding and perseverance, thoroughness as well as an avowal of the principle of rule by the leader."[17]

Lück obviously considered the Germans intrinsically superior to the Poles.

Moreover, Lück maintained further that the Germans were likewise superior to the Poles in the realm of action:

"The German proceeds slowly but considers well and carries out his plans with a sense of order. The Pole on the other hand reflects on many plans at once . . . rushes with great enthusiasm to carry them out but then runs aground often because of a lack of tenacity and endurance. . . . The German is the organizer who puts things in order, the Pole the organizer of disorder. The Pole goes by way of feeling to understanding while for the German the process is reversed—via understanding to feeling. On the attack, the Pole is not a bad soldier—ready to sacrifice himself and daredevilish—but he fails in all deliberation at the necessary technical aspects and can only barely stick it out. He also lacks a sense of time and space. . . . Under German guidance he is a good worker just as he is generally a bad one in freedom (licentiousness). . . . Under foreign leadership his good side is developed."[18]

Lück concluded by portraying what he considered to be the essential difference between the German and the Polish peoples:

"The Germans are a people of the thinker and inventor while the Poles are a people of the storyteller and imitator. The Germans appear to be coarse in their criticism and love of truth. The Poles gladly give and receive polite words and compliments. The average Pole knows all but understands nothing. . . . In all that the Pole says and writes, there is seldom a clear division line between reality and fantasy."[19]

In essence, if Lück could not deny that the Poles had reestablished their state and had incorporated formerly Prussian territories in it, he could cast doubt at least on whether it should have happened and whether the Polish state would endure.

In another long book published in 1943 that was considered scholarly, Lück summarized his views on the proper role in Central Europe that he felt the Poles should take subsequently. After stating that there were two types of Poles, a small minority which listened to reason and accepted German ways, and a large majority which instinctively rejected everything German,[20] Lück continued his comments:

"so it came to the September of 1939 in which the Polish hatred of Germans realized itself in the murder of thousands of innocent Germans, in which however Poland's fate was also finally sealed. The 'myth' was, as so often before, dethroned by the rugged reality."[21]

At this point, it should be noted that what to Lück was a myth—a Polish insistence on Poles deciding the fate of Poland which Lück could only dismiss as an irrational hatred of Germans—was to the Poles "rugged reality." What to Lück was "rugged reality"—the superiority of the Germans—was to the Poles a myth. This difference in perception may well be repeated in other intergroup relationships. In this case, Lück finished with these words:

"Has the Polish people become more mature as a result of these experiences? We do not believe so. Poland was always the promised land of intrigues, myths, and legends hostile to the German. In regard to this, nothing will change in the future. The Great German *Reich* must draw the necessary consequences in the interest of its own security."[22]

Since these words were used to justify mass murder as well as other deeds of oppression, these comments can only be regarded as inhuman. They also reveal how perceptions can be used to rationalize the most brutal of behavior. The moral, if history contains any, might be that humans should be careful of their words and thoughts because their ideas and expressions could be translated by others into action.

With these words Lück had summarized the dominant interwar, non-Nazi view of the Pole, also enunciating the logical conclusion drawn from it. But there was more to this view than just these sentiments. This view purported to trace the actual consequences of the Pole's lack of substance in world history.

The nationalistic publicists who had advanced this view began by contending that since the Pole was incapable of either establishing or maintaining his own state, a Scandinavian called Dago had assumed the Polish name of Mieszko and had founded the first Polish state.[23] Of course, many scholars have contended that the creator of the first Slavic state was a Scandinavian, and there are also many others who are just as certain that Samo, the creator of the first Slavic state, was not Slavic. But to the nationalistic Germans, Mieszko had to have been a Scandinavian. It seemed impossible to the Germans that the Poles could have created their own state.

This low opinion of Polish capabilities failed to improve as the nationalistic German publicists shifted their studies to the medieval period. According to the writer Franz Lüdtke, Boleslaw, who followed Mieszko to the Polish throne, was a non-Pole who gave the Polish nation the obsessive political goal of becoming a Great Power, not through its own strength but by exploiting non-Polish peoples.[24] Many of the German nationalists thought that the first great Polish success had occurred in the Middle Ages when men of German energies brought progress to Poland.[25] And supposedly success had followed success. Dietrich Schäfer called the University of Cracow a German university while he and many others claimed that

Copernicus was a German who, by an accident of place of birth, brought fame to Polish lands.[26] Lück even added that a German, Hannike von Ryge, deserved credit on the Lithuanian side for creating the Polish-Lithuanian Commonwealth.[27]

The German nationalists then complained that the Poles not only failed to appreciate these German achievements but even discriminated against German colonists. As was discussed briefly in Chapter I, the Poles resented the Germans. In Karl Aspern's words, the Poles considered the Germans to be "unwelcomed intruders."[28] So the Poles simply assimilated these "intruders" and assumed responsibility for their own affairs. Of course, in the present age of decolonization, the newspaper reader can readily understand the medieval Poles' apprehension as they witnessed their subordination to a foreign element, but writers of the Schäfer-Lück type took the view that for the Poles to conduct their own affairs amounted to the surrender of the Polish state to forces of confusion and inability. According to a great many German writers, when the Poles not only no longer welcomed German immigration but also greatly restricted the possibilities of an autonomous German community in Poland, they had sealed their doom, with partition an inevitable result.

How then did this school of thought explain the Poles' reemergence as an independent political force in the Napoleonic period? In 1911 Lehmann had looked back a century and credited the Prussians. He contended that from 1793 to 1806 the Prussians had provided the Poles with elements of culture that the Poles used to strengthen their community.[29] Schäfer even implied that a German had inspired the writing of the Polish national anthem, commenting that "an enthusiastic German was able to write 'Poland is still not lost!' "[30] Thus, from Schäfer's point of view, even Poles such as Józef Wybicki would be unable to compose even the Polish national anthem without German assistance.

Lück concurred that inspiration derived from a German source was necessary for the Poles to make substantial achievements. A case in point was Lück's evaluation of Adam Mickiewicz, one of the most prominent 19th-century Polish poets:

"The influences of German literature on the work of Adam Mickiewicz have long since been established. In "Dziady" we find elements from "Werthers Leiden," Schiller's "Amelie," "Jüngling am Bache," and "Don Carlos," further from the novel "Valerie" by Frau von Krudener from which "Gustav" comes. The improvisations of Konrad allow themselves to be compared to Goethe's "Prometheus" and the hunter's song is an imitation from the libretto of Weber's "Freischütz." In "Konrad Wallenrod" we recognize Schiller's republican tragedy, "Die Verschwörung des Fiesco zu Genua". . . . The famous "Oda do Młodości" is related to many poems of Schiller such as the "Ideale" and "An die Freude," the ballet "Świteź" to the "Taucher".... Also one can hear Goethe's lyrical poetry in many poems of Mickiewicz. The "Sonety Krymskie" are animated by "Westöstlichen Divan." "[31]

In short, Lück implied that the works of Mickiewicz would have been impossible without German sources of inspiration. Of course, the literary scholar may object that Lück confused creative influence with slavish imitation and that he ignored Polish and Russian influences on Mickiewicz's work. But for Lück, any similarity between the work of Mickiewicz and that of another author such as Schiller was sufficient cause for him to deny that Mickiewicz had creative powers at all.

Lück had thus attempted to deny the acknowledged creativity of Mickiewicz, naively assuming he could discredit Mickiewicz's abilities merely by demonstrating a similarity between his work and that of a German. This technique of explaining away Polish successes by denying that the Poles themselves could have created whatever body of Polish cultural material had been produced had resulted in a total denial of the creative elements of Polish culture. Käthe Schirmacher wrote in 1923:

"But the Poles? What have they accomplished? What does their literature, art, music weigh on the scale of world history? It is all second-hand without the creative energy of the new, of the pioneer, or the finisher. Each people has to choose between its own culture, foreign culture, and no culture. The Pole destroys foreign culture. He creates none of his own."[32]

Thus, the nationalistic German writers of the period following the First World War fulfilled the mandate which the German public had given them "to explain away" Polish successes and to show how incorrect it was to credit the Polish people with any creative abilities.

When they focused their attention on nonliterary subjects, these nationalistic German writers also explained away the nonliterary Polish successes. Regarding Upper Silesia, Wilhelm Volz wrote that "the forest is Polish and the culture is German."[33] Concerning the land along the Vistula, which flows through Warsaw, Poland's modern capital, Erich Keyser wrote that "there is along the Vistula no monument and no work of art, no canal and no dike, no castle and no church, no city design and no village sketch which have not been created by Germans."[34]

But the most important task was to explain away the restoration of Poland. Walther Recke concluded that the new Poland was merely the product of a series of accidents.[35] Rolf Wingendorf called the new Poland a gift from the heavens that the Poles could not have obtained through their own efforts. Moreover, Wingendorf concluded that since the Poles were not capable of creating their own state, they would be incapable of maintaining the state. Instead, he felt that the state institutions such as the army and the bureaucracy would have to maintain themselves and create whatever unity Poland would have.[36] Furthermore, Wingendorf asserted that the state lacked a principle since it was not a result of Polish actions and ideals, and he claimed that the state would have to oppress national minorities in order to create some unifying principle for the Poles. This oppression thus would help to create a Polish nationalism based on hatred of the foreigner.[37] This, then, was Wingendorf's concept of the new Poland.

Wingendorf's representation of the new Poland was remarkable in its divergence from reality. It revealed how he had transformed historical facts into a myth. Wingendorf was historically correct when he stated that the Poles needed an incredible coincidence—the collapse of two mighty empires at the same time—to achieve a fully independent state. But he was wrong in denying the Poles any credit for this achievement. First of all, from 1795 on, the Poles had kept alive not only their vision of an independent Poland but also the "Polish question." If the Poles had not demanded their independence, fought for it, and skillfully employed their diplomatic assets, the Allies might well have forgotten to resurrect the "Polish question" at Versailles. Secondly, the Poles had organized that state which Wingendorf found to be viable. Lastly, the Poles did not lack for ideas. They had two competing concepts—that of ethnic Poland and that of historic Poland or Poland in its borders of 1772. The conflict between the two accounted for much of the substance of the Wingendorf charge concerning a "Polish struggle against national minorities" as well as his allegation that the Poles lacked a positive focus.[38]

Whatever the reasons for such twisted views, this sort of mythmaking flourished in the descriptions of life in interwar Poland. For example, Herman Rauschning, who was to become president of Danzig's senate in 1933 and who was to flee to Switzerland in 1936, told a tale whose type would become familiar in nationalist writings on almost any former German territory. Rauschning described a Polish meeting which had been held in June of 1921 in the city of Posen. It seems that at this meeting a speaker had risen and told all those present that it had been an error to force the Germans to leave and that the hatred of the Germans which the priests and government had encouraged should stop.[39] Rauschning who reported applause at these remarks, suggested that the Poles really liked Germans and implied that the Poles really wanted Germans back as their masters. While Rauschning's German audience very probably would have liked to accept his account as true and significant, it is doubtful that the Poles in Posen would have truly preferred their old subordination to the Germans. Moreover, many tall tales of this type were circulated after the Second World War. The Poles, it was charged by German nationalists, really did not want the lands east of the Oder—Neisse line. It was alleged that the Poles thought they had stolen these lands and that it had been a mistake to expel the Germans. Yet a quarter of a century's experience has demonstrated the falsity of such stories.

At this point it is clear, then, that the German nationalistic writers had constructed a myth of the Pole in which the Pole was credited with no independent or self-governing capabilities. Yet these writers did find substantial drives and capabilities in the Poles that they regarded as significant even if they deplored them. These authors did consider the Poles as something more than, at best, incapable, dependent creatures.

These German nationalists found much in the Poles that to their minds was vile. Käthe Schirmacher, whose work was quoted earlier, commented in 1926 that "the Poles are a bestial people . . . still not satisfied after their robberies against the German."[40] Others among these nationalist historians and journalists not only agreed with her but also joined in spreading the message to all who would listen.

Karl Schöpke, for example, looked as far back as 12th-century writings for evidence of Polish bestiality. He found it in a quote from the priest Helmond who had asserted that "the Czechs and the Poles to be sure are brave in battle, but in plundering and robbing they display the most extreme cruelty."[41] Lüdtke added more historical events to buttress this allegation of Polish bestiality. He referred to "barbaric cruelty" by the Poles at the battle of Gilgenburg at the turn of the 15th century.[42] Lüdtke and Laubert also aided the building of this negative stereotype by labeling the murder of Protestants at Thorn (in 1724) as a characteristic example of Polish cruelty.[43]

The stereotype of the brutal Poles was traced further. The accusation of Polish bestiality in the present was supported not only by writers but also by average citizens. For example, in 1921 a group of Upper Silesia exiles complained to the *Reichskanzler* of Polish brutality in the struggle then raging over the future of their province.[44] In a 1930 letter to the chancellor, an officers' association likewise expressed bitterness over the Poles' "war of annihilation" against the German community in Poland. This group also feared that the Poles would attack East Prussia next after liquidating the German community within their borders.[45] It is apparent that this charge of Polish brutality seemed to be accepted by a great many types and groups of Germans, ranging from historians to writers, and exiles to army officers.

The German nationalists discovered another Polish quality that they considered equally undesirable—the ability to hate. The German nationalists seemed able to discover this hatred by the Poles in all places and at all times. For instance, when the Bromberg police inspected Polish songbooks in May of 1918 in accordance with their regular work schedules, they found the presence of what they reported as a "national hatred."[46] Actually, what they had found was a strong devotion by the Poles to the Polish national cause. However, such a devotion was accounted by most German nationalists as "hatred" of the Germans. The way in which some German writers managed to develop this theme is interesting since many German nationalists contended that the Polish press was responsible for the development of this "hatred." As a matter of fact, these Germans did not think that the Poles were capable even of hating without instruction. Indeed, Walter Günzel and Berthold Wiegand had attributed the 1906 school strike in Posen to the work of the Polish press.[47]

Upon reflection, it can be seen that these claims blended easily into the image already developed of the incapable, wild, and bestial Pole who was unable to create anything lasting but who could burst out in a fit of rage and display the utmost cruelty. This allegation that the Pole needed the press to stir up his brutal nature was necessary to support Grolman's and Bismarck's claim that the average Pole was a man who cared little for the "national" cause and thus had to be goaded into action by agitators. Therefore, it is obvious how the existence of Polish mass hatred and the claim of Polish passivity can be made to fit together. Moreover, this completed portrait was coherent because it was a description of the peasant who was a rough human being not only unable to better himself but also subject to wild outbursts of fury.

The German nationalistic writers continued to stress the peasant image by emphasizing the Poles' religious devotion since traditionally a peasant people believes in religion. Laubert had even called the Poles the Spaniards of the east.[48] The Pole's commitment to Catholicism and his resultant "Catholic mission" also were supposed to demonstrate the truth of Friedrich Schinkel's assertion that "every religious nationalism necessarily has an aggressive tendency."[49] Schinkel added also that the Poles had felt a special inner compulsion to conquer their neighbors because they wished to make them Catholic—which he implied also meant turning them into Polish Catholics. To Germans like Laubert and Schinkel, religion thus had transformed the Polish peasants into crusaders.

Not content with making these assertions, some German nationalists extended their assumptions by contending that when the Poles finally won their own independence, they would immediately desire to rule other peoples.[50] In fact, the *Tägliche Rundschau* in 1920 equated the intensity and fanaticism of what it had termed Polish "imperialism" with the disturbances brought on by a mental disorder,[51] and Laubert had concurred.[52]

Once again the German writers sought to trace the unfolding of this trait in history. Laubert began, appropriately enough, with Mieszko, with whom he considered that Polish imperialism had originated.[53] Laubert's work also asserted that this imperialism had been strengthened by Miesz-ko's successor Bolesław.[54] Then the Jagiellonian dynasty replaced the Piasts, and as Lück put it, a Polish "Drang nach Osten" began.[55] The Poles polonized the Lithuanians, White Russians, and Ukrainians. In the words of one author, the Poles gave notice to the world that they "are given to take no notice [of the wishes] of the minorities."[56] In the words of the minister of the interior in 1919, "we indeed know from historical as well as practical experience how ruthlessly the Poles do violence to members of other nations who have been handed over to their power."[57] He was at that time describing the kind of Polish action taking place in the territories that were to become part of the new Polish state.

To the Germans, their experiences in this transfer of sovereignty in the eastern provinces during the interwar period seemed to confirm not only that the Poles were bestial but also that they were motivated by a religious imperialism. During the First World War Schäfer lamented that the Germans' 600-year residence in the east meant nothing to the Poles, who continually treated them as second-class citizens,[58] but the Germans truly became second-class citizens when the war ended. Indeed, over three-quarters of a million of them fled westward. In their eyes Poland had become a "typical robber-state."[59] Other Germans, reflecting the anxieties of this experience, reported that Poland planned further robberies. Friedrich Wilhelm von Oertzen, a critical German commentator, observed that a Polish priest in an ethnically mixed area was quietly polonizing his spiritual flock. This priest had allegedly told a family that had no strong national feeling but intended to send its children to a German school that "because you do not want to accustom yourself to using Polish, you are worse than a Bolshevik."[60]

There is one further point that needs to be reemphasized. No matter how many successes the Poles achieved in reestablishing their state, most Germans still refused to recognize that the Poles should be granted a reputation as a competent people and thus be permitted any real freedom of action. They believed, as Adalbert Forstreuter put it in 1940, that "the existence of Poland as a state had continually rested on the weakness of one of the two neighbors."[61] Since both the Soviet Union and Germany had been weak in the 1920s, he considered that Poland had been permitted to enjoy an "unhistorical" existence. Therefore, as Erich Marcks had noted in 1920, Poland had become "this most unnatural state."[62] Clearly implied was the view that, if Poland wished to continue to exist and hoped to become a "natural" state, it would have to recognize the limits of that role and become the puppet of one or the other of the two immediate neighbors.

But in the eyes of most German observers, Poland had failed to acquiesce to the logic of its geographical position. For example, Lüdtke called

Poland a "vassal" of France,[63] and Recke recognized Poland as "the most important part in the French system of an eastern barrier against Germany."[64] Laubert likewise looked at the new Poland but saw only "the old French policy of encirclement, only not merely political but also economic."[65] Then when Poland fell in 1939, Wilhelm Schüssler imagined that "the English-French military camp on the Vistula is annihilated."[66] In the eyes of these Germans, Poland had disregarded its geographical limitations and thus deserved to perish.

The Germans were convinced both before and after 1918 that they knew how the Poles should act, and when the Poles did not conform to German expectations, the Germans accused them of folly and even treason. Some writers like Rudolf Haider even considered this "Polish treason" to be natural.[67] After all, he argued, was not treason the weapon of the weak? Had not Adam Mickiewicz in his "Konrad Wallenrod" confirmed the truth of this assertion? Therefore, although that man of the minority Helmut von Gerlach condemned this way of thinking, most writers simply expected the Poles to submit and, without too much thought, called it treason when they did not.[68]

This then was the image of the Pole during the time of German bitterness. Nationalistic German writers had created the image of a man who refused to follow his assigned geographical and historical role. The writers had tried to picture the Pole as an incapable peasant who needed the firm leadership of the German community. These German writers had really believed that the Pole was a peasant. They were also sure that he had all of the peasant's characteristics, ranging from a lack of culture to a lack of ability, from a religious fervor to wild outbursts of a suppressed bestiality. Some might even attribute to him the peasant's ingratitude and lack of loyalty. And these writers asked, as had Arndt, how could such a man be included among the significant figures in world history? Since the answer obviously was that he could not be, they were enraged that the Poles controlled territories that formerly were German. And they were certain that they had demonstrated the injustice of the loss of these territories to Poland's control.

At this point, it would be well to discuss the image of the German—especially the inhabitant of the eastern provinces—that was developed by the German publicists. Just how did these nationalistic German politicians, authors, and newspapermen assess the stake of the German people in the issue of control over the German-Polish borderland?

As far as the German interests were concerned, it was widely believed by most Germans who discussed political affairs at all that the dispute over possession of the Baltic coastline had resulted in "a struggle for existence" between the German and the Polish peoples.[69] It was believed further that the Polish view stemmed from a Polish resentment against the German people, a hostility that had become permanent when the Teutonic Knights cut Poland off from the sea.[70] The German people had also expressed a permanent interest in controlling the land along the Baltic connecting East Prussia with the central German lands. The German position remained constant from Frederick the Great's policy towards Poland in the 1770s to Clausewitz's rejection of an independent Poland a half century later and further to the dispute over Danzig in the 1920s and 1930s. If there were a choice possible between Polish access to the sea and the contiguity of German state territory so the argument went, then the choice must be made in accordance with German state interests.

Even granting that there was a German interest present in the question of territorial links along the Baltic, some skeptics of this claim of an eternal German-Polish hostility wanted to know if there were any other reasons for Germany to become involved with the east. A Pole named Feldman had answered "no" in a work he had published claiming that in an age of considerable population growth Germany's interest should be focused on the colonial world.[71] Unfortunately for his purposes, however, most of the German nationalistic writers disagreed with this view.

The nationalists stated that security was a major reason for Germany to be involved in the east. Seven years before the First World War, Ernst Hasse had written that Germany needed at least her current borders for a measure of security. Then after the war, Erich Marcks wrote that Germany's reduced borders were "impossible."[72] Both of these writers would have agreed that concepts of security could be reflected in frontier lines in terms ranging from the optimum military border—the frontier that would serve as the best possible defensive line against a Russian attack—to the minimal defensive line necessary for the safety and prosperity of the Germans. While Hasse and Marcks might not have agreed precisely on what constituted the optimum German frontier, they both agreed that the pre-1914 frontier was the minimal German border.

The struggle over security, however, did not have to be restricted to military strategy. In 1913 a Prussian bureaucrat asserted that the contemporary nationality strife throughout Europe was actually a struggle over food supplies.[73] If this contention were accepted, then the need for security would demand that a nation control its own food supply. And as Helmut von Gerlach reported, the province of Posen was an important source of potatoes, grain, and sugar.[74] Although Gerlach himself refused to use this observation to argue for war with Poland, many German nationalists were agreed that the renewed German possession of the lost eastern provinces would, as Richard Nitschke contended in 1940, help to "guarantee the accessibility of food to the German people."[75]

There are other meanings ascribed to security. It could mean a nation's ability to live according to its own national customs and preferences. For example, the Hakatist journal *Die Ostmark* contended that many people failed to realize a very important reason for continued German control of the eastern provinces. They failed to recognize that the agricultural east was needed to maintain an equilibrium within Germany—in order for the agrarian community to stay in balance with the industrial west.[76] In other words, they did not see that if the eastern agricultural provinces were lost, Germany's internal balance between eastern Prussian agricultural provinces and western Rhenish industrial provinces also would be lost. If this were to happen, *Die Ostmark* feared that Germany's unique national life would disappear.

For these reasons that were related essentially to defense or security, German nationalists considered it necessary to maintain the German position in the east. They all wanted to defend their people and their society from an external economic and military attack and from a violent internal transformation. But other German nationalists looked at the east from a more aggressive perspective.

These Germans saw the eastern provinces—indeed, all of East Central Europe—as an area in which the German people must fulfill their destiny. They shared an almost mystical conviction that the German people had tasks to perform in the east. For example, in 1904 Erich Schmidt had projected the medieval movement of Germans to the east as basically a fulfillment of German destiny.[77]

Other German writers expressed pride in previous German accomplishments in East Central Europe. In fact, in 1939 Wilhelm Schüssler attributed the development of the area to German actions.[78] Schüssler stated that the medieval German colonists in Poland were instrumental in bringing the fruits of civilization to the area and pointed out that these colonists had engaged in peaceful settlement.[79] He emphasized that these Germans had carried no sword, had killed no enemies, and had violated no laws. Instead they had prospered through their own labor and had earned what they possessed. Perhaps it was to impress upon the schoolchildren the "German" qualities of Poland and other areas of East Central Europe that schoolteachers in the 1930s were instructed to emphasize the German feats of medieval colonization.[80]

This idea that the German achievements had established a German claim to territories in the east led to the assertion that the Germans deserved to play the decisive role in the provinces they controlled because they had formerly brought culture to barbaric areas such as Posen or West Prussia. Laubert, for example, wrote that Prussia had splendidly fulfilled her cultural mission in the east and that the Germans, through the actions of the Prussian state, had earned a moral right to a lasting possession of the eastern territories.[81] Ilse Rhode likewise asserted the Germans' moral right to these possessions in the east because they were the bearer of culture and the mainstay of the area's economic life.[82] Max Weber reached the conclusion that economic achievement in West Prussia went hand in hand with the presence of the Germans, while Erich Keyser asserted that the Germans' economic achievements had given them a right to control West Prussia.[83] To state it simply, most Germans were agreed that the German community had accomplished a great deal in the east and that, as Bülow had asserted, these German accomplishments had established a sound German *political* right to the area.[84]

To buttress this claim, German nationalists writers were prepared to cite an entire list of historical specifics—beginning, for example, with the claim that in the 9th century Germans had given the Poles the basic elements of their public and private life, including Christianity.[85] In the medieval period the Germans gave the Poles the Madgeburg law code and an urban life. Later, the writers asserted, the Germans brought the rule of law to Posen and developed an unmatched prosperity in this province.

In the end, it is probable that even many ill-educated men and women throughout Germany came to believe that the Poles were in debt to the higher German culture. And they wondered why the Poles had proven to be so ungrateful. Likewise, it is probable that the average Germans believed that the German presence was needed to maintain an adequate culture in the east. Perhaps this was why it was possible for a Nazi functionary to declare after the defeat of Poland in September, 1939, that "the land must quickly receive once again its old face of high culture."[86]

Despite the way the Nazis used this sentiment in justifying Hitler's attack on Poland, it should be noted that many Germans throughout Germany and especially in the eastern provinces sincerely believed that German achievements had given the Germans a moral right to retain and even expand their position in East Central Europe. Moreover, they based this judgment on realities. The province of Posen enjoyed a more efficient administration under Prussian rule than it had under the Poles. The Prussian Germans enjoyed a higher standard of living than the Poles did. And in proportion to their numbers, the Germans on the whole belonged more to the "employer" category, while the Poles belonged more to the "employee" category.[87]

Furthermore, many journalists and historians have repeated Schmidt's assertion that the Germanic tribes had preceded the Slavs who did not come until the 6th century A.D. Indeed, some writers even elaborated upon Schmidt's claim of the initial Germanic settlement. Franz Lüdtke, for example, wrote of "northern tribes" being in the area by 3000–2000 B.C.[88] Erich Reimers stated that Indo-Germanic or Indo-European tribes were established there by 2000 B.C.[89] Kurt Tackenberg placed Germanic tribes in the area by 500 B.C.[90] And some historians and writers were inspired to make even greater claims. Karl Schöpke placed Germanic tribes in all of eastern Europe, including the Ukraine, White Russia, and Rumania.[91] However, all agreed that the first appearance of the Slavs had occurred only after the restless Germanic tribes had moved against the Roman Empire.[92]

There existed, then, among those nationalitic Germans throughout Germany who were interested in these eastern provinces, a strong and well-buttressed sense of being in the right. Utterly convinced of the strength of the German claim to rule in the east, they brooked no questioning of that claim. They were outraged whenever their claim was denied, even if it were only ignored through disinterest. Ironically, nowhere was this more true than in their relationship with their fellow countrymen. When confronted by the lack of concern by the average Germans, or the too-busy government officials, the nationalists felt an overpowering sense of shock.

For example, in 1940 Berthold Wiegand, reflecting on the prewar period, recorded that "at that time, the totality of German public opinion could not understand the Polish problems and the danger of the Polish agitation."[93] Another author wrote that "the echo in that nation remained weak, where it did not ring hostile and mocking."[94] Laubert commented that "the German people bears its rightful measure of guilt for the catastrophe."[95] He also contended that "for the majority of Germans, the east was constantly a detestable foster-child."[96] And Franz Lüdtke made what was, for a German nationalist, the damning admission that "for the West German, the eastern provinces counted as Polish; in reality, they have never been Polish."[97]

As this comment by Lüdtke indicated, not only did most western- and central-area Germans ignore the east, but some Germans even belittled the German heritage there. In 1938 a German writer reflected this disparagement in his comment that "for centuries in Germany, one had looked upon the eastern provinces as unimportant, lacking in culture, and reactionary."[98]

The German nationalists uncovered other obstacles to a strong German position in the east. One of the major ones was the alleged deficiencies in the Germans, but these were the result largely of the idealized overexpectations of the nationalists. Nevertheless, in Franz Lüdtke's judgment the German community had continually displayed a tendency to permit dissension to undermine its strength and thus had allowed the enemy to triumph.[99] The individual German, as in the case of Nikolaus von Renys at Tannenberg in 1410, could even betray the German cause.[100] According to Laubert, over four centuries later in the 19th century the German was still betraying his cause, this time through an apathy that enabled the Poles to win in communal elections.[101] In 1886 Bismarck had deplored the lack of development of a strong German national feeling.[102]

Another area in which the German nationalists considered their people inadequate was in the field of communications. Kurt Lück had contrasted the respective abilities of the Germans and the Poles to wage campaigns of propaganda and finally had concluded that "the Pole is . . . the born pro- pagandist, not only in personal but also in the great political affairs . . . while the German of the East lacks the oratorical talent to propagate correctly truths and profundities."[103] The irony of this charge is that, if Lück were right, the Germans in the East not only were incapable of defending their position but also were incapable of stating it.

To compound this nightmare of the nationalists, the government did not provide effective assistance when the Germans in the east failed to complete their tasks. Indeed, both the nationalists of the pre-Nazi era and the later Nazis charged that the government was just as incompetent as its people. Laubert, for instance, condemned the government for not proceed- ing according to a plan, for pursuing a zigzag course, and for dilettantish behavior.[104] In 1941 the *Festgabe für Heinrich Himmler* summarized the Nazis' evaluation of the previous German defense against the Poles:

"The German defense against the Polish attack was conducted under unfa- vorable conditions: without a sustaining idea; without a powerful, resolute leadership; without sufficient legal authorizations; borne by a weak popu- lation not prepared to fight."[105]

It could be said that the nation had simply failed to live up to the noble standard that, as the earlier German nationalists had claimed, its earlier achievements demanded. To the nationalists this later turn of events still could not negate the Germans' moral right to govern the east since the Germans' achievements in the area kept that claim strong regardless of whatever failings the Germans might have had. Yet to the nationalists the ugly possibility did exist that the peasant-Pole might use the Germans' failings to rob him of his lands. The Pole might just passively watch the German destroy his own position.

Among the few Germans who did not participate in this nationalistic reaction to Germany's loss of the First World War was Helmut von Ger- lach. During the period 1918–1919 Gerlach had refused to aid those Germans resisting the transition to Polish rule, and during the interwar period he had held membership in the pacifist German League for Human Rights.[106] For these acts, he was denounced in the 1930s and early 1940s as a "so-called German," as "a parasite of the people," and as a state secretary who had forgotten his duties to his own people.[107]

Then he wrote *Der Zusammenbruch der deutschen Polenpolitik*. This book was even more revolutionary than his refusal to aid the German partisans. In effect he challenged the German moral claim to the eastern provinces that was based on superior German achievement:

"Poland was not partitioned because it was incapable of putting its state in order but because it had three mighty neighbors who conducted their affairs according to the principle of "I am big and you are small." Acts of [Prussian] violence have laid the groundwork of Prussian-Polish and later German-Polish relations.[108]

Gerlach further decried the "perfidy" of a Prussian king who had signed a treaty of alliance with Poland in 1790 and then participated in the second partition of Poland in 1793.[109] It was thus the Prussian who had allegedly carried German deeds of violence and disloyalty to the east while the Pole had merely become the innocent victim of Prussian will. According to Gerlach, Prussia had brought to the east only the higher culture of German power politics.

But only rarely was Gerlach's attitude shared by other writers. While Johannes Guttzeit agreed with him, the vast majority of post-1918 historians-journalists-publicists-politicians did not.[110] In 1917 Otto Hoetzsch, for instance, had blamed Poland's decline on the introduction of the elective monarchy.[111] Therefore, what happened in 1772, 1793, and 1795 could only be classified as a mercy killing. This majority view of Polish history was, in effect, considered adequate justification for Prussian actions and, against the lonely voices of Gerlach and his few friends, further suggested that Poland's decline had compelled Prussia to act without any consideration of a neighbor's feelings or past accomplishments.

In the end the vast majority of interwar, non-Nazi writers simply concluded that German rule in Prussia was necessary since the Poles were peasants and the Germans represented culture. And the nationalistic writers came to this conclusion despite the fact that it was based on a myth about the Pole. In 1892 a conference of the Polish intelligentsia had been held in Culm. Moreover, the Hakatists had acknowledged the existence of a Polish middle class before Germany lost the First World War.[112] Even though it was true that the Poles were primarily an agrarian people, that fact in no way allowed a scholar, as opposed to a mythmaker, to overlook the existence of a dynamic and productive Polish urban class.

Yet the nationalistic German writers of the period following the First World War had to overlook the existence of this Polish urban class since the task demanded of them by German public opinion was to explain away Germany's defeat in the First World War and to make illegitimate the consequences of that defeat. And the restoration of Poland was such a consequence. By proclaiming that the Poles were essentially incapable and brutal, these nationalistic writers presented a reason that to them made Germany's defeat seem incredible. Moreover, by asserting that the Germans had a moral right to the formerly Prussian territories which had become part of the new Polish state, these writers presented a reason why

Poland's restoration was also not legitimate—regardless of whatever flaws there might have been in the Germans. Polish achievements had to be overlooked by these publicists and politicians, journalists and historians. The Poles had to be portrayed as incapable and brutal peasants for only in this way could the psychological and emotional needs of the post-First World War Germans be appeased.

As a last point it might be well to pose this mythical image of the Pole against the realistic achievements of the Polish state during the interwar period. The reconstruction efforts included a currency reform, with a stable Złoty following the Grabski financial reform of 1924; and at least a beginning was made in agrarian reform. Industrial development included a projected central industrial district and the development of the port of Gdynia, which had been a fishing village; and educational developments included new and restored universities. There was a strong gain in international respect for Polish cultural life (Paderewski's and Reymont's efforts are only two examples). If Poland had remained essentially rural and if Poland had proved to be much weaker in military and industrial power than either Germany or the Soviet Union, these features were true also of the rest of East Central Europe. But these facts did not prevent either the nationalists or the Nazis from having their own views on the place of Poland in world history and in contemporaneous European politics.

Notes

Note: A Polish discussion of these problems is found in Jan Chodera, *Literatura niemiecka o Polsce w latach 1918–1939* (Katowice, 1969). A North American account of the diplomatic history of this period is found in Harald von Riekhoff, *German-Polish Relations 1918–1933* (Baltimore and London, 1971).

1. Ludwig Bernhard, *Die Polenfrage* (München and Leipzig, 1920), p.90.
2. Geheimes Preussisches Staatsarchiv, Rep. 6B, Nr. 186, Landratsamt Meseritz, Acta betreffend: Polen-Aufstand. Bürgermeister Tirschtiegel to Landrat Meseritz of January 20, 1923.
3. In *Polen-Deutschland* (München, 1966), Jobst Gumpert reported that between 1922 and 1933 there were three possibilities of a Polish attack (p.160).
4. Hans Roos, *Polen und Europa* (Tübingen, 1957), pp.41–42; Erich Keyser, *Geschichte des deutschen Weichsellandes* (Leipzig, 1940), p.167.

5. Manfred Laubert, *Die Verwaltung der Provinz Posen 1815–1847* (Breslau, 1923), p.312. Also see Manfred Laubert, *Eduard Flottwell. Ein Abriss seines Lebens* (Berlin, 1919), *Vorwort*.

6. Manfred Laubert and Clemens Brandenburger, *Polnische Geschichte* (Berlin and Leipzig, 1927), p.40.

7. Franz Lüdtke, ed., *Deutsche Ostmark Liederbuch des deutschen Ostbundes* (Berlin, 1925), p.4.

8. Erich Matthias, *Die deutsche Sozialdemokratie und der Osten 1914–1945* (Tübingen, 1954), p.64; Gustav Stresemann, *Vermächtnis* (Berlin, 1932–1933), II, 172; Carola Stern, *Ulbricht* (Frankfurt am Main and Berlin, 1966), p.53.

9. Friedrich von Rabenau, *Seeckt. Aus seinem Leben 1918–1936* (Leipzig, 1940), p.316.

10. Generaloberst Hans von Seeckt, *Moltke. Ein Vorbild* (Berlin, 1931), pp.56–58.

11. Bernhard, viii.

12. Ludwig Bernhard, *Zur Polenpolitik des Königreichs Preussen* (Berlin, 1923), pp.15–16.

13. Herbert Czaja and Gustav E. Kafka, *Deutsche und Polen* (Recklinghausen, 1960) p.69.

14. Gumpert, p.166.

15. Geheimes Preussisches Staatsarchiv, Rep. 6B, Nr. 77, Landrats-Amts Meseritzer Kreises, Acta betreffend: die staatliche Unterstützung deutscher Aertze, Apotheker, Rechtsanwälte. Abteilung für Kirchen- und Schulwesen to Landrat Meseritz of January 20, 1933, reported Kinkhöffel's observation of November 17, 1932.

16. Felix-Heinrich Gentzen and Eberhard Wolfgramm, *"Ostforscher"– "Ostforschung"* (Berlin, 1960), p.87.

17. Kurt Lück, *Der Lebenskampf im deutsch-polnischen Grenzraum* (Berlin, 1943), pp.54–55.

18. Ibid.

19. Ibid.

20. Kurt Lück, *Der Mythos vom Deutschen in der polnischen Volksüberlieferung und Literatur* (Leipzig, 1943), pp.18–22.

21. Ibid., p.484.

22. Ibid.

23. See p.3.

24. Franz Lüdtke, *Ein Jahrtausend Krieg zwischen Deutschland und Polen* (Stuttgart, 1941), p.51.

25. One example is Rudolf Kötzschke and Wolfgang Ebert, *Geschichte der ostdeutschen Kolonisation* (Leipzig, 1937), p.101.

26. Dietrich Schäfer, *Osteuropa und wir Deutschen* (Berlin, 1924), p.78; Kötzschke and Ebert, p.118; Erich Keyser, *Westpreussen* (Würzburg, 1962), p.13; and Kurt Lück, *Deutsche Aufbaukräfte in der Entwicklung Polens* (Plauen i. Vogtland, 1934), pp.159–262. All concur that Copernicus was a German.

27. Lück, *Deutsche Aufbaukräfte* p.51.

28. Karl Aspern, *Geschichte der Polen* (Regensburg, 1916), p.24.

29. Max Lehmann, *Historische Aufsätze und Reden* (Leipzig, 1911), p.98.
30. *Schäfer*, p.94.
31. Lück, *Deutsche Aufbaukräfte* pp.399–400.
32. Käthe Schirmacher, *Unsere Ostmark* (Hannover and Leipzig, 1923), p.33.
33. Wilhelm Volz, *Die völkische Struktur Oberschlesiens* (Breslau, 1921), p.10.
34. Keyser, *Weichsellandes*, p.132.
35. Walther Recke, *Die polnische Frage als Problem der europäischen Politik* (Berlin, 1927), p.355.
36. Rolf Wingendorf, *Polen. Volk zwischen Ost und West* (Berlin, 1939), p.108.
37. Ibid., pp. 67, 190.
38. Ibid., p.191. Poland had disappeared from the map between 1772 and 1795; moreover, frontiers of this time were not ethnic boundaries. What frontier then should the Poles claim? Those attracted to historical and legal justification pointed out that a claim to the borders of 1772 would be justified since this was the border before illegal acts of aggression resulted in Poland's partition. Those attracted to the new idea of national self-determination wanted frontiers which would include all Poles whether or not they lived on territories within the Poland of 1772.
39. Hermann Rauschning, *Die Entdeutschung Westpreussens und Posens* (Berlin, 1930), p.289.
40. Käthe Schirmacher, *Ostfragen Schicksalfragen* (Stolp, 1926), p.5.
41. Karl Schöpke, *Deutsche Ostsiedlung* (Berlin and Leipzig, 1943), p.22.
42. Lüdtke, *Ein Jahrtausend Krieg*, p.78.
43. Ibid., p.130. Manfred Laubert, *Deutsche und Polen im Wandel der Geschichte* (Breslau, 1921), p.14; Wilhelm Volz, ed., *Der ostdeutsche Volksboden* (Breslau, 1926), p.327 [Laubert authored this particular article in Volz's work].
44. Bundesarchiv Koblenz, R43/I/119, Reichskanzlei: auswärtige Angelegenheiten. Vereinigte Verbände Heimatstreuer Oberschlesier Landesverband: Gross-Thüringen kr. Erfurt to the Reichskanzlei of June 18, 1921.
45. Bundesarchiv Koblenz, R43/I/125, Reichskanzlei: auswärtige Angelegenheiten. Reichs-Offizier-Bund E.V. to the Reichskanzler of November 29, 1930.
46. Geheimes Preussisches Staatsarchiv, Rep. 30, Nr. 696, Königlich Preussische Regierung zu Bromberg, Acta betreffend: Agitationen des Polenthums. Allgemeine Vorgänge. Städtischer Polizei-Verwaltung (Bromberg) to Regierungs-Präsident of May 12, 1918.
47. Walter Günzel, *Die nationale Arbeit der polnischen Presse in Westpreussen und Posen zur Zeit der Kanzlerschaft Bülows 1900–1909* (Leipzig, 1933), p.37; and Berthold Wiegand, *Die antideutsche Propaganda der Polen von 1890* (Danzig, 1940), p.112.

48. Laubert, *Wandel*, p.13.
49. Friedrich Schinkel, *Die polnische Frage als Problem der preussisch-deutschen Nationalstaatsentwicklung* (Breslau, 1932), p.23.
50. Dietrich Schäfer, *Die Neugestaltung des Ostens* (München, 1918), p.16.
51. Bundesarchiv Koblenz, R43/I/118, Reichskanzlei: auswärtige Angelegenheiten. *Tägliche Rundschau*, No. 502, November 3, 1920.
52. Manfred Laubert, *Die preussische Polenpolitik von 1772–1914* (Cracow, 1944), pp.178–179.
53. Laubert, *Wandel*, p.3.
54. Ibid., p.4.
55. Lück, *Lebenskampf*, p.22.
56. Franz Wagner, *Was wird aus unserer Ostmark?* (München, 1918), p.5.
57. Geheimes Preussisches Staatsarchiv, Rep. 30, Nr. 753, Königlich Preussische Regierung zu Bromberg, Acta betreffend: Der polnische Aufstand und die Ueberleitung an Polen. Minister des Innern to Regierungspräsidenten of Allenstein, Danzig, Marienwerder, Bromberg, and Oppeln of June 17, 1919.
58. Dietrich Schäfer, *Das deutsche Volk und der Osten* (Leipzig and Dresden, 1915), p.33.
59. Wilhelm Volz, *Die wirtschaftsgeographischen Grundlagen der oberschlesischen Frage* (Berlin, 1921), p.88.
60. Friedrich Wilhelm von Oertzen, *Polen an die Arbeit* (München, 1932), p.29.
61. Adalbert Forstreuter, *Deutsches Ringen um den Osten* (Berlin, 1940), p.244.
62. Erich Marcks, *Ostdeutschland in der deutschen Geschichte* (Leipzig, 1920), p.59.
63. Lüdtke, *Ein Jahrtausend Krieg*, p.180.
64. Walther Recke, *Versailles und der deutsche Osten* (Hamburg, 1935), p.121.
65. Laubert, *Wandel*. p.30.
66. Wilhelm Schüssler, *Mitteleuropa als Wirklichkeit und Schicksal* (Köln, 1939), p.60.
67. Rudolf Haider, *Warum musste Polen zerfallen?* (Berlin, 1940), p.23.
68. In *Der Zusammenbruch der deutschen Polenpolitik* Hellmut von Gerlach states: "Man hat sich wiederholt auf den törichten Standpunkt gestellt: mit den Polen verhandeln wir nicht, das sind Hochverräter" (p.19).
69. Even such a vigorous opponent of the nationalists as Hermann Wendel in his *Die preussische Polenpolitik in ihren Ursachen und Wirkungen* (Berlin, 1908), used such a phrase in discussing the conflict (p.8).
70. For examples, see Bettina Kronacher, *Der deutsche Lebensraum in der Geschichte* (Frankfurt am Main, 1938), p.74; Dietrich Schäfer, *Das deutsche Volk*, p.19; and Eugen Kalkschmidt, *Deutsche Sendung im Ostland* (Köln, 1936), p.31.

71. Wilhelm Feldman, *Deutschland, Polen und die russische Gefahr* (Berlin, 1915), p.71.

72. Ernst Hasse, *Deutsche Politik* (München, 1907), I, Part 1, 39; Erich Marcks, p.57.

73. Geheimes Preussisches Staatsarchiv, Rep. 30, Nr. 688, Königlich Preussische Regierung zu Bromberg, Acta betreffend: Förderung des Deutschtums. Bromberg Regierungspräsident to Oberpräsident of April 9, 1913.

74. Gerlach, p.13.

75. Richard Nitschke, *Die deutschen Ostgebiete an Warthe und Weichsel* (Breslau, 1940), p.16.

76. *Die Ostmark*, No. 9, September, 1909 [found at Geheimes Preussisches Staatsarchiv, Rep. 30, Nr. 686, Königlich Preussische Regierung zu Bromberg, Acta betreffend: Die deutsche Sorge].

77. Erich Schmidt, *Geschichte des Deutschtums im Lande Posen unter polnischer Herrschaft* (Bromberg, 1904), p.16.

78. Schüssler, p.9.

79. See pp.3–4.

80. Willi Czajka, ed., *Der deutsche Ostraum im Unterricht* (Breslau, 1935), "aus den Richtlinien für den Geschichtsunterricht" [from the Guiding Principles for History Instruction].

81. Laubert, *Polenpolitik*, pp. 176–177.

82. Ilse Rhode, *Das Nationalitäten-Verhältnis in Westpreussen und Posen zur Zeit der polnischen Teilungen* (Breslau, 1926), p.64.

83. Max Weber, *Gesammelte Politische Schriften* (München, 1921), p.10; Erich Keyser, *Die Bedeutung der Deutschen und Slawen für Westpreussen* (Danzig, 1919), p.11.

84. Fürst von Bülow, *Deutsche Politik* (Berlin, 1917), p.258.

85. Laubert, *Wandel*, p.4. In essay after essay in Albert Brackmann, ed., *Deutschland und Polen* (München and Berlin, 1933) there is evidence of Polish debts to German culture.

86. Nitschke, p.14 [Greiser was the speaker].

87. In *Die Ausbreitung der Polen in Preussen* (Leipzig, 1913), Waldemar Mitscherlich states: "Der soziale Aufbau der Deutschen und Polen ergibt ein relativ starkes Uebergewicht der Deutschen in der Unternehmerschicht und eine ausgesprochene Schwäche in der untersten sozialen Klasse, während für die Polen das Entgegengesetzte gilt" (p.178).

88. Franz Lüdtke, *Die deutsche Ostgrenze* (Breslau, 1940), p.2.

89. Erich Reimers, *Der Kampf um den deutschen Osten* (Leipzig, 1939), p.9.

90. Kurt Tackenberg, *Germanen und Slawen zwischen 1000 vor und 1000 nach Beginn unserer Zeitrechnung* (Bonn, 1940), pp.3–34.

91. Schöpke, p.14.

92. In 1882 Max Beheim-Schwarzbach, in *Die Besiedelung von Ostdeutschland durch die zweite germanische Völkerwanderung* had placed Germanic tribes on the Volga. In 1894 Friedrich Seiler, in *Die Heimat der Indogermanen*, had established the end of the Germanic

settlement in middle Russia where the steppe turns into forest. Later, a complication appeared. Other scholars asserted that a Lusatian culture had established itself before either Germanic or Slavic tribes appeared. This discovery though simply recast the old controversy. "Was this Lusatian culture," they asked, "related to the Poles or the Germans? " Professor Kostrzewski of Posen insisted on a relationship to present-day Poles while German writers from Kurt Pastenaci to Bolko von Richthofen to Wolfgang La Baume disputed this contention.

93. Wiegand, Vorwort.
94. Kalkschmidt, p.61.
95. Laubert, *Wandel*, p.26.
96. Laubert, *Polenpolitik*, p.177.
97. Franz Lüdtke, *Sturm über der Ostmark* (Bielefeld and Leipzig, 1927), p.4.
98. Curt Hermann, *Die deutsche Ostgrenze im Wandel zweier Jahrtausende* (Breslau, 1938), pp.15–16.
99. Lüdtke, *Ein Jahrtausend Krieg*, p.22.
100. Ibid., p.81.
101. Manfred Laubert, *Skizzen zur Posener Stadtgeschichte vor 100 Jahren* (Posen, 1940), p.60.
102. *Stenographische Berichte über die Verhandlungen des Landtages*, Haus der Abgeordneten, 1886, I (January 28, 1886), 171.
103. Lück, *Lebenskampf*, p.55.
104. Laubert, *Polenpolitik*, pp.41, 175.
105. *Festgabe für Heinrich Himmler* (Darmstadt, 1941), p.119.
106. Kurt Grossmann, "A Chapter in Polish-German Understanding: The German League for Human Rights," *The Polish Review*, 15, No. 3 (Summer, 1970), p.37.
107. Recke, *Versailles*, p.18; Lüdtke, *Ein Jahrtausend Krieg*, p.162; Wingendorf, p.53.
108. Gerlach, p.5.
109. Ibid.
110. Johannes Guttzeit, *Geschichte der deutschen Polen-Entrechtung* (Danzig, 1927), p.50.
111. Otto Hoetzsch, *Polen in Vergangenheit und Gegenwart* (Berlin, 1917), p.28.
112. DZA Merseburg, A.b. Vereine und Gesellschaften polnischer Zunge (Rep. 77, Tit. 862, Nr. 11, Band 3). Report of Polizeirath Zacher of July 10, 1892. Franz Wagner, *Heinrich von Tiedemann zu seinem 70. Geburtstage* (Posen, 1913), p.7.

The Nazis—
From Friendship to Slaughter

The post-First World War German nationalist writers had attempted to make the loss of formerly Prussian territories to Poland seem illegitimate. They had hoped to manage this by picturing the Poles as brutal and incapable human beings whose historical accomplishments revealed their inferiority to the Germans. However, these writers were merely publicists or literary writers. That is, they had no actual responsibility for ruling over large areas in which Poles lived. Therefore, what these nationalist writers would have done had they had the power to issue edicts in a conquered Poland must remain an open question. On the other hand, that the Nazis did conquer Poland in 1939 and did commit mass murder in Poland is well known. The question arises concerning what was the relationship between the nationalists and the Nazis. Did the German nationalist writers who expressed the bitterness of Germany's defeat in the First World War influence the Nazis to murder and loot in Poland? What responsibility, if any, do these writers bear for Nazi atrocities in Poland?

The importance of this question is underlined by the fact that the Germany of February, 1933, consisted of essentially the same human beings as the Germany of 1932 or the Germany of 1930. But there was an obvious difference. In 1933 the Nazis were in control of the government while leaders of the other parliamentary parties were rapidly losing all influence. But the Germans' bitterness at losing the First World War remained. The poison unleashed by the defeat in the war had not been purged by Hitler's victory. Instead, his government could then channel this bitterness as it saw fit.

What were the Nazi goals? Hitler's government wished to eliminate all independent parties and organizations within Germany and to promote its own program not only in Germany but throughout the world. As a result of the first goal, the *Ostmarkenverein* was liquidated. As a result of the second goal, the Poles became a subordinate issue because Hitler had established almost ten years earlier that the Polish issue would be considered only after more important tasks had been accomplished. In his *Mein Kampf*, Hitler had indicated little about the Poles except that germanization in the 19th century had been a "racial" error and that Poland in the interwar period was acting as a lackey of France.[1] As a result, there was little alternative to treating the Poles cynically in accordance with larger, and more immediate, Nazi goals.

What were these immediate goals? A look at the *Völkischer Beobachter*, the self-proclaimed mouthpiece of the Führer and his party,[2] quickly reveals the nature of these tasks. In reading the newspaper, the present-day scholar would have to agree with the conclusion of the diplomat of 1933 that the Nazis wanted most of all to make credible Hitler's pledges of peaceful conduct toward all groups and nations except, naturally, Jews and communists. "Peace" propaganda was the first concern of the Nazis, especially because they wished to erase the image then current in Germany and Europe of Hitler as an extremist.

When the Nazis began in earnest to develop their "peace" propaganda, they published in August, 1933, an article hailing the signing of a Danzig-Polish accord and labeling this agreement a "step towards a relaxation of tensions."[3] In September *Gauleiter* Forster, professing a desire to settle all remaining points of contention, called for a treaty between Danzig and Poland.[4] In an official interview in October, Hitler assured a British journalist whom he permitted to question him that although the Versailles settlement needed revision, Germany would not go to war with Poland just to change some lines on a map.[5] Then the Nazis scored a marked success when Poland, partly out of a desire to act as a major power independent of France, cooperated in lending respectability to Hitler. Germany and Poland signed a 10-year nonaggression treaty on January 26, 1934. The next day, the *Völkischer Beobachter* celebrated the event as the "first great success" of the Nazis' "peace" campaign.[6] Two years later, the party paper was still calling the treaty an example of the peaceful settlement of international disputes.[7]

At times the *Völkischer Beobachter* considered Poland to be more than a tool for convincing the world of Hitler's reasonableness. The newspaper noted that the countries appeared to have much in common. For example, there was a parallel German-Polish attitude toward their territorial disputes with Lithuania and Czechoslovakia. The Germans had a territorial dispute with Lithuania over the Memel territory and the Poles with Lithuania over Wilno. The Germans had a territorial dispute with Czechoslovakia over the Sudetenland and the Poles with Czechoslovakia over parts of southern

Silesia. Germany and Poland not only were hostile toward the Lithuanian and Czechoslovakian states created in the postwar settlement, but both Germany and Poland also wanted territories that these states either possessed or claimed. Germany and Poland were thus, in a sense, revisionist, both inside and outside of Europe. The *Völkischer Beobachter* even claimed in 1936 that Poland's desire for colonies had brought the Polish state down on the revisionist side in the world.[8]

Germany and Poland also appeared to have a common enemy in the Bolsheviks. An SA man could tell his Polish guests in 1938 that Poland and Germany constituted the bulwark for Europe against the Bolshcviks.[9] Even as late as February 28, 1939, the *Völkischer Beobachter* had praised Poland as a comrade against the "Jewish Bolshevism" and generously recognized that only a long, common border with the Soviet Union precluded Poland's formal entrance into the anticommunist camp.[10]

Besides anticommunism, the two countries had, at least in part, another attitude in common—antisemitism. While this is not to suggest that the Nazi murders of Jews can be equated to the Polish dislike and harassment of the Jews, it is true that the *Völkischer Beobachter* emphasized in its columns such incidents as the bombing of synagogues and shops in Poland.[11] The paper also reported demands of Polish nationalist organizations that the international community finance Polish Jewish emigration.[12] The paper used a black headline with a red underline in reporting the prevention of "Jewish high treason" by the Warsaw police.[13]

On May 26, 1936, the *Völkischer Beobachter's* headline read "Poland on the way to a Führer state." The newspaper periodically, if cautiously, reviewed the Polish progress toward a Hitler-style state.[14] For example, the paper stated that Fascist ideology had played a limited role in Pilsudski's coup of 1926 but that Poland since that time had been developing in a manner more consistent with National Socialist thought.[15] In May, 1934, the *Völkischer Beobachter* had characterized the Polish state as lacking in Fascist orientation. Economically it was developing very slowly, progressing satisfactorily in foreign policy, watching its parliament die, and remaining unconsolidated because of its minorities. Yet in the paper's view, Poland had been freed from the so-called evils of parliamentarism.[16] And, as the paper wrote after Pilsudski's death, the influence of the old soldier would insure the continuation of his program although Poland, since it was not a National Socialist state, was not unifying as effectively as Germany had.[17]

Thus, to the *Völkischer Beobachter*, the Poles were to be congratulated because they were, in the semiofficial eyes of the Nazi party's newspaper, no longer "incapable" or "brutal." In October, 1933, the party newspaper provided another and more immediate reason for respecting the Poles. In a comparison of German armed forces and those of selected third countries

published by the *Völkischer Beobachter*, the figures showed an overwhelming Polish superiority on the land and in the air, which indicated
that Poland had become a serious military factor in Central Europe.[18] In
November the Polish air force again was called a serious threat,[19] and the
paper recognized that such an air force should be praised by a party
controlling a neighboring country. And on a lighter note, the paper reported in December that a soccer match against the Poles which Germany had
won by a score of 1−0 had proved to be the most difficult of the last four
German matches (with Belgium, Switzerland, Norway, and Poland).[20]

After Germany and Poland had signed the nonaggression treaty of January, 1934, the *Völkischer Beobachter* had less reason to publish evaluations of Polish military capabilities. Instead, the paper turned to printing
informative and positive feature stories about Poland. In September, for
example, a group of German journalists ventured to Poland and not only
reported favorably about a land which was moving forward in its reconstruction but also praised Orbis, the Polish travel organization, for its
effective handling of their travel arrangements.[21] In October the *Völkischer Beobachter* called Warsaw a sober city and Poland a country which was
secure against economic crises because of the separation of its rural economy from world trade.[22] The next month a journalist praised not only
Polish graciousness but also the high Polish birthrate.[23] Also in November,
the SA choir welcomed a delegation of Polish visitors to Berlin with the
Polish national anthem, and in December the *Völkischer Beobachter* favorably commented in detail about the musical accomplishments of two visiting Polish artists.[24]

But there were two sides to Nazi public comments. Even though they
promoted friendly relations with Poland, the Nazis also expressed a German resentment stemming from the First World War. For example, on
September 7, 1933, while one story in the *Völkischer Beobachter* reported
an increase of antisemitism in Poland, a second wondered if the Poles were
dreaming of attacking the German port of Stettin.[25] Two weeks later, the
newspaper criticized Polish authorities who had compelled German
children to attend Polish-language schools.[26] Six weeks after that, the
paper complained of Polish harassment of German businesses.[27] After the
signing of the German-Polish treaty of 1934, the *Völkischer Beobachter*
expressed hope for a period of Polish indifference toward the Germans
living in Poland. It wished that the German community could be permitted
to catch its breath after fifteen years of turmoil.[28] But within two years
the paper was again complaining of Polish expropriations of German landed holdings.[29] And later in 1936 it devoted its front page to accounts of
anti-German demonstrations in Gdingen and to assertions that the Poles
wished to polonize all Germans living in Polish Pomerania.[30]

At this point, the reciprocal nature of nationalist demands and government actions should be noted. The nationalistic demands by German or Polish groups were genuine. Yet the respective governments tried to intensify and channel them as objects to be manipulated so that both foreign and governmental policies could be served. The columns of mixed opinion about the German-Polish situation printed in the *Völkischer Beobachter* reflected this interaction of genuine passion and governmental convenience.

This interaction presented the diplomat of the time with an analytical problem. How could a foreign observer know which of the newspaper columns were inserted to placate domestic pressures and which ones were designed to advance governmental policies? Since the *Völkischer Beobachter's* opinions consisted of a mixture of sympathy for the Poles and vehement complaints of a Weimar vintage, it not only failed to provide guidance to foreign observers but also failed to communicate the real attitude of the Third Reich's leadership toward the Poles. Did the party leaders regard the Poles as anything more than unimportant objects to be used as *Staatsraison* dictated?

In order to attempt an answer, it is necessary to return to 1933 to try to uncover what, if any, elements of Nazi doctrine might have surfaced in German thought about the Poles up to 1938. The views expressed at the daily press conferences in Berlin are of interest in this examination. The daily conferences were held at Goebbels' ministry for the "enlightenment of the people and propaganda." Excerpts were dispatched to the chief editors of newspapers not able to send representatives to Berlin. The entire German press thus knew what the government wished to be printed. And on June 8, 1934, the government made it very clear that the press would have to follow its "suggestions." It mentioned in its announcement that any journalist who violated the rules of the conference not only would be excluded from the gathering but also would face legal proceedings.[31]

Four journalists—Karl Brammer, Theo Oberleitman, Fritz Sänger, and Gottfried Traub—were able to preserve their collections of notes from these conferences. These notes are to be found at the *Bundesarchiv Koblenz.* Brammer, by the way, edited the *Korrespondenz Brammer* during the Nazi period while Oberleitman and Traub did not have their own newsletter. Sänger worked for the well-known *Frankfurter Zeitung.* The combined accounts of these journalists, which can be read in the Koblenz archives, enable the researcher to know the government's demands of the press and the semipublic reasons stated for its decrees.

Perhaps the most general but the clearest comment on policy toward Poland comes from Brammer's notes. Brammer had reported that the press was advised on March 15, 1934, that authoritative circles both in the party and in the foreign office did not plan to handle Czechoslovakia in the same way as Poland.[32] It was thus evident either that Poland occupied a lower priority than Czechoslovakia in Nazi planning or that the Nazis genuinely envisioned a different role for Poland than that assigned to Czechoslovakia. However, the instructions to the press failed to resolve this question.

These instructions and other official statements only confirmed what the columns of the *Völkischer Beobachter* had suggested that the Nazis would placate the Poles. For instance, several weeks after Hitler's appointment as chancellor, some Nazi party people had outraged the official Polish representation in Germany. In response, Chancellor Hitler's office promptly assured the German foreign ministry that the Führer would issue a party order prohibiting similar actions in the future.[33] One possible motivation was revealed four days later when the press conference was told that speculation was running rampant in Italian circles that the Poles would occupy East Prussia.[34] Another possible motivation was revealed when the journalists at the daily Berlin press conference were "asked" to refrain from comments which would injure the Polish-Danzig relationship.[35] After all, Germany was still unarmed whereas Poland possessed a decisive military advantage in the Danzig area. Besides, whether motivated by a desire to win Poland for the anticommunist crusade or to save Poland for later destruction, Germany needed peace in the Baltic. The press was even instructed on March 15, 1934, to refrain from printing accounts of Polish measures injurious to the German.[36]

From that time on until 1939, the Nazi government's message remained the same. The *Bund Deutscher Osten*, for example, was obliged to recognize the priority of German-Polish peace at the same time that its representative supported its activities "to defend the German."[37] The *Deutsches Nachrichtenbüro* applauded the German-Polish relationship for providing Europe with an unusual sense of security as well as a model for the peaceful solution of disputes.[38] In February, 1935, the Germans even founded a "German-Polish Institute" in Berlin which offered speech courses and lectures on Polish subjects. More than once Hitler's office approved subsidies of 2000 marks to keep the project financially solvent.[39]

The following actions of the ministry "for the enlightenment of the people and propaganda" substantiated further the Nazi government's determination to remain on good terms with Poland by placating the Poles. In April, 1936, for example, these watchdogs of the press denounced newspapers (located mainly in the eastern border area) which had printed articles hostile to Poland.[40] And all newspapers were reminded by the ministry that in reporting anti-German actions in Poland they had to honor the German-Polish treaty of 1934.[41] Therefore, only the news media that had obtained special permission could publish their accounts of events such as the Polish expropriation of German landed property;[42] even though the press could regret anti-German measures, it was told at the Berlin press conferences to avoid expressions such as the "Polish war of extermination against the Germans."[43] Therefore, when the Polish state was prosecuting some young Germans because they had founded a secret society, the Berlin spokesman of the propaganda ministry instructed the press to express the hope that the Polish authorities would recognize the essentially peaceful motives of these young people.[44] The press was also informed that a newspaper article insulting to Polish religious feeling had necessitated a government apology to the state of Poland, together with a pledge that legal proceedings would be undertaken against those responsible for this "outrage."[45] A *Landgerichtsrat* assured his superior that the expulsion of a visiting Polish Jew from a courtroom should be understood as contempt for the Jew and not for the Pole.[46] The Berlin propaganda authorities further instructed the press to publicize only the "positive" events such as Polish actions taken against communists or Jews and to support the current Polish government.[47] These propaganda officials later announced that they would insist on a prepublication examination of all stories concerning the German minority in Poland.[48]

The Berlin propaganda authorities had demonstrated such zeal to preserve German-Polish friendship that on February 18, 1938, they complained that the German press had followed too completely their instructions to avoid publishing stories which might irritate the government of Poland. They chided the press for completely ignoring, for example, the effects of landed expropriations in Poland. The spokesman for the propaganda ministry then advised the press to mention the effects of such expropriations and authorized a few newspapers to write "cautiously" about the entire problem.[49] In another instance on February 24, 1938, the officials in the local propaganda office at Halle-Merseburg had been so convinced by the Berlin officials of the need to preserve German-Polish friendship that they had the secret police confiscate a newspaper because of the paper's anti-Polish articles. Even though the Berlin authorities reprimanded the local office for its action, this episode demonstrated how far the German government's desire to preserve good relations with Poland had influenced the ranks of the various German bureaucracies.[50]

The propaganda ministry's concern was also evident in its requests that the press praise selected Polish personalities. For instance, at the daily Berlin press conference, the ministry's spokesman asked interested newspapers to celebrate the Polish foreign minister Józef Beck's fifth anniversary in office by hailing his successful efforts to establish good relations with Poland's neighbors. The ministry especially requested that the newspapers praise Beck's establishment of an independent Polish foreign policy.[51] Later, the ministry requested that the German press report favorably on the twelfth anniversary of the Polish president's accession to his office.[52] The ministry even requested that the German press publish favorable accounts of the performances given by a visiting Polish ballet company.[53]

Yet merely documenting German government actions which resulted in the favorable reporting of Polish activities does not demonstrate the motives of the Hitler government. And Brammer's records and those of the other journalists help only in part. In 1936 Brammer suggested that the Führer had signed the 1934 treaty with Poland in order to deprive France of her "natural" ally.[54] Citing the propaganda ministry's statements at the Berlin press conference, Brammer reported that the Danzig compromise had secured Germany's northeastern flank and thereby had made it possible for Germany to move against Czechoslovakia.[55] But these reports fail to reveal what in 1936 Hitler's government had planned for Poland.

Instead, at the Berlin press conferences, all the old stories appeared and reappeared. For example, Professor Theodor Oberländer, who was later to be accused of war crimes by the Poles, warned the Berlin journalists—in tones reminiscent of the Hakatists—that Germany could not afford to underestimate the Polish challenge.[56] Dr. Werner Markert informed these journalists that the state of Poland was form without content.[57] The propaganda ministry was pleased that the Poles had followed a German example while the Latvian German leader asserted that history had shown the Slavs dependent upon the Germans for peace and progress.[58] The old journalistic and scholarly disputes over the national origins of Copernicus and Veit Stoss reoccurred—with the propaganda ministry in Berlin indignantly maintaining the obvious German character of both.[59] Even the old nationalist lament of the prewar period was voiced at these Berlin press conferences when the propaganda ministry criticized the German newspapers for calling the German Upper Silesians "Poles" just because they spoke a Polish dialect.[60]

Since most of the comments made at the Berlin press conferences belonged to the Weimar vintage, the non-Weimar substance of the propaganda ministry's announcements was disappointingly meager. In a demonstration of a parallel German-Polish course, for instance, the ministry's spokesman did mention in March, 1938, that a Polish invasion of Lithuania would precipitate a German occupation of the Memel territories, but this was not a revealing commentary on the German-Polish relationship.[61] Another rather unimportant commentary came when the propaganda ministry requested the press not to support too vigorously Poland's demand for the international financing of the Polish Jews' emigration. As the German government remarked sardonically, Germany and Poland in this respect were export competitors.[62] One illustration of this was the German government's demand, on the one hand, for the deportation of all Polish Jews then residing in Germany, and the Polish government's hesitation, on the other, for taking them back.[63]

Then in January, 1939, the German foreign minister, Joachim von Ribbentrop journeyed to Warsaw to participate in the celebration of the fifth anniversary of the German-Polish treaty. Marking this anniversary, the *Völkischer Beobachter* praised that continuous cross-fertilization which was supposed to have taken place between the Germans and Poles in the borderlands of the east.[64] In February the press received word that when Heinrich Himmler went hunting in Poland, he would hold discussions with the chief of the Polish security police.[65] Also, at the end of that month, the propaganda ministry instructed the press not to publish accounts of anti-German demonstrations in Poland because the old policy of maintaining German-Polish friendship still held sway.[66]

As the first quarter of 1939 came to an end, the ministry of the interior did report that a German official had repeated to a Polish delegation the old clichés of Dietrich Schäter and Manfred Laubert[67] to the effect that the Germans had come east before the partitions, that the Germans had enriched Polish lands.[68] He even added a touch of Kurt Lück with the assertion that the Poles had come to dislike the Germans solely because these outstanding citizens had been elevated to the status of a living example of achievement which the individual Pole had been asked to emulate.[69] Even so, none of this was particularly threatening.

On April 7 the situation quickly changed beyond all recognition. That Poland was to be treated like Czechoslovakia was first discovered by the rank and file of the party on April 7 when the *Völkischer Beobachter's* headline exclaimed that a Polish organization had demanded the conquest of German territories where Poles lived or could live.[70] The news media then began a Czechoslovakia-type (1938) campaign of repetitive stories of Polish aggression and brutality. Then on April 28 Hitler annulled the German-Polish treaty. He said that since Poland had unilaterally violated the treaty which he and the honored Piłsudski had concluded, the treaty's validity had lapsed.[71] In a message to the Polish government, Hitler reiterated that Poland— without having a single reason to do so—had betrayed the treaty with Germany. This betrayal consisted of Poland's alliance with the English and aiding the English policy of "encirclement."[72]

Since German journalists had been given advance warning of a future German-Polish conflict, for them only the exact timing of the clash had been uncertain. And they were thus scarcely surprised at the turn of events. On December 16, 1938, the journalists had been informed at the daily Berlin press conferences that some people foresaw a showdown with Poland by summer. Yet this time, they had been cautioned, might prove to be somewhat premature especially since the exploitation of a favorable moment would play a decisive role in timing the showdown. No one could forecast exactly when such a moment might come.[73] As it turned out, the projections of a summer date proved to be very accurate.

The propaganda content of the "summer campaign" was not exceptional. But one interesting feature was an official insistence by Hitler's government that Poland had betrayed its great founder. On May 5, Joseph Goebbels stressed that Piłsudski, besides being a great soldier, had always been a great realist; and Poland had presumably lost that sense of realism when the state had lost Piłsudski.[74] After Poland had fallen, the *Völkischer Beobachter* reminisced that Piłsudski would never have dreamed of marching to Berlin. Presumably, under the leadership of Piłsudski, Poland had experienced a physical rebirth, but after the death of Piłsudski, it became evident that the new state had not experienced a spiritual rebirth.[75] And after the September campaign in the best tradition of Grolman, Treitschke, and Bismarck, the average Pole was supposed to have said that Piłsudski would never have allowed a German-Polish war.[76]

A propaganda thrust like that employed in the 1938 Czechoslovakian campaign consisted of a series of aggression and horror stories in the mass media. According to the propaganda ministry's spokesman, what the Poles published was "baiting" whereas what the Germans published was "propaganda."[77] Thus, typical stories in the *Völkischer Beobachter* recounted the growth of Polish war-baiting and dwelled on accounts of Polish lust for German lands and acts of horror involving innocent Germans living in Poland.[78] Regarding tactics, the ministry advised Berlin journalists in May to print these stories on the second page without too much elaboration because it was essential that the papers avoid giving the impression that a decisive moment was near.[79] Indeed, on June 8 the government spokesman reported not only the government's determination to settle the Polish issue but also the possibility of a later, localized resolution.[80] But in the meantime, the terror stories were continued in the mass media.

On June 21 the *Völkischer Beobachter* warned Poland that the needs of the English "encirclement policy," and not Polish wishes, would determine Poland's future relations with the Soviet Union.[81] The enthusiastic diversion of this flood of journalistic propaganda into anti-English channels was striking, but the reasons behind it were less clear. At the daily press conference on July 6, the propaganda ministry's spokesman suggested the use of four slogans. Two were "encirclement" and "England fights to the last Frenchman and Pole."[82] Furthermore, on August 3 the press was ordered to use the slogan, "England attempts to stir up Poland against us."[83] Perhaps the Hitler government had a far firmer grasp of its policy vis-à-vis England. Perhaps Hitler's propaganda ministry simply concluded that it could better manipulate a deeper well of German antipathy toward England than could be mustered aginst Poland. And obviously England was the more important foe.

In any event, the summer campaign of propaganda was continued in the news media. The propaganda ministry ordered the publication of stories about Polish terrorizing of Germans.[84] In August the ministry advised the German press that they could print stories about Polish threats against Germany on the first page.[85] Yet on August 11 during the ministry's

Berlin press conference, the newspapermen were cautioned that the most biting tone should be avoided because the tempo of the campaign would have to be increased later.[86] However, by August 18 the campaign had reached such a high pitch that the *Völkischer Beobachter* was asserting that the Poles had already named mayors for German cities which they would attempt to seize.[87] Perhaps all that could be done to increase the pace of the campaign was to state on August 21 that large groups of Polish-speaking citizens of Poland were not really Poles—finally a hint of racism—and that they wished to be freed of the Polish yoke.[88] In any event, on August 29 the people involved in the propaganda campaign concluded that the pressure of events had made the credibility of German claims less significant. At this point, what was more important was victory in the war of nerves against Poland.[89]

Other themes of the August propaganda campaign were significant because they revealed how the Hitler government had employed traditional German images of the Pole to further its own ends. On August 4 the *Völkischer Beobachter* wrote about the traditionally peaceful relationship between Germany and Poland. This relationship, the newspaper asserted (in tones reminiscent of nationalist German writers during the Weimar period), had always benefited the Pole.[90] On August 9 the *Völkischer Beobachter* reminded its readers that German architects, sculptors, and painters, as well as German musicians, had contributed greatly to "Polish" achievements in these fields.[91] On August 20 Dr. Wilhelm Koppen wrote in the party paper's columns that the resurrection of the Polish state had led to a decline in the area's living standards, culture, bureaucratic efficiency, economic achievement, and general organization. In the manner typical of the German nationalist in the interwar period, Koppen went on to contend that the clash between Polish illusions of achievement and actual Polish activity had resulted in an unhealthy tension which made Poland a dangerous source of unrest for all of Europe.[92] On August 22 the newspaper continued its campaign with a traditionally nationalist assertion that the Germans in the 13th century had founded the cities of Poland.[93] On August 26 Wallenstein's 1632 letter was put forward denouncing the Pole's lack of discipline.[94] On the following day, Poland stood accused of having neglected the natural wealth of her western territories and of having proved to be incapable of developing the area's industry.[95] Two days later, Albert Brackmann and his colleagues confirmed once again, in the columns of the *Völkischer Beobachter*, the German quality of the so-called Polish corridor.[96] On August 31 the *Völkischer Beobachter* concluded the month by acclaiming German superiority in the martial arts and denouncing Polish "baiting" and the Polish annihilation of the German community within its borders.[97]

Since the Nazis' party newspaper used so many traditional themes in its

August propaganda campaign, it was appropriate that the issue of the *Völkischer Beobachter* containing Ernst Moritz Arndt's comments on the Poles' essentially worthless character was on the presses at the same time that the armored cruiser *Schleswig-Holstein* opened fire on Polish positions on September 1.[98] The Nazis had skillfully used these traditional negative assessments of the Poles which the name of Arndt symbolized.

Interestingly enough Hitler's government and the Nazi officials were still using the traditional anti-Polish themes of the Weimar period even after the conquest of Poland during the first weeks in September. For example, on September 19, in Danzig, Hitler cried that the Prussian territories which had been given to the Poles after the First World War had owed their cultural development to German creative energy and diligence. He added that the Poles had proved to be incapable of preserving the cultural level which the Germans had created.[99] On September 23 the report of a flight over southern Poland asserted that when the orderly landscape became disorderly, the Polish-inhabited area had been reached.[100] Gustav Freytag had adduced similar "evidence" in the previous century. In November the *Völkischer Beobachter* returned to the tradition of Grolman's and Bismarck's 19th-century negative assessments and again portrayed the Pole as a passive man willing to accept German leadership and incapable of understanding why a war had been fought.[101] In 1940 a *Völkischer Beobachter* social analysis, if slightly modified, again was patterned after 19th-century views of the Poles. The peasant was loyal, but the intelligentsia caused difficulties for the German and produced that often-described Polish "hatred" which had become part of the Weimar myth of the Pole.[102] The *Völkischer Beobachter* also claimed, just as Bismarck had, that the Polish workers appreciated the Germans' just administration.[103] Alfred Rosenberg then wrote in its columns about a Polish hatred caused by the Pole's inferiority complex while Goebbels later termed the Pole incapable of creating a state.[104]

At this point, the question posed at the beginning of this chapter reappears. What was the relationship between Nazi thought and deeds and those of previous German nationalists? In the context of this study, an additional question is raised. Did the Nazi leaders actually subscribe to the Weimar myth of the Pole and act accordingly, or did they merely exploit the Weimar myth of the Pole because the ministry had concluded that the German people would be responsive to such a stream of propaganda? Since a review of the press's writings for the period produced very little evidence with which to resolve this question, it might be concluded from an analysis of these writings that the Nazis had no specific perception of the Polish problem as a separate political and cultural issue.[105] This conclusion, supported by the fact that the Nazi ideology was not at all systematic, leads to still another question. How can the historian explain the Nazis' mass slaughters in Poland if he concludes that the Nazis had no specific concept of the Poles and no special plans for them?

An examination of the pronouncements of the propaganda officials could be expected to provide some assistance in answering these questions. Unfortunately, for the most part these officials preferred to employ tested methods of manipulating public opinion. For instance, one of their methods was to proclaim the cruelty of the Poles and conclude that a "humane" treatment of them therefore would be incomprehensible to the German people.[106] Then in order to make their prediction come true, they would discourage any individual activities such as the collection of old clothing for Polish laborers in Germany.[107] However, since manipulation and revenge are not peculiar to the Nazis, these tricks fail to shed light on Nazi motivation or on the Nazi-German nationalist relationship.

The press instructions by the propaganda officials at the daily Berlin press conferences in October, 1939, offered somewhat more assistance. On October 20 an old theme reappeared. The press officials ordered the newspapermen to mention Poland only in the context of "German order against Polish disorder."[108] On October 24 a new theme appeared at the Berlin news conference.[109] The propaganda ministry spokesman began by ordering the German newsmen to write as little as possible about Poland because such articles on the Poles could be used abroad to harm German interests. They might even provoke an anti-German attitude in American public opinion. But when the government did permit the publication of articles on Poland, the journalists were expected to manipulate and reinforce the "instinctive aversion" that Germans supposedly felt for Poles. In fact, the concept of the Pole was to be linked with the images of the Jew and the gypsy, and all three groups relegated to the category of inferior peoples. Here, then, was a forthright statement that the Nazi government officials recognized a deep-seated anti-Polish feeling in the Germans and proposed to channel it to their own use in support of Nazi objectives. To strengthen that support, the officials were therefore anxious to intensify the German anti-Polish feeling.

The propaganda ministry's instructions to the Berlin news corps touched on two topics of further interest. First, although these German journalists were aware of Polish resistance to German rule, the Nazi government forbade them to write articles about it. Thus, unless he had served in Poland and had come in contact with the Polish resistance movement or unless he knew someone with this experience, the average German would know virtually nothing about the Polish resistance movement.[110] Even though Polish pilots were bombing Berlin from bases in Britain, the average German would know nothing about it.[111]

In fact, the German journalists had even been told not to discuss Polish writings or activities in either the past or the present.[112]

The second topic of interest had to do with Nazi priorities. When the Hitler regime was clearly in trouble after the defeat at Stalingrad, the spokesman of the propaganda ministry had attempted to buttress Hitler's militarily vulnerable empire by having the Berlin journalists stress the antisemitism theme.[113] With the very survival of their crumbling regime threatened in 1944, the officials of the propaganda ministry intensified the already heavy campaign of antisemitism.[114] This activity by the propaganda ministry revealed how relatively unimportant anti-Polish feeling was to the Nazi ideology. In their calculations, the Nazis did not consider anti-Polish or anti-Slav feeling to be the basis for, or even at the root of, Nazi appeal.

A more effective approach to determining Nazi-nationalist relationships would be the analysis of Hitler's actions and words in his role as the Nazis' leader. At the beginning of his period of power, the Austrian Hitler seemingly regarded the Poles more highly than did most of his fellow noncountrymen. Hitler's German predecessors had refused to bargain with Poland because they had hoped the state would be at most a temporary nuisance on the European scene, but Hitler dealt with the Poles. He signed a treaty with them on the basis of equality and celebrated Poland's good fortune in having a leader like Piłsudski. Hitler also delivered Poland from the stigma of impermanence which previous German diplomacy had hoped to make Poland's continuing cross. Furthermore, in the judgment of at least one respected contemporary historian, Hitler might have genuinely admired Piłsudski's qualities of leadership and hoped that he could gain Polish support for his anti-Soviet course.[115] If this judgment is accurate, it follows that Hitler could very well have viewed Poland, at least in the beginning, as a permanent feature of the European state system and have considered the Poles as a people of substance capable of loyalty and achievement.

After Piłsudski's death, the Poles could have disappointed Hitler sufficiently that, without a particular commitment toward Poland, he reacted accordingly. In any event, it is an undisputed fact that his signature on the nonaggression treaty proved worthless. Well-equipped by the factories of industrial Germany, his armies attacked a people once viewed as a potential ally. A minor official in Hitler's regime, Max Freiherr du Prel, not only declared that the collapse of Poland was the necessary result of Poland's abandonment of Piłsudski's policy,[116] but he also edited a book which denied even the existence of a Polish people.[117]

This sequence of events brought out another dimension of Hitler's relationship to the German nationalists and added a possible reason for the Nazi slaughters in Poland. When a politician switches positions so drastically as Hitler did vis-à-vis Poland, he usually suffers public embarrassment because of his shift. He may react by attempting to demonstrate his consistency. He may even deny that he has changed positions. Even if he is a dictator, as Hitler was, he will want to show that he has always been doctrinally correct.

Hitler's utterances about the Poles provided him a way of salvaging his image. First of all, in January, 1935, Hitler told a correspondent from the *Gazeta Polska* that the concept of "race" constituted the fundamental analytical tool of National Socialism. Since "race" was ideologically essential to National Socialism, Hitler saw the Polish issue in "racial" terms. Since "blood" and only "blood" determined a group's identity under this view, Hitler totally rejected the practice of attempting to strip a group's nationality from it by teaching its members a new language.[118] In fact, in his so-called "second book," Hitler labeled the germanized Pole a national liability since this individual weakened the racial purity of the German *Volk*.[119] Hitler therefore concluded that a Nazi state would not even wish to make Germans out of Poles.[120] Racially, a German was a German and a Pole was a Pole.

Even so, the question of what constituted a Pole to Hitler and the Nazis remained a problem. Since the Nazis regarded a man's race as all-important, they had considered the Poles from this viewpoint. In a partial evaluation of the German nationalist-Nazi relationship, it is evident that the Nazis, unlike the nationalists, did not search Polish history for evidence to demonstrate that the Poles were incapable, treasonous, or hate-filled. For the Nazis, a simple examination of the Polish race would reveal all that they needed to know. And it revealed, as Hitler privately put it, that the Polish people consisted of a thin, Germanic ruling class with "dreadful material" underneath.[121]

The implications of Hitler's assertion were many. For example, from a military standpoint, Hitler considered it unlikely that the German occupation would encounter a significant mass-resistance movement.[122] He did, however, expect the inferior Polish masses to act in an uncivilized manner toward the Germans.[123] Consistent with this view, Hitler decreed that the "dreadful material" be put to work in Germany at jobs too mundane for the Germans and that the Polish intelligentsia be eliminated.[124] This sentiment reveals a reason for the Nazis' brutal treatment of the Poles. And above all, Hitler firmly ruled that the Germans could not engage in sexual relations with the Poles since such acts would add Germanic blood to the Polish nation and thus replenish the pool from which the Polish leadership could come.[125]

At this point, the evidence is sufficient to see how the Nazis could use these views to justify their great policy reversal of 1939 and to demonstrate that Hitler really had no policy switch in regard to the Poles. Hans

Joachim Beyer actually undertook the task of explanation in two books. In the first, written under the influence of the 1934 nonaggression treaty, Beyer stressed the great amount of German blood in the Pole. He even suggested that the Poles possessed so much German blood that racially speaking the political elites of the two countries possessed approximately the same strength.[126] Therefore, he could admit and explain the great Polish achievements of constructing a state, an army, and a modern industry by pointing to this German blood. For the Nazis, the concept of German blood likewise provided an acceptable racial basis for an alliance between the Third Reich and Poland.

In Beyer's second book, which was written under the impact of war, German blood again provided a basis for condemnation. Beyer did not disown the findings of his first book or retract his 1935 praise of the Polish elite. Instead, he simply denied that it was in any way Polish. He devoted over twenty pages to a "list of leading politicians and military men of non-Polish origin." He wondered if Piłsudski might better be called "King of Lithuania" than a Pole. And he found the Polish enemy, as had Flottwell and Ganz, in the Polish women who could employ their powers of attraction to make foreign men so forget their own national tasks as to enrich the Polish blood supply.[127] Beyer then concluded, like Hitler, not only that the most vital German interest in Poland was to prevent the loss to the Poles of another drop of German blood but also that no specific Polish people existed. Beyer so despised the Poles that, without their foreign elite, he could view them as nothing more than a collection of various blood mixtures having only the Polish language in common.[128]

These words were used to justify an attack on Poland in 1939 because Poland was presumed to be no longer governed by a German and Lithuanian elite. And these words by Beyer were also strongly reminiscent of the Weimar technique of crediting all Polish achievements to the German or the Scandinavian or some other Nordic or northern man. Beyer's second book merely revealed that, by using this technique, all remaining substance could be drained from the Poles. Each and every Polish achievement thus found its way onto the lists of accomplishments of some other people. Each and every capable Polish leader in whatever field was placed on a list of another nation's talent. In the end, since nothing remained, Beyer could conclude that there was no Polish nation—that the people called "Poles" were merely some mountain folk and some city people around Cracow who shared the same language.

However, the same difficulty which plagued the German nationalist writers faced Beyer. To make his case sound convincing, he would have to explain the origins of this common language and why, if everything else Polish turned out to be such shadows, the language persisted so tenaciously under such adverse circumstances. To answer these questions, Beyer would also have had to emulate the Hakatists and acknowledge a tough and capable foe. This he refused to do. Like the German nationalist writers, Beyer preferred to explain away or deny Polish achievements rather than explain the reasons for their occurrence.

At this point, three statements can be made concerning the sources of Nazi policy toward the Poles. First, despite some similarity in techniques used, the evidence clearly shows that the Nazis' emphasis on "race" discredits any claims of continuity from the Hakatists and other German nationalists to the Nazis. Although the justly celebrated Professor Witold Jakóbczyk of the Adam Mickiewicz University in Poznań has suggested a continuity between earlier Hakatist plans to raise Polish orphans as Germans and the Hitler plan of reclaiming the Poles of German blood for the German race,[129] it should be repeated that Hitler explicitly condemned the nationalists' plan.

The second point about the sources of Nazi policy is that some Nazis did consider the Poles racially rich enough to warrant a lasting German-Polish alliance. Alfred Rosenberg, the self-proclaimed chief theorist of the Nazi movement, speculated in 1934 on a German-Polish-English alliance against the Soviet Union.[130] Even as late as 1939, a memorandum from Rosenberg's office praised the Poles' not inconsiderable Nordic blood.[131] And the party paper, the *Völkischer Beobachter*, also nominated the Poles for informal membership in the anticommunist alliance. Therefore, the Nazi leadership was fragmented on the issue of the Poles as well as on other policies.

As a third point about the sources of Nazi policy, there were two reasons why it was so difficult to uncover a specific Nazi image of the Pole. On the one hand, the Nazi leaders disagreed with one another. The ideology they had in common was incomplete and garbled. Also they used various themes of popular resentment in their public statements. On the other hand, as the spokesman of the propaganda ministry said in Berlin on October 24, 1936, it would not be in the German interest to publish stories detailing that only a narrow class maintained the Polish state.[132] Therefore, the Nazi standpoint remained largely hidden.

Of course, the Nazi point of view quickly became known after Hitler's armies had attacked and conquered Poland. The Poles had also been the victims of a prearranged Soviet attack. As agreed upon in the negotiations preceding the signing of the German-Soviet pact in August, 1939, the Soviet forces crossed the Polish eastern frontier and, in another partition of Poland, occupied the ethnically non-Polish eastern provinces. Moreover, this partition extended to the Baltic states. Here most of the Germans who lived in areas destined to come under Russian control took advantage of the German government's desire to have them "return home" and moved west.

But what of the Poles? The Nazis first had to decide what to do with the Polish laborers who had been permitted to work in Germany before the war. In this regard, the letter of September 9 from the *Reichssicher-heitshauptamt* to the local police was both ludicrous and terrifying. This letter not only asserted that Poles had threatened their German co-workers but also "beseeched" the local police to arrest such threatening Poles and arrange for their confinement in Dachau.[133] A week later, Himmler ordered the internment of all male Poles in the age group from 15 to 65. Of course, like the German landowner of the 19th century, Himmler exempted those Poles whose labor was required for continued and uninter-rupted production in agriculture, weapons procurement, and mining.[134] Finally, in the interest of increased production Himmler's office in Febru-ary, 1940, ordered the release of the interned Poles, with the exception of spies and Jews.[135]

The next problem for the Hitler government was the organization of territories. Hitler's initial response on September 25 was to order the creation of four military districts (West Prussia, Posen, Lodz, and Cracow) which would themselves bear the costs of their occupation.[136] He next decreed on October 19 that the military occupation would end at mid-night on October 25.[137] Dr. Hans Frank, a long-time Nazi and a leading official of the Reich, received the commission to organize and head the civilian administration in the conquered areas.[138] In 1940 Frank an-nounced that a Polish state would never again grace the map of Eu-rope.[139] Moreover, his bureaucracy did not become that of an independ-ent Polish state at any point in time, nor did his bureaucracy rule in the formerly German territories which had come under Polish rule after the First World War. Effective November 1, 1939, a *Reichsgau* West Prussia and a *Reichsgau* Posen, as well as the enlarged provinces of Silesia and East Prussia, graced a new German map showing the complete reversal of the decisions reached at Versailles.[140] In addition, all Polish place names in these lands lost their validity.[141] Finally, in April, 1941, the Nazis celebrated the return of these lands to the Reich by founding a German university in Posen.

But how was the individual Pole in these lands to be treated? Martin Bormann concisely summarized the Nazi high command's single guideline when he wrote that Germany had an interest only in the Poles' physical labor.[142] Therefore, the Jewish Poles and all members of the Polish intelligentsia would be transported from the new additions to the prov-inces of East Prussia and Silesia and from the new provinces of Posen and West Prussia to Dr. Frank's *Generalgouvernement*, which consisted of those formerly Polish territories not incorporated in either Germany or the Soviet Union. The presence of the remaining Polish laborers in the new German territories posed a dilemma since the Nazis were torn between an obvious need for Polish labor and an ideological desire for a "pure" German territory. Indeed, the planning department of the SS staff for colonization developed a plan for the expulsion of all Poles from these new German territories and the introduction of short-term Polish laborers from the *Generalgouvernement*. The department also developed plans for the expulsion of landless Poles from these new German territories and the transformation of the presumably better disciplined Polish landowners into landless, agricultural laborers who, it was hoped, would vanish when the Germans could replace them.[143] Since production took precedence over theory in this instance, these plans were ignored by Hitler and his government because the Nazis lacked sufficient manpower to implement all their schemes at once.

The Poles thus remained. And the dilemma of the Nazis also remained since they wished, on the one hand, to treat the Poles as nothing but beasts, and, on the other, they needed to favor the continued existence of a Polish community in the interest of public order. As a grotesque example of this dilemma between lack of interest in the Polish community's welfare and a concern for the preservation of public order, a state attorney complained that the medical authorities' disinclination to waste time doing dissections on Poles might well have been justified racially but that this refusal hindered the authorities in their quest to preserve order. These officials, in many cases, needed medical findings to be able to prove that a crime had been committed or in order to catch a criminal.[144]

This conflict, concerning stability in the Polish community, reached its greatest intensity in the *Generalgouvernement*, in the areas where the greatest number of Poles lived. The Nazi high command was adamant that the *Generalgouvernement* where twelve million Poles lived would one day be a German land "like the Rhineland" with a population of four to five million Germans.[145] This goal obviously implied the annihilation of the Polish population. But the local officials also had to prod the Poles to develop ever greater productivity. In hopes of gaining more productivity immediately, these officials attempted to boost Polish morale by such actions as revoking an edict prohibiting performances of Chopin's works.[146]

Two conferences in 1942 further demonstrated the contradictory aspects of future plans and present necessities. On March 10 Dr. Frank first contended that the Poles were enemies of the Germans "unto death" while, at the same time, he admonished that Polish acts of sabotage could not preclude a search for reasonable exchanges with trustworthy Poles.[147] Then on August 15 he described what he considered the "peculiar" reality of the Polish lands. These lands were eventually to become completely German territories, but at the time the Poles needed to be permitted to work in peace and quiet.[148] Unfortunately for Dr. Frank's hopes, the high command, far removed from the everyday problems of motivating millions of people to work, had no understanding of his concerns. Instead, they wondered why a brutal exploitation of the Poles based upon overwhelming German force would not extract from the land everything that was needed.

As their conference of April 20, 1943, at Cracow revealed,[149] the shattering defeat at Stalingrad intensified both the concern and the dilemma of Dr. Frank and his subordinates. First, Dr. Frank reported that an attempt had just been made on the life of the state secretary for security affairs, a man named Krüger. Dr. Frank had remarked that this had been the first attempt to murder a leading official. Sobered by this news, Dr. Frank's subordinates proceeded to condemn the policy of the Nazi high command. The official who was responsible for propaganda, a man named Ohlenbusch, suggested that the discovery at Katyn of the graves of Polish officers (supposedly murdered by the Soviets) offered the German government opportunity to alter its Polish policy without a loss of face. Ohlenbusch added that his last visit to Berlin had been discouraging in this regard. Another speaker, the *SS Brigade Führer* Dr. Schöngarth, demanded that, in view of the German need for Polish assistance, the Nazis should summon the necessary courage to change policy. He thanked fate that the discoveries at Katyn offered the possibility of gaining active Polish assistance against the Soviets. A third speaker by the name of Gerteis reported that in the first quarter the railroad security units had suffered 354 dead and 100 wounded. Gerteis further contended that his 3500 men could not possibly protect the more than 4200 miles of track, and he eloquently implied that as a minimum, Polish neutrality would be required for a successful supply of German forces. Eichholz, the man responsible for education, added that underground Polish schools were spreading rapidly, especially in the large cities. Thus, it would be foolish, with inadequate manpower and more pressing demands, to try to destroy the Polish character of the Polish-inhabited *Generalgouvernement.* To these men, the contradiction between the hopes for an all-German territory in the *Generalgouvernement* and the current need for Polish assistance had proved to be a chasm they could not bridge.

On June 19, 1943, Dr. Frank did present these conclusions to Hitler[150] as he issued a plea for a drastic change in the German policy toward the Poles. Beginning in the traditional fashion, he offered the usual critique of the Polish situation. That is, he wrote about an ignorant mass of Poles led by a narrow group of ambitious but incapable power-seekers. Then he added that, since the masses had not been responsible for the Polish power "madness," the German occupation had erred in offending their national feelings. No gain for Germany, he contended, had come from inadequate rations, arbitrary seizures of property, mass arrests and executions, a severely curtailed Polish cultural life, the closing of Polish schools, the exclusion of Poles from the administration of the land, measures directed against the Catholic church, and other invasions of privacy. In fact, argued Dr. Frank, these measures had drawn the masses closer to the resistance forces. But since an opportunity had now presented itself—the discovery of the mass graves at Katyn—Germany could appeal for Polish support against the Soviets without having to acknowledge previous error. To be sure, Dr. Frank did confess, if privately, Nazi error; and he even concluded in his report to Hitler that Nazi rule had produced a measure of Polish unity previously unknown in Polish history, which was being directed against Germany.

Yet for all his eloquence and evidence, Dr. Frank failed to secure Hitler's approval for a program which would bridge the gap between the present Nazi needs and the hopes for all-German territories. The officials at the party and the government headquarters refused to think about the Poles except as objects to be brutally exploited. Thus Dr. Frank, at a press reception on October 23, 1943, complained that the Polish laborer in Germany was constantly being linked by the Berlin propaganda ministry to the Jew and gypsy. But despite the fact that the discontinuation of such a propaganda tactic would have been only the merest concession to the Poles, the propaganda officials hesitated to permit it. Almost a half year passed before Himmler agreed to make even the slightest concession to placate the Poles—by not referring to them as fit companions for Jews and gypsies.[151] In the end, Dr. Frank could only hope that the Poles, even without the inducement of German concessions, would give up their hopes for independence and ultimately agree that their future could best be preserved under the rule of the Germans.[152]

Dr. Frank's fantasy of securing Polish support against the Soviet Union without the bribe of substantial concessions failed to materialize. Instead, a Polish resistance movement grew in importance. The top leadership in the Nazi high command knew of its scope and impact from the very beginning even as it tried to ignore that movement in its press commentary. The reports of Polish resistance crossed the desks of the top Nazi officials early in the Nazi occupation of Poland and continued to come. For instance, Hitler's office received word on February 21, 1940, of increasingly frequent acts of violence in Polish areas.[153] On May 4, Himmler advised Göring of the murder of policemen and various acts of sabotage, including the placing of explosives on train tracks.[154] On November 29, the minister for justice learned of an intense Polish propaganda and organizational effort.[155] He learned further that the Poles continued to hope for the restoration of their state.[156] He and Hitler had also received various reports of increased Polish sabotage.[157] Although many Nazi officials preferred to believe that the Polish resistance fighters were "professional criminals," they knew of the resistance to German rule.[158] But they refused to allow men like Dr. Frank to make concessions to the Polish community in an attempt to defuse the resistance movement. Their hopes for an all-German territory where Poles were then living took precedence over the solving of their current problems.

Present reality and future hopes also clashed in the concept of German blood. According to Nazi theory, German blood had created everything of substance in Poland. Therefore, its recovery would both diminish the creativity of the Poles and enrich the Germans. As a result, the Nazis clung to the hope that the German blood could be regained from the Polish community. The difficulty, however, lay in transforming this hope into a viable program.

A Nazi report on November 25, 1939, rather than presenting such a program, merely asserted that the Poles were racially a mixture of nothern or Nordic blood (especially in the western areas where Prussia had ruled), eastern blood, East Baltic blood, Mongolian blood, and Jewish blood. It further contended that the men and women of German blood were the bearers of that Polish-Catholic tradition which had to be destroyed if they were to come home to their own people,[159] although a method of bringing them back to the German community was not provided.

Himmler issued his decree of September 12, 1940, in response to his obligation to help fortify the position of the German people in the formerly Polish provinces of Germany which had been newly annexed. Himmler attempted to set up a program of returning German blood to the German people with an elaborate system of classification. His decree contended that there were four main groups of people in the Polish lands.[160] According to Himmler, the first group contained those men and women of German blood who possessed both German citizenship and full civil rights. The second contained men and women of German blood who lacked full civil rights and had to be reeducated to the meaning of their German heritage. The third contained people of at least some German blood who could be regained for the German nation. They would receive German citizenship on recall and would be regermanized in the old German territories. The fourth consisted of those persons of non-German blood. The primary difficulty with Himmler's classification system, however, was the inability of Himmler's subordinates to determine a person's group placement. Himmler's subordinates received their only help on November 14 when Himmler's office issued a list of instructions concerning the germanization of Polish families.[161] His first instruction specified that entire families were to be chosen since the appearance of a single good-looking individual would fail to establish the presence of German blood for a whole family. Only the presence of a healthy attitude, diligence, cleanliness, and physical health in an entire family was supposed to justify the assumption that German blood was present. Moreover, that family should stand out in its environment. Then even if no one in the family knew German or even if someone in the family had an unfavorable political past, the family could be selected for category three and guided toward the goal of German citizenship.

Yet there were other difficulties. As Himmler conceded, some men or women, although identified as having German blood, might prefer to remain Poles. In many cases, they might actively struggle for the Polish cause. Rather than being able to guide such people back to the German community, Himmler found it necessary to restrain them from contributing to the enemy's cause.[162] Himmler considered these to be renegades because they had challenged the validity of blood as the determinant of nationality. But even these experiences failed to shake Himmler's belief in blood.

In another area, Nazi hopes of purity in bloodlines were also thwarted by actual events. Since the Nazis had presumed that the main task in the east was to prevent German blood from enriching the Polish lines, the Germans were not permitted to marry Poles. In fact, Germans who had sexual relations with Polish or Czech women were subject to immediate dismissal from government service, as well as other penalties.[163] Yet many German males ignored the strictures about blood and forced Polish women whom they supervised at work to engage in sexual relations. The farmer's son and the supervisor on the job proved to be the worst offenders.[164] When offenses became known, the government reacted swiftly. The penalties for women for these activities consisted of a three-week jail sentence as well as a new job (with a concentration camp available for repeaters). For men, sentences of at least three months were prescribed, with the added prospect of fines and the loss of Polish laborers.[165]

But again, events did not go according to script. There was continual contradiction of Nazi hopes by actual conditions. A local official in Posen, for example, complained to Berlin officials about financial corruption. This problem was prevalent in areas settled by Germans from pre-1937 Germany. These men had travelled to those areas Hitler had annexed in 1939, in the hope of reaping easy riches.[166] The public trustees who had come to these areas not only practiced nepotism but also exploited their public position for private gain.

In addition to the tensions developed between Nazi policies and German conduct, some of the more traditional disputes persisted. For instance, the German nationalist writers of the Weimar and pre-Weimar periods had claimed that Copernicus was German. At the 400th anniversary of Copernicus's death the German press was expected to emphasize his German nationality.[167] Even though the anniversary occurred after the battle of Stalingrad, Goebbels found time to intervene personally and request the presence of a minister of the Reich at the official celebration in Königsberg.[168] Dr. Frank, for his part, asserted that Copernicus's life made legitimate the German rule in the east and further announced that a university named for Copernicus would rise in Cracow after the war.[169] Dr. Frank also denounced the Polish attempts to claim Copernicus.[170]

Other parts of the Weimar myth of the Pole also persisted. German officials complained that order, cleanliness, hygiene, and proper transportation had to be brought to the eastern area by the Germans.[171] A year after the victory over Poland, a pamphlet was issued which probably was authorized by Himmler's office to encourage German immigration to the east. The enthusiastic author of this pamphlet wrote that German achievement in the east had made these lands rightfully German.[172] In 1941 Dr. Frank had insisted that the non-German was the stranger in the land.[173] In 1942 the official organ *Deutsche diplomatisch-politische Korrespondenz* asserted an instinctive Polish hatred of Germans.[174] In 1943 this paper condemned the presumed Polish insanity that made the Poles dream fantastic dreams of expansion.[175] And the Nazi regime continued to conduct its affairs under these delusions until it completely collapsed in May, 1945.

In considering once again, and for the last time, the questions which underlie this chapter, the reader should find that these conclusions seem justified by the evidence presented. First of all, although the public statements of Nazi officials until the end of Hitler's Reich used the Weimar myth of the Pole in various ways, the myth did not guide their actions. Hitler's inspiration in judging the Poles was primarily racial in focus. The German nationalists therefore had no direct responsibility for Nazi behavior in Poland. On the other hand, because of the impact of the Weimar myth of the Pole, the Nazis could take advantage of it to act freely in Polish matters without any fear of adverse reactions from the German people. To this extent, the negative assessments of the Pole in the Weimar myth are responsible for the Nazi slaughters in Poland. These negative attitudes not only permitted but even encouraged a tremendous brutality towards the Poles. Of course, it should also be noted that the existence of a tight police rule and a controlled press likewise made possible the unrestrained actions of the Hitler regime.[176]

It seems probable that the problem of the Poles was of secondary concern to Hitler and that Hitler and the Nazis actually had no specific policy toward the Poles. In the end, the Nazis attacked the Poles because the political situation in Europe seemed to them to require such action. Why then did the Nazis slaughter so many Poles during their years of power in Poland? One possible answer is the common accusation that the Nazis were brutal men and that brutal men do brutal things. Another answer is that the vehemence of the Polish resistance movement provoked such reprisals. A third answer, one which has already been discussed in this chapter, is that the Weimar myth of the Pole had made Polish lives seem cheap. To the degree that this explanation is valid, and only to the degree to which this explanation is valid, the German nationalist writings of the pre-Hitler period can be considered partially and unwittingly to have made possible and even probable Nazi atrocities against the Poles.

Notes

Note: An interesting Polish discussion of German-Polish relations from 1933 to 1938 is found in Marian Wojciechowski's *Stosunki polsko-niemiecki, 1933–1938* (Poznań, 1965).

1. Adolf Hitler, *Mein Kampf* (München, 1935), pp.429–430, 748.
2. *Völkischer Beobachter*, No. 31, January 31, 1936.
3. Ibid., No. 220, August 8, 1933.
4. Ibid., No. 262, September 19, 1933.
5. Ibid., No. 293, October 20, 1933.
6. Ibid., No. 27, January 27, 1934.
7. Ibid., No. 26, January 26, 1936.
8. Ibid., No. 280, October 6, 1936.
9. Ibid., No. 258, September 15, 1938.
10. Ibid., No. 59, February 28, 1939.
11. Ibid., No. 45, January 14, 1936.
12. Ibid., No. 282, October 8, 1936.
13. Ibid., No. 232, August 20, 1937.
14. Ibid., No. 147, May 26, 1936.
15. Ibid., Nos. 358, 359, and 360; December 24, 25, and 26, 1933.
16. Ibid., No. 139, May 19, 1934. In *Der deutsche Osten* (Berlin, 1936), by Karl Thalheim and Arnold Hillen Ziegfeld, Otto Hoetzsch also agreed (p.224).
17 *Völkischer Beobachter*, No. 133, May 12, 1936.
18. Ibid., No. 293, October 20, 1933.
19. Ibid., No. 332, November 28, 1933.
20. Ibid., No. 339, December 5, 1933.
21. Ibid., No. 271, September 28, 1934.
22. Ibid., No. 286, October 13, 1934.
23. Ibid., Nos. 308 and 309, November 4 and 5, 1934.
24. Ibid., No. 305, November 1, 1934; Nos. 350 and 351, December 16 and 17, 1934. In 1935 this flood of praise continued as Germans from Poland graciously thanked the Poles for having made their

journey to the new Germany possible. Next, a delegation from the *Hitler-Jugend* went to Warsaw and praised the Polish desire for a clear understanding with Germany. Then Pilsudski died and Hitler personally sent a telegram of condolence to Poland while Walther Schmitt for the *Völkischer Beobachter* characterized the deceased Polish leader as the "father of the entire nation."

From 1936 to 1938 this praise of many things Polish was continuing. For instance, in May, 1936, Warsaw University swimmers were praised for their performance in a meet with Berlin swimmers while in July the Polish dance troupe aroused official enthusiasm. In 1937 a headline announced that Polish boxers had continually improved, and the story related that these Polish chaps always gave the German lads a difficult time. In fact, only the Germans' better training discipline was supposed to have prevented a Polish victory. In January, 1938, three photographs of the Polish ballet company graced the pages of the *Völkischer Beobachter*, and the story revealed that under the sponsorship of Ambassador Lipski and Propaganda Minister Goebbels, the Polish dancers would perform for the benefit of German charity. In November the Polish boxer again won praise as a man who traveled from triumph to triumph.

25. Ibid., No. 250, September 7, 1933.
26. Ibid., No. 264, September 21, 1933.
27. Ibid., Nos. 309, 310, November 5 and 6, 1933.
28. Ibid., No. 53, February 22, 1934.
29. Ibid., No. 50, February 19, 1936.
30. Ibid., No. 316, November 11, 1936.
31. Bundesarchiv Koblenz, Sammlung Sänger (Z Sg. 102, Nr. 1), letter of June 8, 1934, from the Reichsminister für Volksaufklärung und Propaganda to the journalists attending the press conference.
32. Bundesarchiv Koblenz, Sammlung Brammer (Z Sg. 101, Nr. 3), Anweisung Nr. 357 of March 15, 1934.
33. Bundesarchiv Koblenz, Reichskanzlei: auswärtige Angelegenheiten (R43 II/1480), Staatssekretär in der Reichskanzlei of March 7, 1933.
34. Bundesarchiv Koblenz, Sammlung Brammer (Z Sg. 101, Nr. 26), Informationsbericht of March 11, 1933.
35. Ibid., Nr. 1, Mitteilungen an die Redaktionen. Nicht zur Veröffentlichung of June 29, 1933.
36. Ibid., Nr. 3, Anweisung Nr. 359 of March 15, 1934.
37. Ibid., Nr. 28, Vertraulicher Informationsbericht of March 7, 1935 [its representative was Professor Oberländer].
38. Ibid., Nr. 28, Koblenz, Deutsches Nachrichtenbüro: Deutsche diplomatisch-politische Korrespondenz (Z Sg. 116, Nr. 1911), *Deutsche diplomatisch-politische Korrespondenz*, January 27, 1936.
39. Bundesarchiv Koblenz, Reichskanzlei: auswärtige Angelegenheiten (R 43 II/1482a), SA Brigade Führer Professor Doktor von Arnim to Hitler of April 27, 1936; reply of Staatssekretär Dr. Lammers of May 5; also see letters of December 12, 1936, and October 4, 1937.

40. Bundesarchiv Koblenz, Sammlung Sänger (Z Sg. 102, Nr. 2), aus der Presse Konferenz of April 4, 1936.
41. Bundesarchiv Koblenz, Sammlung Traub (Z Sg. 110, Nr. 3), Streng vertraulich–nur zur Information of December 18, 1936.
42. Ibid., Nr. 4, Streng vertraulich–nur zur Information of March 11, 1937.
43. Ibid., Nr. 5, Streng vertraulich–nur zur Information of June 3, 1937.
44. Ibid., Streng vertraulich–nur zur Information of July 8, 1937.
45. Bundesarchiv Koblenz, Sammlung Sänger (Z Sg. 102, Nr. 6), aus der Presse Konferenz of September 6, 1937.
46. Bundesarchiv Koblenz, Reichskanzlei: auswärtige Angelegenheiten (R43 II/1482a), Dr. Emmert, Landgerichtsrat to Oberlandesgerichtspräsident, Nürnberg of November 26, 1937.
47. Bundesarchiv Koblenz, Sammlung Traub (Z Sg. 110, Nr. 6), Streng vertraulich–nur zur Information of December 17, 1937; Bundesarchiv Koblenz, Sammlung Brammer (Z Sg. 101, Nr. 31), Informationsbericht Nr. 185 of December 17, 1937.
48. Bundesarchiv Koblenz, Sammlung Traub (Z Sg. 110, Nr. 8), Streng vertraulich–nur zur Information of May 30, 1938.
49. Ibid., Nr. 7, Streng vertraulich–nur zur Information of February 18, 1938.
50. Bundesarchiv Koblenz, Reichsministerium für Volksaufklärung und Propaganda (R55, Nr. 443), report of February 24, 1938.
51. Bundesarchiv Koblenz, Sammlung Traub (Z Sg. 110, Nr. 6), Streng vertraulich–nur zur Information of October 30, 1937.
52. Ibid., Nr. 8, Streng vertraulich–nur zur Information of June 3, 1938.
53. Ibid., Nr. 7, Streng vertraulich–nur zur Information of February 12, 1938.
54. Bundesarchiv Koblenz, Sammlung Brammer (Z Sg. 101, Nr. 29), Privater Sonderbericht of October 17, 1936.
55. Ibid., Informationsbericht of July 10, 1936.
56. Bundesarchiv Koblenz, Sammlung Traub (Z Sg. 220, Nr. 1), Streng vertraulich–nur zur Information of March 8, 1935.
57. Bundesarchiv Koblenz, Sammlung Brammer (Z Sg. 101, Nr. 31), Informationsbericht of October 26, 1937.
58. Bundesarchiv Koblenz, Sammlung Traub (Z Sg. 110, Nr. 6), Streng vertraulich–nur zur Information of December 16, 1937; Bundesarchiv Koblenz, Sammlung Brammer (Z Sg. 101, Nr. 33), Informationsbericht of December 8, 1938.
59. Bundesarchiv Koblenz, Sammlung Brammer (Z Sg. 101, Nr. 9), Anweisung Nr. 496 of April 13, 1937; Bundesarchiv Koblenz, Sammlung Sänger, (Z Sg. 102, Nr. 11), aus der Presse Konferenz of July 5, 1938; and Bundesarchiv Koblenz, Sammlung Traub (Z Sg. 110, Nr. 9), Streng vertraulich-nur zur Information of July 7, 1938.
60. Bundesarchiv Koblenz, Sammlung Traub (Z Sg. 110, Nr. 7), Streng vertraulich–nur zur Information of January 19, 1938.
61. Bundesarchiv Koblenz, Sammlung Brammer (Z Sg. 101, Nr. 11),

report of March 15, 1938.

62. Bundesarchiv Koblenz, Sammlung Brammer (Z Sg. 101, Nr. 12), Anweisung Nr. 78 of January 24, 1939.

63. Bundesarchiv Koblenz, Reichssicherheitshauptamt (R58/270a), Der Reichsführer SS und Chef der Deutschen Polizei of May 8, 1939, and July 3, 1939.

64. *Völkischer Beobachter*, No. 26, January 26, 1939.

65. Bundesarchiv Koblenz, Sammlung Sänger (Z Sg. 102, Nr. 14), aus der Presse Konferenz of February 17, 1939.

66. Bundesarchiv Koblenz, Sammlung Traub (Z Sg. 110, Nr. 11), reports of February 25, February 27, February 28, March 1, and March 8, 1939.

67. It is a debated question to what degree an author is responsible for the use others make of his words. Certainly neither Schäfer nor Laubert were Nazis.

68. Bundesarchiv Koblenz, Reichskanzlei: auswärtige Angelegenheiten (R 43 II/1482b), Reichsminister der Innern to Reichskanzlei of March 29, 1939.

69. Ibid.

70. *Völkischer Beobachter*, April 7, 1939, No. 97.

71. Ibid., No. 119, April 29, 1939.

72. Ibid.

73. Bundesarchiv Koblenz, Sammlung Traub (Z Sg. 110, Nr. 10), Streng vertraulich—nur zur Information of December 16, 1938.

74. *Völkischer Beobachter*, No. 125, May 5, 1939.

75. Ibid., No. 282, October 9, 1939.

76. Ibid., No. 301, October 28, 1939.

77. Bundesarchiv Koblenz, Sammlung Brammer (Z Sg. 101, Nr. 10), Anweisung Nr. 960 of July 28, 1937.

78. *Völkischer Beobachter*, Nos. 124 and 126; May 4 and 6, 1939.

79. Bundesarchiv Koblenz, Sammlung Sänger (Z Sg. 102, Nr. 16), aus der Presse Konferenz of May 8, 1939.

80. Bundesarchiv Koblenz, Sammlung Brammer (Z Sg. 101, Nr. 34), Informationsbericht Nr. 55 of June 8, 1939.

81. *Völkischer Beobachter*, No. 172, June 21, 1939.

82. Bundesarchiv Koblenz, Sammlung Oberleitmann (Z Sg. 109, Nr. 1), July 6, 1939.

83. Ibid., Nr. 2, August 3, 1939.

84. Ibid., Nr. 1, July 20, 1939.

85. Ibid., Nr. 2, August 8, 1939.

86. Bundesarchiv Koblenz, Sammlung Brammer (Z Sg. 101, Nr. 13), Anweisung Nr. 850 of August 11, 1939.

87. *Völkischer Beobachter*, No. 230, August 18, 1939.

88. Bundesarchiv Koblenz, Sammlung Oberleitmann (Z Sg. 109, Nr. 2), August 21, 1939.

89. Bundesarchiv Koblenz, Sammlung Brammer (Z Sg. 101, Nr. 13), Anweisung Nr. 923 of August 29, 1939. In July the *Völkischer Beobachter* had also summoned the non-Nazi past to march in its

campaign of words against Poland. On July 2 the paper called Copernicus a symbol of the Germans' cultural work in the east; it asserted furthermore that this cultural work was so firmly identified with the territory that the Poles had to resort to the falsification of the national origins of Copernicus in order to appear at home in the area. Nineteen days later, the words of Frederick the Great's time joined the fray when a report of the 1770s once more depicted the desolation and disorder of 18th-century Poland. On July 30 Wilhelm Jordan, another voice from the past, spoke nationalistic words from the hectic days of 1848, telling the masses of 1939 that Poland was the German's enemy unto death and that a justified and healthy egoism should dictate German policy towards the Pole.

90. *Völkischer Beobachter*, No. 216, August 4, 1939.
91. Ibid., No. 221, August 9, 1949.
92. Ibid., No. 232, August 20, 1939.
93. Ibid., No. 234, August 22, 1939.
94. Ibid., No. 238, August 26, 1939.
95. Ibid., No. 239, August 27, 1939.
96. Ibid., No. 241, August 29, 1939.
97. Ibid., No. 243, August 31, 1939.
98. Ibid., No. 244, September 1, 1939.
99. Ibid., No. 263, September 20, 1939.
100. Ibid., No. 266, September 23, 1939.
101. Ibid., No. 319, November 15, 1939.
102. Ibid., No. 14, January 14, 1940.
103. Ibid., No. 79, March 19, 1940.
104. Ibid., No. 147, May 26, 1940; and No. 78, March 19, 1941.
105. Martin Broszat, *Nationalsozialistische Polenpolitik 1939–1945* (Frankfurt am Main and Hamburg, 1965), p.12.
106. Bundesarchiv Koblenz, Sammlung Oberleitmann (Z Sg. 109, Nr. 3), September 8, 1939, and September 23, 1939.
107. Ibid., Nr. 11, May 21, 1940.
108. Ibid., Nr. 4, October 20, 1939.
109. Ibid., October 24, 1939; Bundesarchiv Koblenz, Sammlung Sänger (Z Sg. 102, Nr. 19), October 24, 1939; Bundesarchiv Koblenz, Sammlung Brammer (Z Sg. 101, Nr. 14), Anweisung Nr. 1306 of October 24, 1939.
110. Bundesarchiv, Koblenz, Sammlung Brammer (Z Sg. 101, Nr. 35), January 20, 1940; and Nr. 17, Anweisung Nr. 630 of July 28, 1940.
111. Bundesarchiv Koblenz, Sammlung Sänger (Z Sg. 102, Nr. 35), aus der Presse Konferenz of November 12, 1941.
112. Bundesarchiv Koblenz, Sammlung Oberleitmann (Z Sg. 109, Nr. 14), August 19, 1940.
113. Ibid., Nr. 42, April 29, 1943.
114. Ibid., Nr. 48, March 2, 1944.
115. Hans Roos, *Polen und Europa* (Tübingen, 1957), p.151.
116. Max Freiherr du Prel, ed., *Das General-Gouvernement* (Würzburg, 1942), pp.16–17.

117. Ibid., pp.27—28.
118. *Völkischer Beobachter*, No. 26, January 26, 1935.
119. *Hitlers Zweites Buch* (Stuttgart, 1961), p.79.
120. Ibid., p.81.
121. Hans-Gunther Seraphim, ed., *Das politische Tagebuch Alfred Rosenbergs* (München, 1964), p.98.
122. Ibid., p.119.
123. Ibid., p.133.
124. Bundesarchiv Koblenz, Sammlung Brammer (Z Sg. 101, Nr. 90), *Die Welt* of September 2, 1947.
125. Henry Picker, ed., *Hitlers Tischgespräche im Führerhaupt-quartier 1941—1942* (Bonn, 1951), p.69.
126. Hans Joachim Beyer, *Aufbau und Entwicklung des Ostdeutschen Volksraums* (Danzig, 1935), pp.117—118.
127. Hans Joachim Beyer, *Das Schicksal der Polen* (Leipzig and Berlin, 1942), pp.130—158. In *Grundzüge der Rassen- und Raumgeschichte des deutschen Volkes* (München and Berlin, 1943), Gustav Paul agreed about Piłsudski (p.218).
128. Beyer, *Schicksal*, pp.157, 13.
129. Seraphim, p.166.
130. Ibid., p.170.
131. Adam Galos, Witold Jakóbczyk, and Felix-Heinrich Gentzen, *Die Hakatisten* (Berlin, 1966), p.242.
132. Bundesarchiv Koblenz, Sammlung Traub (Z Sg. 110, Nr. 3), Streng vertraulich—nur zur Information of October 24, 1936.
133. Bundesarchiv Koblenz, Reichssicherheitshauptamt (R58/270a), letter to local police of September 9, 1939.
134. Ibid., letter to local police of September 16, 1939.
135. Ibid., letter to local police of February 5, 1940.
136. Bundesarchiv Koblenz, Reichskanzlei: Krieg (R43 II/647), Erlass des Führers of September 25, 1939.
137. Ibid., Erlass des Führers of October 19, 1939.
138. Bundesarchiv Koblenz, Kanzlei des Generalgouverneurs: Tagebuch (R 52/II/174), Vorbemerkung.
139. Ibid., Nr. 178, speech of July 25, 1940.
140. Bundesarchiv Koblenz, Reichskanzlei: Krieg (R43 II/646a), Erlass des Führers of October 8, 1939.
141. Ibid., Nr. 646b, Reichsminister des Innern (Frick) to local officials of December 29, 1939.
142. Bundesarchiv Koblenz, Reichskanzlei: auswärtige Angelegenheiten (R 43 II/1484), Bormann to Oberkommando der Wehrmacht of November 9, 1940.
143. Bundesarchiv Koblenz, Reichskommissar für die Festigung deutschen Volkstums: die Ansiedlung der Umsiedler im Warthegau (R49/Anhang I/34), report of SS-Ansiedlungsstab Planungsabteilung of February 28, 1941.
144. Bundesarchiv Koblenz, Reichsjustizministerium (R22/3372), Generalstaatsanwalt (Kattowitz) to Staatssekretär of May 14, 1941.

145. Bundesarchiv Koblenz, Kanzlei des Generalgouverneurs: Tagebuch (R52/II/181), talk of March 26, 1941.
146. Ibid., Nr. 234, meeting of July 22, 1941.
147. Ibid., Nr. 190, meeting of March 10, 1942.
148. Ibid., Nr. 194, talk of August 15, 1942.
149. Ibid., Nr. 244, meeting of April 20, 1943.
150. Bundesarchiv Koblenz, Kanzlei des Generalgouverneurs: Berichte des Generalgouverneurs (R52/II/12a), Frank's letter to Hitler of June 19, 1943.
151. Bundesarchiv Koblenz, Kanzlei des Generalgouverneurs: Tagebuch (R52/II/208), press reception of October 23, 1943, and Nr. 245, meeting of April 19, 1944.
152. Ibid., Nr. 244, meeting of October 26, 1943.
153. Bundesarchiv Koblenz, Reichskanzlei: Krieg (R43/II/647a), letter of February 21, 1940, from the Generalbevollmächtigte für die Reichsverwaltung to the Reichskanzlei.
154. Ibid., Himmler to Göring of May 4, 1940.
155. Bundesarchiv Koblenz, Reichsjustizministerium (R22/3383), Reichsstatthalter (Posen) to Reichsminister der Justiz of November 29, 1940.
156. Ibid., letter of April 3, 1941.
157. Bundesarchiv Koblenz, Reichskanzlei: Krieg (R43/II/647a), Reichskanzlei to Reichsminister der Justiz of May 27, 1941.
158. Bundesarchiv Koblenz, Reichsjustizministerium (R22/3383), Reichsstatthalter (Posen) to Reichsminister der Justiz of September 25, 1943.
159. Bundesarchiv Koblenz, Reichskommissar für die Festigung deutschen Volkstums (R49/75), report of November 25, 1939.
160. Bundesarchiv Koblenz, Reichskanzlei: Krieg (R43/II/646), Himmler's decree of September 12, 1940.
161. Bundesarchiv Koblenz, Reichskommissar für die Festigung deutschen Volkstums (R49/Anhang III/Nr. 160), Richtlinien für Eindeutschung polnischer Familien.
162. Bundesarchiv Koblenz, Reichskanzlei: Reichsangehörigkeit (R43/II/136), Himmler's letter of February 16, 1942.
163. Bundesarchiv Koblenz, Reichskanzlei: auswärtige Angelegenheiten (R43/II/1484), Chef der Reichskanzlei to Bormann of June 15, 1940.
164. Bundesarchiv Koblenz, Reichssicherheitshauptamt (R58/270a), Anlage to the Runderlass of September 3, 1940.
165. Ibid.
166. Bundesarchiv Koblenz, Reichsjustizministerium (R22/3383), Reichsstatthalter (Posen) to Reichsminister der Justiz of July 31, 1940.
167. Bundesarchiv Koblenz, Sammlung Oberleitmann (Z Sg. 109, Nr. 42), Tagesparole des Reichspressechefs of May 13, 1943.
168. Bundesarchiv Koblenz, Kanzlei Rosenberg (NS 8/241), Aktennotiz of May 17, 1943.
169. Bundesarchiv Koblenz, Kanzlei des Generalgouverneurs: Tagebuch

(R52/II/Nr. 202), remark of May 24, 1943.

170. Bundesarchiv Koblenz, Institut für Deutsche Ostarbeit Krakau (R52/IV/95), *Krakauer Zeitung* of May 25, 1943, No. 123.

171. Bundesarchiv Koblenz, Reichsjustizministerium (R22/3383), Reichsstatthalter to Reichsminister der Justiz of April 27, 1940.

172. Bundesarchiv Koblenz, Reichskommissar für die Festigung deutschen Volkstums: die Ansiedlung der Umsiedler im Warthegau (R49/Anhang I/nr. 34), *Ein Jahr deutsche Ostsiedlung!*

173. Bundesarchiv Koblenz, Kanzlei des Generalgouverneurs: Tagebuch (R52/II/185), talk of September 12, 1941.

174. Bundesarchiv Koblenz, Deutsches Nachrichtenbüro: Deutsche diplomatisch-politische Korrespondenz (Z Sg. 116/1925), issue of September 1, 1942, no. 136.

175. Ibid., nr. 1928, issue of April 28, 1943, no. 4.

176. The police did uncover, and take action on, German activities which aided the Pole. For instance, the police rebuked judges who gave light sentences to Polish defendants, Catholics who permitted Polish laborers to use the Sunday mass as an opportunity to visit each other and exchange experiences, Catholics who collected clothes for the Pole and even shared their rations with the Polish laborer, and Catholics and intellectuals who remained unimpressed by government propaganda about Soviet slaughters of Polish officers because the German government had done the same thing. For details see *Meldungen aus dem Reich* issued by Der Chef der Sicherheitspolizei und des SD of August 21, 1941, Nr. 213; September 25, 1941, Nr. 223; November 6, 1941, Nr. 235; August 20, 1942, Nr. 310 and April 19, 1943, Nr. 377. Most of these documents can be found in Heinz Boberach's edition of *Meldungen aus dem Reich (Neuwied and Berlin, 1965)*, pp.188–191, 289–292, 383. All of these documents can be found in National Archives, American Committee for the Study of War Documents, Reichsführer SS und Chef der Deutschen Polizei (Cat. 39, T–175, Roll 261, 263, 265).

CHAPTER FIVE
1945–1973

Toward a New
German–Polish Relationship

The continual conflict of historical continuity versus historical change occurred in a much changed setting in the period after the Second World War. In every aspect of German life, the defeated Germans had to consider whether their old traditions had led to the disaster that was Adolf Hitler. They also had to question whether their old traditions were still viable in a transformed world. Germany's partition complicated the matter because of the dilemma of the two distinct settings in which these considerations had to take place. But they did take place, and they also covered all aspects of German life. After the defeat of the Nazi regime, the Weimar myth of the Pole was subject to this general reexamination. With respect to the Germans' traditional relationship to the Pole, two epochal events provided the setting for a transformed German-Polish relationship following the Second World War. The first concerned German-Polish borders. The Poles' attachment to the winning side resulted in a gain of German lands. When the Second World War ended, the armies of the Soviet Union stood on the soil of East Central Europe. For reasons of their own, which included a desire to make Poland dependent on Soviet power, the Soviets wished to extend Poland's western frontier to the Oder and Neisse rivers while incorporating in their state the former Polish eastern provinces and the former Prussian territories around Königsberg.[1] Since the Soviet armies were in actual possession of these territories, the Western Allies had little choice but to acquiesce. At the 1945 Potsdam Conference the United States, the United Kingdom, and the Soviet Union agreed provisionally to these new borders pending a final peace treaty which would be binding on all issues.

Once again the Germans awoke after a world war to discover that the Poles were in possession of a considerable amount of lands which formerly were Prussian. They also had to come to grips with another and more frightening reality: expulsion. At Potsdam the Allies had maintained the objective of removing Germans from other European states and thus preventing a future German leader from using the presence of Germans abroad as an excuse for aggression. The Allies therefore concluded that all Germans living either within the interwar borders of the East Central European states or on the lands given to Poland and the Soviet Union should be resettled in the newly diminished Germany. From the new Polish territory alone more than seven and a half million men, women, and children came west. They brought with them very few possessions but many tales of lost homes and of death and humiliation along the way. In comparison to the situation after the First World War, the number of displaced Germans this time was more than tenfold the number who had fled during the period 1919–1923.

But there was also a significant qualitative distinction between the two movements. After the Second World War, there was a profound difference in German consciousness. The Germans were fully prepared for defeat; the German armies, far from being intact on foreign lands, had disintegrated. Their cities had suffered the bombs of enemy planes, the shells of enemy artillery, and occupation by enemy troops. Their leaders had committed suicide or had been taken captive or had succeeded in escaping either to a new identity or to another country. And the policies advanced by their leaders had been so thoroughly discredited that, after this war, the Germans had to cope mainly with feelings of guilt instead of resentment or bitterness. In these circumstances they could not be aroused easily by the plight of the expellees even though in 1950 one out of every seven West Germans came from the New Poland while still others came from Soviet or Czech, Hungarian, or Balkan territories.

Two other circumstances also worked against the intensification of anti-Polish feelings. The first, the foreign control of Germany, precluded the dissemination of anti-Polish diatribes or the organization of anti-Polish groups. It also kept the Germans so busy wondering how to cope with the demands of the conquerors that they had no time except for immediate problems. The second, the physical devastation of rump Germany, caused many West Germans to view the expelled Germans as a threat to their own interests. They were wondering how West Germany's very limited resources should be used to meet the overwhelming needs of both themselves and the new expellee arrivals. In fact, as U. W. Kitzinger reported, many West Germans in condemning the amount of aid which was given the expellees, asked these questions:

"Why is every second farm on the new polder given to a refugee?
"Why is there no cheap housing being built for native inhabitants?
"Why cannot a native inhabitant open any competitive business? Because
he does not get the cheap credits available to a refugee."[2]

Therefore, when for the first time in history Polish achievements became
significant in everyday, practical terms to Germans in all parts of Germany, these Germans were in no mood to assess the Poles' positive or
negative characteristics.

In 1949 the issue of the Poles' successes did enter West German public
life when the United States, the United Kingdom, and France permitted
the formation of a West German state—the Federal Republic of Germany.
Since in this state all sorts of political parties could be formed, an expellee
party competed for voter support. This party (the BHE, or the Union of
Those Expelled from Their Homes and Deprived of Their Rights) militated
in all parts of West Germany against what had happened in the German-
Polish borderlands, demanding that the provisionally accepted Potsdam
settlement of 1945 be nullified.

An examination of the BHE program reveals two major demands. The
BHE, stressed in its foreign policy that the West German government not
only should refuse to recognize the new German-Polish border but also
should strive to change it. The party thus seemed to insist that all Germans
unite in a campaign to negate the Polish successes contained in the
Potsdam accords. In domestic affairs, the BHE demanded even greater
subsidies for the expellee. This demand revealed that the BHE was, at least
in part, an interest group which used elections to secure additional governmental assistance for its members. But when the government and the
general rebirth of the West German economy had greatly improved the
expellees' economic position in West Germany and when the major parties
had absorbed the expellee foreign interests into their programs, the need
for a separate BHE disappeared. Consequently, the BHE failed to elect any
deputies to parliament.

Despite the basically self-defeating nature of the BHE, two aspects of
the party's history are important for the light they shed on the West
German-Polish relationship. First, the BHE secured considerable governmental financial and social assistance for the expellees. This support
ranged from partial compensation for lost possessions to preferences in
areas such as bank loans, housing, and a certain proportion of places in the
secondary schools, as well as benefits such as scholarships for expellee
children in the universities. Yet the more assistance the party secured for
its members and the more the expellees were integrated in West German
society, the less credible became their expellee identity and the more

unreal became their insistence that they wished to return to their former lands then under Polish rule.[3] In a sense, their fairly remarkable domestic success undermined the credibility of their demands that the new German-Polish border be negated. This led the major parties in the 1950s to conclude that they could gain expellee votes by voting monies for expellee subsidies and making their foreign policy pronouncements favorable to permitting expellees to return to their former homes if they wished. There was little real bitterness in West Germany concerning the German-Polish border debate, at least in comparison to that of the Weimar period. Instead, the parties in West Germany merely insisted that the Potsdam accords were provisional and that the new German-Polish border on the Oder and Neisse rivers was not final. Moreover, this generalized unwillingness of the parties to consider recognizing the new German-Polish relationship continued into the 1960s virtually unchallenged by West German politicians.

As a matter of fact, only rarely did the West Germans consider either the achievements or the failures of the Poles and their state. These Germans considered it absurd to spend time thinking about the Poles as long as the Soviet Union controlled almost all of East Central Europe. They doubted that it made any sense to consider the Poles at all as long as Soviet power was considered dominant in Central Europe.

In East Germany (or the central area of Germany before the Second World War), events progressed in a far different manner. The new German Democratic Republic was dependent politically, militarily, economically, and culturally upon the Soviet Union, which contended that the Oder-Neisse line was the German-Polish frontier. Therefore, the East German government speedily recognized the Oder-Neisse line in 1950. Both East German-Polish cooperation in various Soviet-sponsored organizations and joint East German-Polish activity followed.

Interestingly enough, from that time to the present the East German and Polish peoples, as a result of this politically imposed coexistence, have come to know each other. For example, since travel in countries dominated by the Soviets has been restricted primarily to nationals of other countries dominated by the Soviets and since travel to the Soviet Union itself has been expensive and limited, many Poles and East Germans have vacationed in each other's country and purchased each other's products. They have read each other's books, if mainly in translation, and watched each other's movies and television programs. They have competed with each other in athletic competitions, and their armies have held joint field maneuvers. Since their leaders have conferred regularly with one another, their policies as well as their lives have, in a real sense, been coordinated. They have come to know one another as citizens and neighbors, not just as foreign workers in a more industrialized country.

In considering the evolution of German-Polish relations after the Second World War, the journalist, scholar, or diplomat has speculated about how the East German-Polish relations would develop were Soviet power removed. The observer could wonder whether they would approximate West German-Polish relations—whether the East Germans, given an opportunity to share in the life of the West, would vacation in Poland, purchase Polish products, read Polish books, watch Polish films, or compete often in Polish athletic competitions. In a sense, the answers to these questions would determine whether a true meeting of the two peoples has taken place along the Oder or whether the present East German-Polish relationship is merely a forced coexistence. Unfortunately for the purposes of historical scientific inquiry, since the Soviets show no signs of relinquishing either East Germany or Poland, the researchers probably will be unable to obtain answers to the questions of mass behavior for a long time.

One can, however, understand more clearly the postwar writer's view of the Pole. Despite the questions that German-Polish relations raise in terms of boundaries or contact between the German and Polish peoples, a different series of issues emerges when the post-1945 image of the Pole in German journalistic, scholarly, and political writings is considered. But first, though, there is a need to understand that in any historical situation elements of the old necessarily coexist with those of the new—even though almost any participant in discussions about German life after 1945 would have been forced to concede that new forces had dominated, and transformed the older ones, so many of which the course of the Second World War had thoroughly discredited. For example, since the Hitler dictatorship had proved to be incompetent, after the war, the old right wing, with its exaggerated nationalism, had virtually disappeared. Moreover, since the old army was discredited after Germany's defeat, the old militarism had also collapsed. The schools and the universities thus received a new message to impart to their students—democracy in West Germany and communism in East Germany. Yet some of the former attitudes remained.

The old was retained in the realm of man and his attitudes. Obviously, not every German who was alive in 1939 perished in the war, nor did every German who was alive in 1939 renounce all of his former ways after the war. Change took place after the war because some ideas were discarded, others were modified, and new tenets were formed out of the dynamic intermixture of the old and the new. Relatively little, though, changed in the minds of some men, and in West Germany some traditionalists could express themselves.

Bolko Freiherr von Richthofen, for one, continued to believe in the Weimar myth of the Pole. As a matter of fact, in 1929 he had helped to elaborate it. He had published a book which energetically attacked the Polish claim that the Slavs had originally settled the German-Polish borderlands. Three decades later, he again offered the reading public a book which maintained a Weimar view of the Pole.

The book began with a brief contribution by Victor Kauder, who was of a traditional mind; that is, he emphasized in Weimar fashion Germany's contribution to the development of Poland and implied that continued German assistance was needed. Kauder repeated in his introduction the Weimar myth of the incapable Pole. He ended by stating again that the Pole wanted to return to Germany those lands which the Potsdam agreement had placed under Polish administration.[4] Poles, according to Kauder, realized that they needed the Germans' creative ability if the Oder-Neisse lands were to produce the wealth of which they were capable.

Then Richthofen reinforced Kauder's contribution by demonstrating that in thirty years his belief in the Weimar myth of the Pole had not wavered. He began by stating:

"The *so-called* [italics added] first partition of Poland was moreover in reality not a partition but a considerable reduction in the size of Poland. It brought Prussia only old Germany territory."[5]

Thus, Richthofen justified the partition of Poland just as writers had done before the Second World War. But what is the difference between a "considerable reduction in size" and a "partition"? Beyond that, what did Richthofen intend to imply by the phrase "so-called"? Certainly, even the most rabid German nationalist of the 1920s had conceded that the Polish state had been partitioned in the 18th century. And while the argument that Prussia had received only German lands was an accepted part of the Weimar Polish myth in addition to its acceptance by German historians, most of the historians had admitted that the Polish state had been the object of aggression even when they were contending that Prussian participation in that aggression was justified by the danger of Russia's gaining complete control over Poland. In short, Richthofen's formulations would have been extreme in the 1920s.

Richthofen further developed his argument by repeating the claim made by Kauder that the Poles did not truly want the Oder-Neisse lands. He again made the familiar contention that the Poles were incapable of developing these lands:

"The Polish intention to bring by their own energy the Polish-administered German lands to a new prosperity and a new culture must be seen as a hopeless endeavor. . . . A great part of the emigrant Polish population in East Germany lacks as before any inner connection with the land and any special drive to pledge themselves to a reconstruction."[6]

In this statement, Richthofen has presented not only the myth of the "incapable" Pole, but he has attributed that incapability to the lack of an "inner connection." Richthofen's use of the phrase "inner connection" appears to be ambiguous and the measurement of its effect on creativity uncertain. For instance, neither Schiller or Goethe nor Heine or Rilke required an "inner connection" with some particular locality in order to write their literary works. The belief that a man's family history has to be rooted in the history of a specific locality before he can act creatively in that locality is not supported by experience. Nor does a Pole moving to a formerly German area have to wait until he feels an "inner connection" before he can begin to provide for himself and his family.

In 1959 the writer Johannes Seipolt contributed to this discussion at a meeting of the Central Committee of German Catholics. In some ways he clarified it, for he not only asserted that the Poles who had moved to the former German lands had suffered both from a bad conscience over the expulsion of the Germans as well as from a feeling that everything was provisional, but he also reported that the Poles were prepared to revise the German-Polish border if the revision would free them from the Russian yoke.[7] The assertion concerning the Poles' bad conscience seems highly improbable. In light of the atrocities committed by Germans in Poland during the Second World War, it seems unlikely to assume that a significant number of Poles would have felt guilty about measures designed to punish Germany or Germans. Also, many of those who settled on the former German lands had lost their own homes in the war. In receiving compensation, they would hardly have suffered from a bad conscience. An examination of the second assertion, however, clarifies the source of the debate. There is a difference between lacking an "inner connection" to an area and worrying about whether a superior force is going to evict you from it. It seems more probable that the Polish settlers had a concrete fear of German power and that this fear had led them to wonder whether they would be able to settle permanently. Finally, even if the Poles were willing to exchange a revised border for freedom from Soviet domination, that presumed readiness in no way demonstrated that the Poles were incapable of developing the Oder-Neisse territories. Any readiness to negotiate would not necessarily imply a desperate internal situation or ultimate domestic failure. Also, it should be emphasized that the Germans have not had the power in the post-Second World War world to free Poland from Soviet domination. Therefore, Seipolt's suggestions that such a German-Polish agreement be reached can be considered only a myth. And he was advancing a myth of German power which was itself unreal in the post-1945 world.

Besides these defects in Seipolt's arguments given to support both this supposed Polish inability to cultivate former German lands and this unlikely Polish desire to return those lands to Germany, there was another reason to doubt his contentions. Seipolt's assertions were also part of the

Weimar myth of the Pole. After the First World War, German nationalist writers had repeatedly asserted that the Pole was incapable and needed German guidance. The following comments are typical of the myth:

"Frequently enough the Poles have expressed their apprehension to their German fellow-citizens over what would be the result for the future of the land of such an extensive loss of the land's German character. Polish workers come to the authorities hoping to get back the German crownland lessee since the new Polish one could not understand how to manage the enterprise."[8]

At that time, such assertions seemed to correspond more closely to the German myth of the Pole than to actual conditions of the period because they implied a Polish preference for remaining a suspect minority in a German state. A quarter of a century later, they seemed more mythical than real.

This myth of the incapable Pole in the post-1945 period was strongly advanced by the *Göttingen Arbeitskreis*, an organization led by Herbert Kraus and dedicated to strengthening German claims to these lands.[9] For example, in a work entitled *Ostdeutschland 1960–61 in der polnischen Presse*, the *Kreis* reproduced published Polish laments over shortcomings in the economy and then, using these reports, suggested that the Poles had totally failed to develop these formerly German territories.[10] But there was a marked difference in climate between 1925 and 1965. Because the climate in 1925 was made bitter by the German defeat in the First World War, the Germans automatically accepted such assertions. But in 1965 Friedrich Zipfel, a reviewer, denounced the *Kreis's* conclusion in *Jahrbuch für die Geschichte Mittel- und Ostdeutschlands*, a West Berlin scholarly journal. After admitting that "naturally there are deficiencies" in any period of reconstruction following major destruction, he charged that the *Kreis* had deliberately reprinted only those sources which indicated bottle-necks in the economy, or failures to meet time schedules, while willfully neglecting those sources which recorded Polish successes in reconstructing a viable economy in a devastated area.[11]

Despite this new criticism, other parts of the Weimar myth of the Pole reappeared. The *Kreis* contended that German tribes had been the first to come to the northern part of the German-Polish borderlands. Moreover, Mieszko was still supposed to have been a Scandinavian.[12] Helmut Carl, author of a history of Poland, speculated that the Pole could not have resisted the "higher civilization" of the German had the First World War not interfered.[13] Flottwell would surely have agreed. Seipolt, who was mentioned earlier, had issued still another warning to the Poles that should they keep the lands east of the Oder-Neisse line, the Germans would revive their old image of the Pole as a "land-robber."[14] Of course, by mentioning the possibility, Seipolt not only kept alive the Weimar myth of Polish aggression but also implied a threat. He further intimated in good Weimar fashion that German approval should be the main criterion by which the Poles should measure their actions or, in other words, that the Poles should recognize their subordinate position in their relations with the Germans. Another writer, Fritz Gause, told the world in a 1952 book that the Oder-Neisse border was an unreasonable result of a policy of conquest.[15]

The Weimar myth of the Pole thus found outlets after the Second World War. Yet this myth encountered serious resistance. Influenced by Germany's 1945 disaster, many Germans consciously wanted to reevaluate traditional historical judgments. Germans such as the writer Jobst Gumpert had to explain the rise of Adolf Hitler and to show why he had been able to act on behalf of Germany.

Gumpert, however, did not consider that Hitler alone had been responsible for the Nazi period, nor did he believe that the Nazi phenomenon was without historical antecedents. On the contrary, sensing that traditional attitudes must have been in some way responsible for the events of the Nazi period, Gumpert concluded that these actions must have been the result of a long historical process which he wished to study and exorcise.[16] Thus, motivated by a need to understand the recent catastrophe and work against a possible recurrence, he undertook to write his book.

In exploring the historical antecedents of the Germans' negative attitudes toward the Poles, Gumpert began with the original settlers dispute. He wondered, for example, what would have happened if every nation had demanded possession of that territory which its ancestors had possessed 1500 to 2000 years before.[17] England, he mused, would have had to be returned to the Celts. Another writer of similar persuasion, Hermann Schreiber, agreed that this quarrel was basically irrelevant.[18] Moreover, again challenging the Weimar myth of the Pole, Gumpert rejected the assertion of the German nationalist that Mieszko was a Scandinavian and dismissed the implication that the Pole was incapable of founding his own state. Although he conceded that individual Scandinavian soldiers-of-fortune might have served in the Polish army, he opposed the nationalist views of Weimar and pre-Weimar Germany by concluding that this fact had no real bearing on the interpretation either of Mieszko's Scandinavian origin or of Polish capabilities, especially since these Scandinavian soldiers-of-fortune had served in numerous armies throughout Europe.[19] And in his book, Gumpert continued to challenge the various unsupported assertions comprising the Weimar myth of the Pole.

In his study, Gumpert demanded new ways to understand the past, and his need for new interpretations was shared by others with a similar focus who searched for new answers and challenged old assertions in their own ways. Martin Broszat, for example, wrote that the Nazis had destroyed the legitimate historical position of the German in the east.[20] His colleague, Golo Mann, concurred with him. Mann went further by commenting in the popular magazine *Stern* that, in comparison to the Nazi occupation of Poland, the subsequent period of the Stalinist rule in Poland was paradise.[21] The leadership of the German Evangelical Church had stressed that Nazi brutality in Poland had invalidated any legal claim the Germans might have had to the Oder-Neisse lands. The leaders of the German Catholic Church, in responding to the invitation of the Polish Catholic hierarchy to visit Poland and to their hopes for mutual forgiveness, replied that the terrible things which had been done in Germany's name would result in difficult consequences for the whole nation. These statements effectively challenged the Weimar belief in the moral right of the Germans to the German-Polish borderlands. Furthermore, Radio Bremen told its listeners that Hitler bore full responsibility for both Poland's absorption in the Soviet bloc and the shifting of Poland's borders westward.[22]

As the postwar German historians, journalists, clergymen, politicians and others sought to understand what Hitler had done in the name of Germany and how he had been able to carry out certain activities, they published new assessments of German-Polish relations. For example, Hans Roos wrote in his *Polen und Europa* that German-Polish discord had resulted in the advance of Soviet power. He hoped that the consequences of this, including the partition of Germany, would lead to a later German-Polish understanding.[23] His hope for a new relationship with Poland was widely shared. Werner Conze, the Heidelberg historian, concluded that "for the first time in the history of the Polish question," the German nation stood no longer "under the obsolete, destructive alternatives: with Russia at the cost of Poland or with the help of Poland against Russia."[24] Moreover, beyond these conclusions was the realization, as Schreiber put it, that while the Germans had the right and duty to discuss the Oder-Neisse border, "it must be clear to us that no border can be a greater injustice than a war which one conducts on account of it."[25] What other sentence could have been a clearer statement of national priorities? [26] Many Germans in responsible positions in Germany society in attempting to develop a new basis for German-Polish relations thus recognized that this effort necessitated a new German image of the Pole.

Gotthold Rhode's revolutionary first sentence in his *Geschichte Polens* revealed a possible direction for German scholars to follow in constructing this new image. The sentence read: "In a manner similar to German and Bohemian history, Polish history begins first in the tenth century. . . ."[27] With this statement, Rhode at the very least suggested an equality among the histories of Poland, Germany, and Bohemia. He explicitly denied that German or Germanic history began many centuries before the Slav had come to Europe. The reader of Rhode's work also would not detect any implication that Slavic history was clearly inferior to German history. Instead, Rhode suggested an equality between the histories of Germany, Bohemia, and Poland. This, in turn, meant a denial of the inequality which was assumed in the Weimar myth. Rhode wrote that "in a manner similar to German and Bohemian history Polish history begins first in the tenth century."

Rhode also poses a problem to the historian's understanding of the relationship between creativity and the environment. In 1941 Rhode published his first book, *Brandenburg-Preussen und die Protestanten in Polen 1640–1740.* In content it was two books. One was factual; the other, consisting of the foreword and part of the conclusion, was primarily propaganda. The young Rhode obviously gave the then ruling party only the barest minimum of public fidelity. A decade and a half later, he followed his first book with a massive study of Poland's medieval role as a bulwark of the occident. Entitled *Die Ostgrenze Polens,* the work would be a credit to any historian as would his *Geschichte Polens* published in 1966. But one does wonder how a man who grew up in Nazi Germany and was educated to a negative view of the Pole could emerge as the most impartial and most impressive interpreter of Polish history Germany has yet had. In Rhode's case there appears to be no apparent explanation except that some creative individuals are able to transcend time and place and local influence.

On the other hand, there is a very strong correlation existing between work and environment in other books of the postwar period. In the atmosphere of the cold war, many authors reacted to Poland in terms of anticommunism. For example, in 1956 after the Poles had won from the Soviet Union the right to change top leadership in the Polish communist party, the government, and the army without prior Soviet approval, one writer who was observing the Polish scene realized that "since October 1956 Europe again knows that Poland still belongs to it."[28] He then recalled that Poland "has for a long time, and this should not be forgotten, made the road to Europe difficult for autocratic Moscow and who has achieved much of significance in the defense against the Turks."[29] Another author who reached a similar conclusion saw in Poland "a people living and thinking in the western European, occidental cultural tradition."[30] Yet since such praise remained largely dependent upon continued Polish defiance of Soviet might, it was likewise dependent on Soviet acceptance of Polish actions.

The current political situation also inspired two further glances at the

Poles. First, the partition of Germany forced some Germans to recognize that the Polish nation had survived over a century of division and stateless-ness.[31] These Germans might well have wondered whether the German nation would be able to survive over a century of division, if not stateless-ness. Secondly, many Germans soon realized that a policy of healing the wounds suffered during the Second World War was incomplete without a reconciliation with Poland. As Konrad Adenauer, the "father" of the Federal Republic of Germany, told General Charles de Gaulle in 1960, Germany wished to have good relations with Poland.[32] Moreover, on the political front, Adenauer approved of the travels of a leading industrialist to Poland in the early 1960s and the trade agreement which was consum-mated in 1963. Motivated by the same desire to heal up the wounds suffered during the Second World War, Willy Brandt publicly worked for a reconciliation between the Germans and the Poles. He wrote that a reconciliation between Germany and Poland would have the same histo-rical importance as the reconciliation between Germany and France.[33] Then in December, 1970, seemingly supported by a West German public opinion which longed for new relationships with Eastern Europe, Chancel-lor Brandt signed a treaty with the Poles in Warsaw.[34] The election results of 1972 confirmed that the West Germans wanted to repudiate the old myths and hatreds and that they were actively rejecting these old tradi-tionalist views.

While the Weimar myth of the Pole had not completely disappeared from post-1945 West Germany, its tenets were being challenged by politi-cians and clergymen, scholars and journalists, and these challenges had won popular support. Most West Germans were realizing that the new factors had made new points of view mandatory. Specifically, they recog-nized that Hitler's policies had resulted in the destruction of the German state, the devastation of German society, the expulsion of Germans from many areas of East Central Europe, the partitioning of Germany, and a widespread hatred of Germans throughout Europe and North America. This realization resulted in the conclusion that Hitler and his policies represented a great disaster for the German people and that the racial and nationalistic beliefs associated with the Nazis therefore needed to be dismissed.

Most West Germans had come to realize also that Hitler's policies had resulted in death camps with full schedules; the murder of many of Europe's Jews; the slaughter of countless Poles and Yugoslavs as well as Russians; the humiliation of the Czech, Dutch, Danish, and Norwegian peoples; the bombing of England; and long lists of victims wherever Hitler's followers had operated. Such a realization produced a feeling of guilt which also resulted in a readiness among West Germans in the post-1945 period to accept the replacement of long-established beliefs.

Along these lines, some West German writers have searched for new paths in the postwar period while others have been caught between recognizing the need for new departures and hesitating to betray old ideas. Still others have doggedly pursued the traditional paths. Yet where the dynamics of the resultant interactions will lead is not yet clear. Thus far it has led to treaties with the Soviet Union and Poland—Brandt's *Ostpolitik*. Even though the Weimar myth of the Pole had been largely discredited, this was not to say that a new image of the Pole had taken its place in West Germany. It may well be that the West Germans will revert eventually to their traditional posture of indifference towards the Poles. Today the treaties with the Soviet Union and Poland represent an attempt by the West Germans to settle some outstanding debts which date from 1945. But it is difficult to forecast what their actions will be once these accounts are settled.

When the new East Germany is discussed, it must be noted first that the communist party considers its teachings valid for each and every aspect of human existence. The party therefore even decrees how the historian or journalist should handle the topic of German-Polish relations. Specifically, since the party views history as a process of class struggle (rather than national struggle), historians are obliged to begin with the premise that the German and Polish working classes, since they both belong to the proletariat, have had no reason to quarrel. Moreover, since the party claims that communists alone can perceive truth because they alone have the scientific theory of Marx to guide them, historians also assume that they can dismiss the findings of previous bourgeois and nationalist writers.

The work of Felix-Heinrich Gentzen reveals what these beliefs in the primacy of class and the infallibility of Marx's teachings have produced. About national enmity he wrote:

"The true history of the German people shows that, besides the persecution and suppression of the Polish people by the ruling German classes which work together with the ruling Polish classes, there are also good traditions: traditions of friendship and common struggle of the working masses of both nations."[35]

Gentzen is thus asserting that the workmen of Poland and Germany supposedly have developed a tradition of friendship while their class enemies supposedly have repressed them. In a later work, Gentzen added:

"The German and Polish working class has been required to offer many and bloody sacrifices until their recognition of the necessity of a friendship between the German and the Polish people became generally accepted and the guiding principle of the policy of both people—and this on the German side only in one part of Germany."[36]

Furthermore, in a summary which many West Germans could accept at face value, Gentzen cleared away the debris of the Weimar myth of the Pole and dismissed the views of his nationalistic predecessors with the following statments:

"There is hardly an area of German history in which consciously or unconsciously so many falsifications and distortions have been undertaken as in the area of German-Polish relations. Beginning with the thesis of the "original Germanic settlement" of the Polish western territories, via the "German plough" and the "German handicraft" which the Germans first had to bring to Poland, via the "Norman blood" of the Polish kings, via the bloom of a Polish renaissance culture in the 16th century which allegedly stemmed from the Germans, to the "German industry" and the German capital in Poland—there is not a positive phenomenon in the history of Poland which does not stem from the Germans. All negative, phenomena however are supposed to have their roots in the "Polish discord," in the "inability to govern themselves," in the "Polish economy" and in the end in a suppression of the German element."[37]

Even though many West Germans could accept the dismissal of the Weimar myth, they were unwilling to accept Gentzen's conclusions in its place. The present political leadership of both Poland and East Germany does have its reasons for wanting Gentzen's substitute accepted by the masses. After all, the two allies of the Soviet Union must cooperate, and negative impressions of each other could only hinder coexistence. The Poles, therefore, have to be convinced that the "socialist" East Germans of today bear no relationship to the sadistic Germans who occupied Polish territories during the Second World War; similarly, the East Germans have to be persuaded that the resolute, creative Poles of today bear no relationship to the "incapable" Poles of yesterday. Scholars like Gentzen, then, must meet these needs.

Yet the West Germans and others outside the confines of the communist bloc are unwilling to accept Gentzen's version of German-Polish relations. They refuse to take Gentzen's viewpoint because he has simply created another myth. For instance, the "Polish ruling classes" did not cooperate with the "German ruling classes." It is assumed that the phrase the "Polish ruling classes" refers to the Polish nobility and "German ruling classes" to those who shared in the Prussian and German state power. In other words, these phrases encompass Polish men like Kościuszko, Piłsudski, and the nobles who left Prussia in 1830 to fight the Russians; they encompass German men like Flottwell, Bismarck, and Bülow. Yet since these two groups fought one another fiercely, Gentzen's attempt to make allies of them is mythmaking.

There was also little actual cooperation between the German and Polish working classes. One of the basic conclusions of this study is that the German man-in-the-street, particularly in Western and Central Germany, has been indifferent to the entire "Polish question." Most of the German factory workers who have lived precisely in these areas of Western and Central Germany have never even met a Pole. Thus, to say that these workers "cooperated" with the Poles is still more mythmaking on Gentzen's part.

Gentzen's other formulations also confirm that he has been constructing a substitute for the Weimar myth of the Pole. For example, when Gentzen considered the question of who first settled the German-Polish borderlands, he refused to conclude as had many West Germans that the problem was without a solution based on hard facts and that the problem lacked present political relevance. Instead, he accepted the old Polish argument, which was the obverse of the traditional German argument. He simply stated that the original settlers were related to the Western Slavs.[38] However, like the makers of the Weimar myth of the Pole, Gentzen could not prove his assertion.

But since evidence, or its absence, seldom bothers the mythmaker, Gentzen proceeded to offer the following solution to the controversy over the emergence of the Polish state:

"This thoroughly natural historical process was dependent upon the development of the productive powers and the alteration of social relations and had not the slightest to do with such "mysterious, mythical forces" as the alleged Norman blood of the Polish Piasts."[39]

This statement also is simple assertion. It may well have been that a Pole seized upon a given degree of social development and formed the Polish state. But Gentzen's formulation fails to prove this. It just mechanically assumes that since a given stage of social development automatically produces a certain result, there would be no need to investigate the human actors who participated in that result.

In continuing to build his myth of the Pole, Gentzen next condemned the partitions of Poland, primarily because Marx and Engels had condemned them.[40] Since the information did not fit into his myth, Gentzen neglected to mention that Marx had written that one must question whether German territory should be given to a people unable to advance from a state of feudalism.[41] In making this statement, Marx was thinking of the Poles.

Gentzen brought his version of Polish history to the present with a stirring account of the Polish resistance movement:

"It is proof of the fabulous vigor of the Polish people [did he mean the Polish proletariat] that despite this great loss of men and tremendous destruction it still organized an active resistance against the bestial German fascism and undermined more and more the dominion of the enemy."[42]

While Gentzen considered his version of Polish history complete, it was in the main unrealistic. Unsupported by evidence, his conclusions were largely myths.

Other pronouncements by East German politicians concerning the problems of German-Polish relations contain the same themes and present the same difficulties. For instance, Walter Ulbricht, the "father" of the German Democratic republic, denounced that constant *Drang nach Osten* which he considered to have benefited the owners of the large estates. While other East German writers agreed with this assertion, no one bothered to prove whether it was true.[43] Otto Grotewohl, for his part, contended that Hitler's reign of terror in Poland had failed to destroy either the Polish people or the presumed friendly relations between the "progressive and revolutionary circles" of the two peoples.[44] While such an assertion had been fitted into the East German communist party's myth of the Pole, there was no evidence to demonstrate that these friendly relations had existed.

In spite of their mythmaking role, men like Gentzen could play an important role in the future evolution of German-Polish relations. In East Germany, they present their views to a captive audience. Moreover, having easy access to important archives and ample opportunity to discuss scholarly issues with Polish historians, they could bring a new sensitivity to German evaluations of Polish history while stimulating in their Polish colleagues a fresh awareness of Polish evaluations of German history.[45]

This progress from myth to myth, with overtones of paradox and uncertainty, is a significant finding of this study of German images of the Pole. The paradox is found in the fact that the East Germans have constructed their own myth of the Pole which is, in large measure, the obverse of the German nationalists' myth of the Pole. There is uncertainty because the West Germans have not yet constructed a new image of the Pole and because the East Germans have an opportunity to create an era of genuine German-Polish cooperation. Inasmuch as this account of the history of the German nationalists' myth of the Pole can only end on these overtones of paradox and uncertainty, it may well be that the legacy of the German nationalists' myth of the Pole will be both an East German myth and a West German indifference.

Notes

1. Many observers believe that the Soviets hoped that the Oder-Neisse line would make permanent the German-Polish hatred and thus cement the Polish dependency upon the Soviet Union.
2. U. W. Kitzinger, *German Electoral Politics* (London, 1960), p.194.
3. Harry Kenneth Rosenthal, "The Integration and Assimilation of the German Expellees," *Polish Review*, 8, No. 1 (Winter, 1963), 78–112.
4. Bolko Freiherr von Richthofen, *Deutschland und Polen. Schicksal einer nationalen Nachbarschaft* (Weener [Osfriesland], 1959), p.7 [his 1929 book was entitled *Gehört Ostdeutschland zur Urheimat der Polen?*].
5. Ibid., p.29.
6. Ibid., pp.45–46.
7. Herbert Czaja and Gustav E. Kafka, *Deutsche und Polen* (Recklinghausen, 1960), pp.96, 95.
8. Hermann Rauschning, *Die Entdeutschung Westpreussens und Posens* (Berlin, 1930), p.89.
9. The *Kreis* was especially active in presenting legal arguments; see *Ostdeutschland* (Kitzingen-Main, 1953), I, Part 1, 3–124.
10. Also see *Ostdeutschland 1958–59 in der polnischen Presse* (Würzburg, 1959).
11. Friedrich Zipfel, review of *Ostdeutschland 1960–61 in der polnischen Presse*, in *Jahrbuch für die Geschichte Mittel- und Ostdeutschlands*, 13 –14 (1965), 635.
12. *Ostdeutschland*, pp.35–36.
13. Helmut Carl, *Kleine Geschichte Polens* (Gütersloh, 1963), pp. 111–112.
14. Czaja and Kafka, p.90.
15. Fritz Gause, *Deutsch-slawische Schicksalsgemeinschaft* (Kritzingen-Main, 1952), p.286.
16. Jobst Gumpert, *Polen-Deutschland* (München, 1966), p.10.
17. Ibid., p.11.
18. Herman Schreiber, *Land im Osten* (Düsseldorf and Wien, 1961), p.26.
19. Gumpert, p.22.
20. Martin Broszat, *Nationalsozialistische Polenpolitik 1939–1945* (Frankfurt am Main and Hamburg, 1965), p.172.

21. Golo Mann, "Mit den Polen Frieden machen," *Stern*, 17, No. 28 (July 7–13, 1964), 29.

22. Radio Bremen, *Begegnung mit Polen* (Bremen, 1963), p.113.

23. Hans Roos, *Polen und Europa* (Tübingen, 1957), p.400.

24. Werner Conze, *Polnische Nation und deutsche Politik im ersten Weltkrieg* (Köln and Graz, 1958), p.405.

25. Schreiber, p.397.

26. Furthermore, some writers contended that the Pole had made excellent use of this time of peace. For example, in *Deutschlands Osten, Polens Westen?* (Frankfurt am Main, 1965) Hansjakob Stehle even asserted that the Pole had been successful in his efforts to make the Oder-Neisse lands Polish. This conclusion certainly shocked the men of the Göttinger Arbeitskreis even as it led to the suspicion that time was on the Pole's side in this old-fashioned territorial dispute.

27. Gotthold Rhode, *Geschichte Polens* (Darmstadt, 1966), p.1.

28. Herbert Ludat, ed., *Liegt Polen noch in Europa?* (Giessen, 1960), p.29; Klaus Zernack was the author cited.

29. Ibid., p.23.

30. Ibid., p.59; Herbert Ludat was the author cited. Also see Karl Hartmann, *Polen* (Nürnberg, 1966), p.x; and Hansjakob Stehle, *Nachbar Polen* (Frankfurt am Main, 1963), p.10.

31. Helmut Fechner, *Deutschland und Polen* (Würzburg, 1964), p.68; and Hans Rothfels and Werner Markert, eds., *Deutscher Osten und Slawischer Westen* (Tübingen, 1955), p.118, with Eugen Lemberg the author cited.

32. Konrad Adenauer, *Erinnerungen 1959–1963* (Stuttgart, 1968), p.45.

33. Willy Brandt, *Friedenspolitik in Europa* (Frankfurt am Main, 1968), pp.114, 115, 154, 122.

34. *Der Spiegel*, No. 31, July 26, 1971, reported that of every hundred expellees only the following number refused to recognize the Oder-Neisse line: in October, 1969, 57; in March, 1970, 50; in June, 1970, 47 and in December, 1970, 34.

35. Felix-Heinrich Gentzen, *Deutschland und Polen* (Leipzig and Jena, 1956), pp.12–13.

36. Felix-Heinrich Gentzen, *Grosspolen im Januaraufstand* (Berlin, 1958), p.260. Also see Felix-Heinrich Gentzen, Adam Galos, and Witold Jakóbczyk, *Die Hakatisten* (Berlin, 1966), p.418.

37. Gentzen, *Deutschland und Polen*, p.7.

38. Ibid., p.14.

39. Ibid., p.17.

40. Ibid., p.60.

41. Wolfgang Hallgarten, *Studien über die deutsche Polenfreundschaft in der Periode der Märzrevolution* (München and Berlin, 1928), p.91. Also see Engel's statement on p.24 of this study.

42. Gentzen, *Deutschland und Polen*, p.103.

43. Walter Ulbricht, *Die Entwicklung des deutschen volksdemokrat-*
    ischen Staates 1945–1958 (Berlin, 1959), p.225; Erhard Moritz,
    Preussen und der Kościuszko-Aufstand 1794 (Berlin, 1968), p.5; and
    Otto Grotewohl, *Im Kampf um die einige Deutsche Demokratische*
    Republik (Berlin, 1959–1964), IV, 522–523.
44. Grotewohl, II, 151–152; II, 89; and IV, 524.
45. A joint East German-Polish historical commission was founded in
    1956.

EPILOGUE

If the course of events in the future cannot be known, the present situation can be described with some confidence; and the evolution of past events is even clearer. The present in the two Germanies is a period of neither Hakatist respect nor Weimar contempt for the Pole. West Germans consider their country's relations with Poland of secondary interest. Even though a treaty with Poland did arouse debate in the Federal Republic, it was the treaty with the Soviet Union that decided the present course of West Germany's relations with the east. Likewise, the Soviet Union basically determines the present course of East Germany's relations with Poland.

A study of the past, for its part, reveals no thousand-year war between the Polish and German peoples. A thousand years of indifference is closer to the mark. After all, mass participation in assigning a stereotype to the Pole first became evident in 1894, and this stereotype was spread to all Germany only after the First World War. While these conclusions may enrage those for whom the brutalities of the Second World War have made overwhelming the need to picture German-Polish hostility as eternal, they are clearly supported by the available evidence.

This is not to say that the German stereotype of the Pole played no part in Nazi activities in Poland. It seems probable that the negative assessments of the Poles made easier the Nazi program of slaughter, for they disarmed potential critics of Nazi genocide. Still, disarming critics is not the same as slaughtering millions of men and women. It is too much to place a major responsibility for Nazi bestialities on pre-Nazi writers, especially since the Nazis had their own sources of inspiration.

Two points should be made regarding the methodology of this study. First, the writings of second-rate journalists furnished far more materials and much greater, and closer, appreciation of mass attitudes than did the works of great men of letters. The great writers wrote little about the daily comings and goings of the Polish community. This community failed to arouse the literary writers sufficiently to permeate their thought. Moreover, the image of the Pole of Schiller, for example, proved to be less important than the caricatures of Poles by minor Prussian officials or Saxon pamphleteers.

Second, and more important, the concept of myth adequately explains the development of the modern German image of the Pole. The implications of this are highly significant, for accepting the mythical side of group relations necessitates a recasting of historical and other forms of analysis. The "facts" thus may not, as a result, square with group attitudes. In short, the historian, in addition to knowing what *was* happening and why, should endeavor to understand what people *thought* was happening and why. Man's consciousness deserves to be studied just as does his material situation.

Studies of man's consciousness are especially important in our age of mass politics. Since the man-on-the-street has psychological as well as material needs and since he may be less aware of his material situation than his leaders, his behavior and its effect on society and government cannot be measured simply by statistical indices of economic performance. If a group's consciousness and material situation are incongruous at points in time, either could still be dominant in a particular historical situation. Thus, both must be assessed if historical events are to be explained.

BIBLIOGRAPHY

1. Archival Sources

Deutsches Zentralarchiv Potsdam

Reichskanzlei
> Nr. 665, Band 9. Acta betreffend: die Polen.
> Nr. 666, Band 10. Acta betreffend: die Polen.

Deutsches Zentralarchiv Merseburg

Ministerium des Innern
> Rep. 77, Tit. 862, Nr. 11, Band 3. Acta betreffend: Vereine und Gesellschaften polnischer Zunge.
> Rep. 77, Tit. 864, Nr. 41. Acta betreffend: die Gründung polnischer Blätter zur Belehrung der Bevolkerung in den polnischen Gebiets-theilen des Landes.
> Rep. 77, Tit. 870, Nr. 47, Adh. A, Band 1. Acta betreffend: die Polenbewegung in der Provinz Westpreussen.
> Rep. 77, Tit. 1083, Nr. 10, Band 1. Acta betreffend: den "Verein zur Förderung des Deutschthums in den Ostmarken."

Preussisches Staats-Ministerium
> Rep. 90a, Abt. B, Tit. 111, 2b, Nr. 6, Bände 102–115. Acta betreffend: die Staatsministerial Sitzungs-Protokolle.

Ministerium der Geistlichen, Unterrichts und Medizinal-Angelegenheiten
> Rep. 76, IV, Sekt. 1a, Abt. 2, Nr. 1, Band 5. Acta betreffend: den erzbischöflichen Stuhl von Gnesen-Posen zu Posen.

149

Wojewódzkie Archiwum Państwowe w Poznaniu

Naczelne Presydium w Poznaniu (Oberpräsidium der Provinz Posen)
OP XXIX D I 32. Acta betreffend: das Ableben des Erzbischofs
Dinder und die Wiederbesetzung des erzbischöflichen Stuhles.

Geheimes Preussisches Staatsarchiv (Berlin-Dahlem)

Königlich Preussische Regierung zu Bromberg
Rep. 30, Nr. 679, Acta betreffend: die Förderung des Deutschtums
in den Ostmarken.
Rep. 30, Nr. 685. Acta betreffend: die Stärkung und Förderung des
Deutschtums in der Provinz Posen.
Rep. 30, Nr. 686. Acta betreffend: die deutsche Sorge.
Rep. 30, Nr. 688. Acta betreffend: Förderung des Deutschtums.
Rep. 30, Nr. 693. Acta betreffend: die erneuerten Bestrebungen für
die polnische Nationalität.
Rep. 30, Nr. 694. Acta betreffend: Agitation des Polenthums.
Rep. 30, Nr. 696. Acta betreffend: Agitationen des Polenthums.
Allgemeine Vorgänge.
Rep. 30, Nr. 701. Acta betreffend: Betheiligung des Katholischen
Klerus and der nationalpolnischen Bewegung.
Rep. 30, Nr. 705. Acta betreffend: Agitation des Polentums. Allge-
meine Vorgänge.
Rep. 30, Nr. 753. Acta betreffend: der polnische Aufstand und die
Uberleitung an Polen.
Rep. 30, Nr. 754. Acta betreffend: Neugestaltung der polnischen
Verhältnisse.
Königlich Preussische Regierung zu Marienwerder
Rep. A181, Nr. 1456–1458. Acta betreffend: die im Jahren 1848
ausgebrochenen Unruhen der polnischen Bevölkerung des hiesigen
Regierungs-Bezirks.
Rep. A181, Nr. 2314. Acta betreffend: die im Jahren 1848 ausge-
brochenen Unruhen der polnischen Bevölkerung des hiesigen
Regierungs-Bezirks.
Landrats-Amts Meseritzer Kreises
Rep. 6B, Nr. 75. Acta betreffend: Förderung des Deutschtums.
Rep. 6B, Nr. 76–77. Acta betreffend: die staatliche Unterstützung
deutscher Aerzte, Apotheker, Rechtsanwälte.
Rep. 6B, Nr. 185–186. Acta betreffend: Polen-Aufstand.
Rep. 6B, Nr. 500. Acta betreffend: die im Jahre 1848 in der Provinz
Posen ausgebrochenen kriegerischen Unruhen.
Landratsamt Strasburg
Rep. A205, Nr. 153, Acta betreffend: die revolutionairen Kund-
gebungen unter der polnischen Bevölkerung der Provinz
1863–1864.

Landratsamt Thorn
   Rep. A207, Nr. 601. Acta betreffend: die polnische Bewegung im
      Kreise Thorn.
Polizei-Präsidium zu Danzig
   Rep. A209, Nr. 1 Acta betreffend: Neuorientierung in der Polen-
      politik.
Königlich Domanien Amts Schöneck
   Rep. A145, Nr. 28. Acta betreffend: die Agitation in Interesse der
      polnischen Nationalität.
Königlich Domanien Amts Tuchel
   Rep. A145, Nr. 31. Acta betreffend: die Errichtung der Liga Polska
      durch den Gutsbesitzer v. Polczynski in kr. Schliewitz 1849.
Magistrat zu Dirschau
   Rep. A308, Nr. 447. Acta betreffend: Organisation und Bekämpfung
      des Polonismus.
Deutscher Volksrat für Westpreussen und Polen
   Rep. A419, Nr. 1—7. Werbelisten.

Bundesarchiv Koblenz

R19/334. Chef der Ordnungspolizei.
R22/3372. Reichsjustizministerium.
R22/3383. Reichsjustizministerium.
R43/I/117—127. Reichskanzlei: auswärtige Angelegenheiten.
R43/II/646—647b. Reichskanzlei: Krieg.
R43/II/650. Reichskanzlei: Krieg.
R43/II/1480—1484b. Reichskanzlei: auswärtige Angelegenheiten.
R49/75. Reichskommissar für die Festigung deutschen Volkstums:
      die Frage der Behandlung der Bevölkerung der ehemaligen pol-
      nischen Gebiete nach rassenpolitischen Gesichtspunkten.
R49/Anhang I/34. Reichskommissar für die Festigung deutschen
      Volkstums: die Ansiedlung der Umsiedler im Warthegau.
R52/II/12a. Kanzlei des Generalgouverneurs: Berichte des General-
      gouverneurs, 1943—1944.
R52/II/174—223. Kanzlei des Generalgouverneurs: Tagebuch.
R52/II/244—246. Kanzlei des Generalgouverneurs: Tagebuch.
R58/270a. Reichssicherheitshauptamt.
Z Sg. 101/1—42. Sammlung Brammer.
Z Sg. 102/1—43. Sammlung Sänger.
Z Sg. 109/1—55. Sammlung Oberheitmann.
Z Sg. 110/1-11. Sammlung Traub.
Z Sg. 116/1911-1929. Deutsches Nachrichtenbüro: Deutsche diplo-
      matisch-politische Korrespondenz. National Archives: American
      Committee for the Study of War Documents.
Reichsführer SS und Chef der Deutschen Polizei: Cat. 39, T-175,
      Roll 261, 263, 265.

2. German Writings Concerned with the Poles

Altkemper, Johannes. *Deutschtum und Polentum in politisch-konfessionel-ler Bedeutung.* Leipzig, 1910.

Arndt, Ernst Moritz. *Polenlärm und Polenbegeisterung.* Berlin, 1848.

———. *Versuch in vergleichender Völkergeschichte.* Leipzig, 1843.

Arnold, Robert Franz. *Geschichte der deutschen Polenlitteratur von den Anfängen bis 1800.* Osnabrück, 1966. [Reprint of 1899 Vienna edition.]

Aschenbrenner, Viktor; Birke, Ernst; Kuhn, Walter; and Lemberg, Eugen. *Die Deutschen und ihre östlichen Nachbarn.* Frankfurt am Main-Berlin-Bonn-München, 1967.

Aspern, Karl. *Geschichte der Polen.* Regensburg, 1916.

Aubin, Hermann. *Die deutsche Leistung in Ostmitteleuropa.* Berlin, 1938.

———. *Die volkspolitische Bedeutung von Gewerbe und Industrie in Ost-deutschland.* Breslau, 1941.

———. *Geschichtlicher Aufriss des Ostraums.* Berlin, 1940.

———. *Von Raum und Grenzen des deutschen Volkes.* Breslau, 1938.

———. *Zur Erforschung der deutschen Ostbewegung.* Leipzig, 1939.

Baske, Siegfried. *Praxis und Prinzipien der preussischen Polenpolitik von 1849–1871.* Hamburg, 1960. [Dissertation.]

Beer, Adolf. *Die erste Theilung Polens.* Wien, 1873.

Beheim-Schwarzbach, Max. *Die Besiedelung von Ostdeutschland durch die zweite germanische Völkerwanderung.* Berlin, 1882

———. *Hohenzollernsche Colonisationen.* Leipzig, 1874.

Berger, Heinrich. *Friedrich der Grosse als Kolonisator.* Giessen, 1896.

Bergmann, Eugen von. *Zur Geschichte der Entwickelung deutscher, pol-nischer und jüdischer Bevölkerung in der Provinz Posen seit 1824.* Tübingen, 1883.

Bernhard, Ludwig. *Die Polenfrage: Das polnische Gemeinwesen im preu-ssischen Staat.* Leipzig, 1910.

———. *Die Polenfrage: Der Nationalitätenkampf der Polen in Preussen.* München and Leipzig, 1920.

———. *Preussische Städte im Gebiete der polnischen Nationalitäten-kampfes.* Leipzig, 1909.

———. *Zur Polenpolitik des Königreichs Preussen.* Berlin, 1923.

Beyer, Hans Joachim. *Aufbau und Entwicklung des ostdeutschen Volks-raums.* Danzig, 1935.

———. *Das Schicksal der Polen.* Leipzig and Berlin, 1942.

———. "Der Ursprung der polnischen Führungsschicht und der Zusammen-bruch des polnischen Staates." *Deutsche Monatshefte*, 7, Nos. 5–6 (November–December, 1940), 220–231.

———. *Die deutsche Einheit des grösseren Mitteleuropa und Ihr Verfall im 19. Jahrhundert.* Posen, 1943.

Beyer, Hermann Wolfgang. *Tausend Jahre deutscher Schicksalskampf im Osten*. Berlin, 1939.

Beyl, Edmund. *Deutsche Polenpolitik im 19. Jahrhundert*. Danzig, 1940.

Bibliographie zur Geschichte der polnischen Frage bis 1919. Stuttgart, 1942. [Bibliographie der Weltkriegsbücherei.]

Biedermann, Gerd S. *Polen im Urteil der nationalpreussischen Historiographie des 19. Jahrhunderts*. Erlangen, 1967. [Dissertation.]

Bierschenk, Theodor. *Die deutsche Volksgruppen in Polen 1934–1939*. Kitzingen-Main, 1954.

Birnbaum, Immanuel. *Entzweite Nachbarn*. Frankfurt am Main, 1968.

Bismarck, Otto Fürst von. *Gedanken und Erinnerungen*, vols. 1–3. New York and Stuttgart, 1922

Bleck, Walter. *Die politischen Parteien und die Posener Frage in den Jahren 1848/1849*. Posen, 1914. [Dissertation]

Boberach, Heinz, ed. *Meldungen aus dem Reich*. Neuwied and Berlin, 1965.

Bock, Wilhelm, *Zur Sprachenfrage in der Provinz Posen*. Berlin, 1917.

Botschaften der Versöhnung. Berlin, 1966.

Botzenhart, Erich, ed. *Freiherr vom Stein*, vols. 1–7. Berlin, 1931–1937.

Brackmann, Albert. *Die Anfänge des polnischen Staates*. Berlin, 1934.

———. *Die Wikinger und die Anfänge Polens*. Berlin, 1942.

———, ed., *Deutschland und Polen*. München and Berlin, 1933.

———, ed., *Germany and Poland in Their Historical Relations*. Munich and Berlin, 1934.

Brandt, Willy. *Friedenspolitik in Europa*. Frankfurt am Main, 1968.

Braun, Friedrich. *Die Urbevölkerung Europas und die Herkunft der Germanen*. Berlin-Stuttgart-Leipzig, 1922.

Bredt, Johann Victor. *Die Polenfrage im Ruhrkohlengebiet*. Leipzig, 1909.

Breyer, Richard. *Das Deutsche Reich und Polen 1932–1937*. Würzburg, 1955.

———, ed. *Probleme der Wissenschaft im heutigen Polen*. Marburg/Lahn, 1968.

Broszat, Martin. *Nationalsozialistische Polenpolitik 1939–1945*. Frankfurt am Main-Hamburg, 1965.

———. *200 Jahre Deutsche Polenpolitik*. München, 1963.

Bülow, Bernhard Fürst von. *Denkwürdigkeiten*, vols. 1–4. Berlin, 1930–1931.

———. *Deutsche Politik*. Berlin, 1917.

Burneleit, Heinz, ed. *Friedrich der Grosse*. Würzburg, 1962.

Carl, Helmut. *Kleine Geschichte Polens*. Gütersloh, 1963.

Caro, Jacob. *Geschichte Polens*, vols. 2–5, Part 2. Gotha, 1863–1888.

Clausewitz, Carl von. *Politische Schriften und Briefe*. München, 1922.

Cleinow, Georg. *Der Verlust der Ostmark*. Berlin, 1934.

———. *Die Polenfrage vor der Entscheidung*. Berlin, 1918.

———. *Die Zukunft Polens*, vols. 1–2. Leipzig, 1908, 1914.

Conrady, Emil von. *Carl von Grolman*, vols. 1–3. Berlin, 1894–1896.

Conze, Werner. *Polnische Nation und deutsche Politik im ersten Weltkrieg*. Köln and Graz, 1958.

———, and Hertz-Eichenrode, Dieter, eds. *Karl Marx. Manuskripte über die polnische Frage (1863–1864)*. 'S-Gravenhage, 1961.

Craemer, Rudolf. *Deutschtum im Völkerraum*. Stuttgart, 1938.

Credner, F. A. *Polnische Revolutionen*. Prague, 1863.

Czaja, Herbert, and Kafka, Gustav E. *Deutsche und Polen*. Recklinghausen, 1960.

Czajka, Willi, ed. *Der deutsche Ostraum im Unterricht. Ein Handbuch für den Lehrer*. Breslau, 1935.

Das östliche Deutschland. Würzburg, 1959.

Das verwirrte Pohlen. Frankfurt and Leipzig, 1711.

Delbrück, Hans. *Die Polenfrage*. Berlin, 1894.

Der Osten, Part 1. *Soldatenbriefe zur Berufsförderung*, vol. 16. Breslau, 1941.

Deutsch-polnische Begegnungen 1945–1958. Würzburg, 1960.

Deutsch-polnische Nachbarschaft als Problem und Aufgabe. Leer/Ostfriesland, 1959.

Deutsche Ostforschung. Ergebnisse und Aufgaben seit dem ersten Weltkrieg, vols. 1–2. Leipzig, 1942–1943.

Deutsche Ostsiedlung im Mittelalter und Neuzeit. Köln, 1971.

Die deutsche Ostmark. Berlin, 1894.

Die deutsche Ostgebiete zur Zeit der Weimarer Republik. Köln and Graz, 1966.

Diels, Paul. *Die Slawen*. Leipzig and Berlin, 1920.

Diewerge, Wolfgang. *Der neue Reichsgau Danzig-Westpreussen*. Berlin, 1940.

Dross, Armin. *Deutschland und Polen in Geschichte und Gegenwart*. Hannover, 1964.

Du Prel, Max Freiherr, ed. *Das General-Gouvernement*. Würzburg, 1942.

Eichler, Adolf. *Deutschtum im Schatten des Ostens*. Dresden, 1942.

Von einen Eingeweihten [By an initiated person]. *Die polnische Frage*. Breslau, 1891.

Emmerich, Werner. *Der deutsche Osten*. Leipzig, 1935.

Epstein, Fritz T. "Friedrich Meinecke in seinem Verhältnis zum europäischen Osten." In *Jahrbuch für die Geschichte Mittel- und Ostdeutschland*, 3 (1954), 119–144.

Erbe und Aufgabe. Düsseldorf and Köln, 1951.

Fechner, Helmut. *Deutschland und Polen*. Würzburg, 1964.

Festgabe für Heinrich Himmler. Darmstadt, 1941.

Flottwell, Edward. *Denkschrift, die Verwaltung der Provinz Posen von Dezember 1830 bis zum Beginn des Jahres 1841 betreffend*. Berlin, 1897.

Forstreuter, Adalbert. *Der endlose Zug*. München, 1939.

———. *Deutsches Ringen um den Osten*. Berlin, 1940.

Freytag, Gustav. *Soll und Haben*, vols. 1—2. Leipzig, 1866.

Friedlaender, Richard. *Deutsch-Polen*. Ratibor, 1916.

Friedrich der Grosse, vols. 1—2. Leipzig, 1886.

Froese, Udo. *Das Kolonisationswerk Friedrichs des Grossen, Wesen und Vermächtnis*. Heidelberg and Berlin, 1938.

Ganz, Hugo. *Die preussische Polenpolitik*. Frankfurt am Main, 1907.

Gause, Fritz. *Deutsch-slawische Schicksalsgemeinschaft*. Kitzingen/Main, 1952.

Geffcken, Heinrich. *Preussen, Deutschland und die Polen*. Berlin, 1906.

Geiss, Imanuel. *Der polnische Grenzstreifen 1914—1918*. Lübeck and Hamburg, 1960.

Gentzen, Felix-Heinrich. *Deutschland und Polen*. Leipzig and Jena, 1956.

———. *Grosspolen im Januaraufstand*. Berlin, 1958.

———; and Galos, Adam; and Jakóbczyk, Witold. *Die Hakatisten*. Berlin, 1966.

Gentzen, Felix-Heinrich, and Wolfgramm, Eberhard. *"Ostforscher"-"Ostforschung"*. Berlin, 1960.

Gerecke, Anneliese. *Das deutsche Echo auf die polnische Erhebung von 1830*. Wiesbaden, 1964.

Gerlach, Helmut von. *Der Zusammenbruch der deutschen Polenpolitik*. Berlin, 1919.

Gisevius, Gustav. *Die polnische Sprachfrage in Preussen*. Leipzig, 1845.

Gollub, Hermann. *Der grosse Kurfürst und Polen von 1660 bis 1668*. Berlin, 1914. [Dissertation].

Grabowsky, Adolf. *Die polnische Frage*. Berlin, 1916.

Grossmann, Kurt. "A Chapter in Polish-German Understanding: The German League for Human Rights." *The Polish Review*, 15, No. 3 (Summer, 1970), 32—47.

Grotewohl, Otto. *Die deutsch-polnische Freundschaft hilft den Frieden in Europa sichern!* Berlin, 1951.

———. *Im Kampf um die einige Deutsche Demokratische Republik*, vols. 1—6. Berlin, 1959—1964.

Gruhn, Albert. *Das deutsche Kapital und der Polonismus*. Berlin, 1895.

Grünhagen, Kolmar. *Geschichte Schlesiens*, vols. 1—2. Gotha, 1884—1886.

Gumpert, Jobst. *Polen-Deutschland*. München, 1966.

Günzel, Walter. *Die nationale Arbeit der polnischen Presse in Westpreussen und Posen zur Zeit der Kanzlerschaft Bülows 1900—1909*. Leipzig, 1933. [Dissertation].

Guttry, Aleksander von. *Die Polen und der Weltkrieg*. München and Berlin, 1915.

Guttzeit, Johannes. *Geschichte der deutschen Polen-Entrechtung*. Danzig, 1927.

Häckel, Manfred. *Für Polens Freiheit*. Berlin, 1952.

Hagemeyer, Hans, ed. *Europas Schicksal im Osten*. Breslau, 1938.

Haider, Rudolf. *Warum musste Polen zerfallen?* Berlin, 1940.

Hallgarten, Wolfgang. *Studien über die deutsche Polenfreundschaft in der Periode der Märzrevolution*. München and Berlin, 1928.

Hampe, Karl. *Der Zug nach dem Osten*. Leipzig and Berlin, 1921.

Handbuch der Politik, vol 2. Berlin and Leipzig, 1912–1913.

Hanel, Egon. *Ueber alles die Wahrheit!* Wurzburg, 1966.

Hannish, Erdmann. *Die Geschichte Polens*. Bonn and Leipzig, 1923.

Hansen, Ernst R. B. *Polens Drang nach dem Westen*. Berlin and Leipzig, 1927.

Hartmann, Karl. *Polen*. Nürnberg, 1966.

Hartung, Fritz. *Polenpolitik*. In *Politisches Handwörterbuch*, vol. 2. Leipzig, 1923.

Hasse, Ernst. *Deutsche Politik*. München, 1907.

Heike, Otto. *Das deutsche Schulwesen*. Dortmund, 1963.

Heinrich Heine's sämmtliche Werke, vol. 13. Hamburg, 1876.

Hensel, Paul. *Die Polengefahr für die masurische Bevölkerung*. Berlin, 1911.

Hermann, Curt. *Die deutsche Ostgrenze im Wandel zweier Jahrtausende*. Breslau, 1938.

Heuer, Reinhold. *Siebenhundert Jahre Thorn 1231–1931*. Danzig, 1931.

Hintze, Otto. *Staat und Verfassung*. Göttingen, 1962.

Historische Kommission für Schlesien. *Geschichte Schlesiens*. Stuttgart, 1961.

Hitler, Adolf. *Mein Kampf*. München, 1935.

Hitlers Zweites Buch. Stuttgart, 1961.

Hodann, Max. *Der slawische Gürtel um Deutschland*. Berlin, 1932.

Hoetzsch, Otto. *Der deutschen Kampf im Osten*. Berlin, 1915.

———. *Osteuropa und deutscher Osten*. Berlin, 1934.

———. *Polen in Vergangenheit und Gegenwart*. Berlin, 1971.

———. *Vorläufige Gedanken zur polnischen Frage*. N.p., December, 1914. [Printed in manuscript form.]

Jablonowski, Horst. *Die preussische Polenpolitik von 1815 bis 1914*. Würzburg/Main, 1964.

Jacobsen, Hans-Adolf, ed. *Misstrauische Nachbarn*. Düsseldorf, 1970.

Jaffé, Moritz. *Die Stadt Posen unter preussischer Harrschaft*. Leipzig, 1909.

Kaindl, Raimund Friedrich. *Polen*. Leipzig and Berlin, 1916.

Kalkschmidt, Eugen. *Deutsche Sendung im Ostland*. Köln, 1936.

Kattner, E. *Deutsche Abrechnung mit den Polen*. Bromberg, 1862.

Kauder, Viktor. *Deutsch-polnische Nachbarschaft*. Würzburg, 1957.

Keyser, Erich. *Danzigs Vergangenheit*. Danzig, 1940.

———. *Das Werk der Deutschen an der Weichsel*. Danzig, 1940.

———. *Die Bedeutung der Deutschen und Slawen für Westpreussen*. Danzig, 1919.

————. *Geschichte des deutschen Weichsellandes*. Leipzig, 1940.

————. *Westpreussen*. Würzburg, 1962.

Kiel, Diethelm. *Die preussisch-deutsche Polenfrage der wilhelminischen Epoche vor 1914*. Tügingen, 1961.

Kirn, Paul. *Politische Geschichte der deutschen Grenzen*. Mannheim, 1958. [Earlier edition in Leipzig, 1934.].

Klessmann, Christoph. *Die Selbstbehauptung einer Nation*. Düsseldorf, 1971.

Knaake, Emil. *Geschichte von Ost-und Westpreussen*. Berlin and Leipzig, 1923.

Knorr, Emil. *Die polnischen Aufstände seit 1830*. Berlin, 1880.

Kohl, Horst. *Die politischen Reden des Fürsten Bismarck* vols. 1–13. Stuttgart, 1892–1905.

Kohte, Wolfgang. *Deutsche Bewegung und preussische Politik im Posener Lande 1848–49*. Posen, 1931.

Kopp, Friedrich. *Deutschland–Europas Bollwerk im Osten*. München, 1939.

Korth, Rudolf. *Die preussische Schulpolitik und die polnischen Schulstreiks*. Würzburg, 1963.

Kötschke, Hermann. *Die deutsche Polenfreundschaft*. Berlin, 1921.

Kötzschke, Rudolf. *Quellen zur Geschichte der ostdeutschen Kolonisation im 12. bis 14. Jahrhundert*. Leipzig and Berlin, 1912.

Kötzschke, Rudolf, and Ebert, Wolfgang. *Geschichte der ostdeutschen Kolonisation*. Leipzig, 1937.

Kranz, Herbert. *Das Buch vom deutschen Osten*. Leipzig, 1941.

Kranz, M. *Neu-Polen*. München, 1915. [Privately printed].

Krische, Paul. *Die provinz Posen*. Stassfurt, 1907.

Krollman, Christian. *Politische Geschichte des Deutschen Ordens in Preussen*. Königsberg, 1932.

Kronacher, Bettina. *Der deutsche Lebensraum in der Geschichte*. Frankfurt am Main, 1938.

Kundgebungen, Beschlüsse und Forderungen des Alldeutschen Verbandes 1890–1902. München, 1902.

Laeuen, Harald. *Polnische Tragödie*. Stuttgart, 1955.

Lange, Friedrich. *Ostland kehrt heim*. Berlin and Leipzig, 1940.

Laubert, Manfred. *Carl von Grolman als Sekundant des Oberpräsidenten Flottwell im Kampf um die Posener Mischehenfrage*. Posen, 1943.

————. *Das Heimatrecht der Deutschen in Westpolen*. Bromberg, 1924.

————. *Der Flottwellsche Güterbetriebsfonds in der Provinz Posen*. Breslau, 1929.

————. *Der Kampf um den Gebrauch der polnischen Sprache auf dem 1. Posener Provinziallandtag 1827*. Posen, 1939.

————. *Deutsch oder slawisch?* Berlin, 1928.

————. *Deutsch und Polen im Wandel der Geschichte*. Breslau, 1921.

————. *Die Anfänge der Posener Generalkommission*. Posen, 1935.

———. *Die Behandlung der Posener Teilnehmer am Warschauer November-aufstand vom 1830/1.* Marburg/Lahn, 1954.

———. "Die Juden der Provinz Posen in Branntweinschank und Hausier-gewerbe bis zum Gesetz vom 23.7.1847." *Deutsche Monatshefte,* 7, Nos. 11—12 (May—June, 1941), 499—533.

———. *Die oberschlesische Volksbewegung.* Breslau, 1938.

———. *Die preussische Polenpolitik von 1772—1914.* Cracow, 1944.

———. "Die Provinz Posen und die polnischen Aufstandsversuche von 1833." *Deutsche Monatshefte.* 6, Nos. 8—9 (February—March, 1940), 285—307.

———. *Die Verwaltung der Provinz Posen 1815—47.* Breslau, 1923.

———. *Eduard Flottwell. Ein Abriss seines Lebens.* Berlin, 1919.

———. *Flottwells Auflassung von Beamtenpflicht.* Posen, 1941.

———. "Minutolis amtliche Berichte und der Aufstand von 1846." In *Werke der Posener Bildenden Kunst.* 1921.

———. *Nationalität und Volkswille im preussischen Osten.* Breslau, 1925.

———. *Ostmärkische Siedlungsprobleme insbesondere der Provinz Posen vor hundert Jahren.* Breslau, 1936.

———. *Skizzen zur Posener Stadtgeschichte vor 100 Jahren.* Posen, 1940.

———. *Studien zur Geschichte der Provinz Posen in der ersten Hälfte des neunzehnten Jahrhunderts.* Posen, 1908.

——— , and Brandenburger, Clemens. *Polnische Geschichte.* Berlin and Leipzig, 1927.

Lauterbach, Samuel Friedrich. *Pohlnische Chronicke, oder Historische Nachricht von dem Leben und Thaten aller Hertzoge und Könige in Pohlen.* Frankfurt and Leipzig, 1727.

Lehmann, Max. *Historische Aufsätze und Reden.* Leipzig, 1911.

Lohmeyer, Karl. *Geschichte von Ost- und Westpreussen.* Gotha, 1908.

Lorenz, Friedebert. *Die Parteien und die preussische Polenpolitik 1885—1886.* Halle, 1938.

Lück, Kurt. *Der Lebenskampf im deutsch-polnischen Grenzraum.* Berlin, 1943.

———. *Der Mythos vom Deutschen in der polnischen Volksüberlieferung und Literatur.* Leipzig, 1943.

———. *Deutsche Aufbaukräfte in der Entwicklung Polens.* Paluen i. Vogtland, 1934.

Luckwaldt, Friedrich. *Deutschland Russland Polen.* Danzig, 1929.

Ludat, Herbert. *An Elbe und Oder um das Jahr 1000.* Köln and Wien, 1971.

———. *Die Anfänge des polnischen Staates.* Cracow, 1942.

———. *Die polnische Geschichtswissenschaft.* Schneidemühl, 1939.

———. *Polens Stellung in Ostmitteleuropa in Geschichte und Gegenwart.* Berlin, 1939.

——— , ed. *Liegt Polen noch in Europa?* Giessen, 1960.

Lüdtke, Franz. *Die deutsche Ostgrenze.* Breslau, 1940.

———. *Du heiliger deutscher Osten!* Breslau, 1940.

———. *Ein Jahrtausend Krieg zwischen Deutschland und Polen.* Stuttgart, 1941.

———. *Preussische Kulturarbeit im Osten.* Leipzig and Berlin, 1915.

———. *Sturm über der Ostmark.* Bielefeld and Leipzig, 1927.

———, ed. *Deutsche Ostmark Liederbuch des deutschen Ostbundes.* Berlin, 1925.

Maass, Johannes. *Dokumentation der deutsch-polnischen Beziehungen 1945–1959.* Bad Godesberg, 1960.

Mai, Joachim. *Die preussisch-deutsche Polenpolitik 1885/1887.* Berlin, 1962.

Mandel, Willi and Ziegfeld, Arnold Hillen. *Unser Osten.* Berlin, 1939.

Mann, Golo. "Mit den Polen Frieden machen." *Stern*, 17, No. 28 (July 7–13, 1964).

Manteuffel-Szoege, Georg Baron. *Geschichte des polnischen Volkes.* Berlin, 1950.

Marcks, Erich. *Ostdeutschland in der deutschen Geschichte.* Leipzig, 1920.

Maresch, Maria. *Aus Polens Geschichte und Kultur.* München-Gladbach, 1916.

Markert, Werner, ed. *Polen.* Köln and Graz, 1959.

Marx-Engels-Lenin-Stalin. Zur deutschen Geschichte, vol. 2, Book 1. Berlin, 1954.

Maxchke, Erich. *Das Erwachen des Nationalbewusstseins im deutsch-slavischen Grenzraum.* Leipzig, 1933.

———. *Der deutsche Orden.* Jena, 1939.

———. *Die treibenden Kräfte in der Entwicklung Polen.* Berlin, 1939.

Massow, Wilhelm von. *Die Polennot im deutschen Osten.* Berlin, 1907.

Matthias, Erich. *Die deutsch Sozialdemokratie und der osten 1914–45.* Tübingen, 1954.

Mayr, Kaspar. *Ist die Verständigung zwischen Polen und Deutschland unmöglich?* Wien, 1931.

Meissner, Boris. *Die deutsch Ostpolitik 1961–1970.* Köln, 1970.

Meyer, Christian. *Geschichte des Landes Posen.* Posen, 1881.

Meyer, Enno. *Grundzüge der Geschichte Polens.* Darmstadt, 1969.

Missalek, Erich. *Das Königreich Polen.* Leipzig and Bielefeld, 1915.

———. *Geschichte Polens.* Breslau, 1911.

Mitscherlich, Waldemar. *Der Einfluss der wirtschaftlichen Entwicklung auf den ostmärkischen Nationalitätenkampf.* Leipzig, 1910.

———. *Die Ausbreitung der Polen in Preussen.* Leipzig, 1913.

———. "Die Irrtümer über das wirtschaftliche Vordringen der Polen." In *Jahrbuch für Gesetzgebung. Verwaltung und Volkswirtschaft im Deutschen Reich*, 35, No. 4 (1911), 51–89.

———. *Die Ostmark, Eine Einführung in die Probleme ihrer Wirtschafts-*

geschichte. Leipzig, 1911.

———. "Die polnische Boykottbewegung in der Ostmark und ihre Aussichten." In *Jahrbuch für Gesetzgebung. Verwaltung und Volkswirtschaft im Deutschen Reich*, 35, No. 3 (1911), 31–65.

Moltke, Count Helmut Karl Bernhard von. *Poland*. London, 1885. [The German original was published in Berlin in 1832.]

Moritz, Erhard. *Preussen und der Kościuszko-Aufstand 1794*. Berlin, 1968.

Müller, Leonhard. *Der Kampf zwischen politischem Katholizismus und Bismarcks Politik im Spiegel der Schlesischen Volkszeitung*. Breslau, 1929.

———. *Nationalpolnische Presse, Katholizismum und katholischer Kleruss*. Breslau, 1931.

Müller, Sepp. *Von der Ansiedlung bis zur Umsiedlung*. Marburg/Lahn, 1961.

Münch, Ingo von, ed. *Ostverträge II. Deutsch-polnische Verträge*. Berlin, 1971.

Munstermann, Wilhelm. *Die preussisch-deutsche Polen-politik der Caprivizeit und die deutsche öffentliche Meinung*. Münster, 1936.

Nasarski, Peter E. *Deutsche Jugendbewegung und Jugendarbeit in Polen 1919–1939*. Würzburg, 1957.

———, ed. *Nachbarn im Osten*. Leer/Ostfriesland, 1965.

Neubach, Helmut. *Die Ausweisungen von Polen und Juden aus Preussen 1885/86*. Wiesbaden, 1967.

Neumann, Friedrich. *Was wird aus Polen?* Berlin, 1917.

Neumann, Rudolf J. *Polens Westarbeit*. Bremen, 1966.

Nieborowski, Paul. *Oberschlesien und Polen*. Breslau, 1922.

Nippold, Friedrich, ed. *Erinnerungen aus dem Leben des General-Feldmarschalls Hermann von Boyen*, vols. 1–3. Leipzig, 1889–1890.

Nitschke, Richard. *Die deutschen Ostgebiete an Warthe und Weichsel*. Breslau, 1940.

———. *Die deutschen Ostgebiete an Warthe und Weichsel*. Breslau, 1942.

Nölting, Wilhelm. *Polen*. Berlin, 1936.

Oertzen, Friedrich Wilhelm von. *Alles oder Nichts*. Breslau, 1934.

———. *Das ist Polen*. München, 1932.

———. *Marschall Pilsudski*. Berlin, 1935.

———. *Polen an der Arbeit*. München, 1932.

Oncken, Hermann. *Bismarck und die Zukunft Mitteleuropas*. Heidelberg, 1915.

Orth, Hans Joachim. *Diesseits und jenseits der Weichsel*. Darmstadt, 1962.

Ostdeutschland. Kitzingen-Main, 1953.

Ostdeutschland 1958–59 in der polnischen Presse. Würzburg, 1959.

Osterroht, Ernst. *Die polnische Frage*. Berlin, 1908.

Partsch, Joseph. *Schlesien*, vols. 1–2. Breslau, 1896–1911.

Pastenaci, Kurt. *4000 Jahre Ostdeutschland*. Leipzig, 1942.

Paul, Gustav. *Die räumlichen und rassischen Gestaltungskräfte der gross-deutschen Geschichte*. München and Berlin, 1938.

Perdelwitz, Richard. *Die Posener Polen von 1815–1914*. Schneidemühl, 1936.

Peter, Egon. *Raubstaat Polen*. Berlin-Leipzig, 1939.

Petzet, Christian. *Die preussischen Ostmarken*. München, 1898.

Pfeiffer, Hans. *Der polnische Adel und die preussische Polenpolitik von 1863 bis 1894*. Jena, 1939.

Picker, Henry, ed. *Hitlers Tischgespräche im Führerhauptquartier 1941–1942*. Bonn, 1951.

Polen, Deutschland und die Oder-Neisse-Grenze. Berlin, 1959.

Polen und Deutsche als Nachbarn. München, 1959.

Puchert, Berthold. *Der Wirtschaftskrieg des deutschen Imperialismus gegen Polen 1925–1934*. Berlin, 1963.

Püschel, Ursula. *Bettina von Arnims Polenbroschüre*. Berlin, 1954.

Puttkamer, Baron Karl von. *Die Misserfolge in der Polenpolitik*. Berlin, 1913.

Rabenau, Friedrich. *Seeckt. Aus seinem Leben 1918–1936*. Leipzig, 1940.

Radio Bremen. *Begegnung mit Polen*. Bremen, 1963.

Ranke, Leopold von. *Geschichten der romanischen und germanischen Völker von 1494 bis 1514*. Leipzig, 1885.

Raschdau, Ludwig. *Der Weg in die Weltkrise*. Berlin, 1934.

———. *Die Ostmarkenfrage*. October 1908 [Special Reprint from *Deutsche Revue*.].

Rauschning, Hermann. *Die Entdeutschung Westpreussens und Posens*. Berlin, 1930.

Recke, Walther. *Der Geburtstag des polnischen Staates* Danzig, 1939.

———. *Die polnische Frage als Problem der europäischen Politik*. Berlin, 1927.

———. *Versailles und der deutsche Osten*. Hamburg, 1935.

———. *Westpreussen. Der Schicksalraum des deutsch Ostens*. Danzig, 1940

Recke, Walther and Wagner, Albert Malte. *Bücherkunde zur Geschichte und Literatur des Königreichs Polen*. Warsaw and Leipzig, 1918.

Rehfeld, Klaus Helmut. *Die preussische Verwaltung des Regierungsbezirks Bromberg 1848–1871*. Köln and Berlin, 1968.

Reimers, Erich. *Der Kampf um den deutschen Osten*. Leipzig, 1939.

Reismann-Grone, Theodor. *Die slawische Gefahr in der Ostmark*. München, 1899.

Rhode, Arthur. *Die evangelischen Deutschen in Russisch-Polen*. Lissa, 1906.

Rhode, Arthur. *Geschichte der evangelischen Kirche im Posener Lande*. Würzburg, 1956.

Rhode, Gotthold. *Brandenburg-Preussen und die Protestanten in Polen 1640–1740*. Leipzig, 1941.

———. *Das Siedlungswerk Friedrichs d.Gr. und die Deutschen aus Polen.* Posen, 1939.

———. *Die Ostgrenze Polens.* Köln and Graz, 1955.

———. *Geschichte Polens.* Darmstadt, 1966.

———. *Völker auf dem Wege. Verschiebungen der Bevölkerung in Ostdeutschland und Osteuropa seit 1917.* Kiel, 1952.

———, ed. *Die Ostgebiete des Deutschen Reiches.* Würzburg, 1955.

Rhode, Gotthold and Wagner, Wolfgang, eds. *Quellen zur Entstehung der Oder-Neisse-Linie.* Stuttgart, 1956.

Rhode, Ilse. *Das Nationalitäten-Verhältnis in Westpreussen und Posen zur Zeit der polnischen Teilungen.* Breslau, 1926. [Dissertation.].

Richter, Friedrich. *Preussische Wirtschaftspolitik in den Ostprovinzen.* Berlin and Königsberg, 1938.

Richthofen, Bolko Freiherr von. *Deutschland und Polen. Schicksal einer nationalen Nachbarschaft.* Weener, 1959.

———. *Gehört Ostdeutschland zur Urheimat der Polen?* Danzig, 1929.

Rjazanov, D., ed. [David Borisovich Gol'dendach], *Karl Marx, Friedrich Engels Briefwechsel*, vol. 3, Part 1. Berlin, 1929.

Roeren, Hermann. *Zur Polenfrage.* Hamm, 1902.

Roos, Hans. *Geschichte der polnischen Nation 1916–1960.* Stuttgart, 1961.

———. *Polen und Europa.* Tübingen, 1957.

Roth, Paul. *Deutschland und Polen.* München, 1958.

———. *Die politische Entiwicklung in Kongresspolen während der deutschen Okkupation.* Leipzig, 1919.

Rothfels, Hans. *Bismarck und der Osten.* Leipzig, 1934.

———, and Markert, Werner, eds. *Deutscher Osten und Slawischer Westen.* Tübingen, 1955.

Sappok, Gerhard. *An Warthe und Weichsel.* Leipzig, 1942.

Schäfer, Dietrich. *Das deutsche Volk und der Osten.* Leipzig and Dresden, 1915.

———. *Die Neugestaltung des Ostens.* München, 1918.

———. *Osteuropa und wir Deutschen.* Berlin, 1924.

———. *Unser Recht auf die Ostmarken.* Berlin, 1920.

Schieder, Theodor. *Das deutsche Kaiserreich von 1871 als Nationalstaat.* Köln and Opladen, 1961.

Schiller-Buch. Dresden, 1860.

Schinkel, Friedrich. *Die polnische Frage als Problem der preussisch-deutschen Nationalstaatsentwicklung.* Breslau, 1932.

———. *Polen, Preussen und Deutschland.* Breslau, 1931.

Schirmacher, Käthe. *Ostfragen Schicksalfragen.* Stolp, 1926.

———. *Unsere Ostmark.* Hannover and Leipzig, 1923.

Schmidt, Erich. *Geschichte des Deutschtums im Lande Posen unter polnischer Herrschaft.* Bromberg, 1904.

Schmidt, Hans. *Die polnische Revolution des Jahres 1848 im Grossherzogtum Posen*. Weimar, 1912.

Schöpke, Karl. *Deutsche Ostsiedlung*. Berlin and Leipzig, 1943.

Schreiber, Hermann, *Land im Osten*. Düsseldorf and Wien, 1961.

———. *Teuton and Slav*. London, 1965.

Schubring, Helmut. *Deutscher Friedenswille gegen polnischen Nationalhass*. Berlin, 1941.

Schumacher, Bruno. *Geschichte Ost- und Westpreussen*. Würzburg, 1958.

Schüssler, Wilhelm. *Mitteleuropa als Wirklichkeit und Schicksal*. Köln, 1939.

Schwidetzky, Ilse. *Die polnische Wahlbewegung in Oberschlesien*. Breslau, 1934. [Dissertation.]

Seeckt, Generaloberst Hans von. *Moltke. Ein Vorbild*. Berlin, 1931.

Seiler, Friedrich. *Die Heimat der Indogermanen*. Hamburg, 1894.

Selchow, Bogislav Freiherr von. *Der Kampf um das Posener Erzbistum 1865*. Marburg, 1923.

Sellin, Fritz. *Die polnische Frage*. Berlin, 1932.

Sello, Landgerichtsrat Artur. *Die polnische Frage*. Berlin, 1922.

Seraphim, Hans-Günther, ed. *Das politische Tagebuch Alfred Rosenbergs*. München, 1964.

Sering, Max. *Die innere Kolonisation im östlichen Deutschland*. Leipzig, 1893.

Simoleit, Gustav. *Ostdeutschland und Osteuropa*. Osterwieck/Harz and Berlin, 1937.

Sohnrey, Heinrich. *Eine Wanderfahrt durch die deutschen Ansiedlungsgebiete in Posen und Westpreussen*. Berlin, 1897.

Spatz, M. *Die Kampforganisationen Neu-Polens*. München, 1910.

Stade, Paul. *Breslau. Ein Schutzwall gegen das Slaventhm*. Hamburg, 1895.

———. *Das Deutschtum gegenuber den Polen in Ost- und Westpreussen*. Berlin, 1908.

Stehle, Hansjakob. *Deutschlands Osten. Polens Wester?* Frankfurt am Main, 1965.

———. *Nachbar Polen*. Frankfurt am Main, 1963.

Stöckl, Gunther. *Osteuropa und die Deutschen*. Oldenburg and Hamburg, 1967.

Stoll, Christian. *Die Rechtsstellung der deutschen Staatsangehörigen in den polnisch verwalteten Gebieten: Zur Integration der sogenannten Autochthonen in die polnische Nation*. Frankfurt am Main and Berlin, 1968.

Stressmann, Gustav. *Vermächtnis*, vols. 1–3. Berlin, 1932–1933.

Tackenberg, Kurt. *Germanen und Slawen zwischen 1000 vor und 1000 nach Beginn unserer Zeitrechnung*. Bonn, 1940.

Thalheim, Karl, and Ziegfeld, Arnold Hillen. *Der deutsch Osten*. Berlin, 1936.

Trampe, L. *Ostdeutscher Kulturkampf*, vols. 1–2. Leipzig, 1907–1908.

Treitschke, Heinrich von. *Das deutsche Ordensland Preussen*. Leipzig, 1916.

———. *Deutsche Geschichte im Neunzehnten Jahrhundert*, vols. 1–5. Leipzig, 1879–1894.

———. *Historische und politische Aufsätze*, vol. 2. Leipzig, 1871.

———. *Zehn Jahre deutscher Kämpfe*. Berlin, 1879.

Trzciński, Julius von. *Russisch-polnische und galizische Wanderarbeiter im Grossherzogtum Posen*. Stuttgart and Berlin, 1906.

Tümmler, Hans. "Die preussische Polenpolitik in der Provinz Posen vom Wiener Kongress bis zum Ausbruch des Weltkrieges." In *Vergangenheit und Gegenwart*, 29, Nos. 11–12 (1939), 578–590.

Turowski, Ernst. *Die innenpolitische Entwicklung Polnisch-Preussens und seine staatsrechtliche Stellung zu Polen vom 2. Thorner Frieden bis zum Reichstag von Lublin (1466–1569)*. Berlin, 1937. [Dissertation.]

Ueber die Darstellung der deutsch-polnischen Beziehungen im Geschichtsunterricht. Braunschweig, 1960.

Ulbricht, Walter. *Die Entwicklung des deutschen volksdemokratischen Staates 1945–1968*. Berlin, 1959.

Urbanek, Viktor. *Friedrich der Grosse und Polen nach der Konvention vom 5. August 1772*. Breslau, 1914. [Dissertation.]

Vallentin, Wilhelm. *Westpreussen seit den ersten Jahrzehnten dieses Jahrhunderts*. Tübingen, 1893.

Voigts, C. von. *Aktenmässige Darstellung der polnischen Insurrektion im Jahre 1848*. Posen, 1848.

Volz, Gustav Berthold, ed. *Die Werke Friedrichs des Grossen*, vols. 1–10. Berlin, 1913.

Volz, Wilhelm. *Die völkische Struktur Oberschlesiens*. Breslau, 1921.

———. *Die wirtschaftsgeographischen Grundlagen der oberschlesischen Frage*. Berlin, 1921.

———. *Oberschlesien und die oberschlesische Frage*. Breslau, 1922.

———, ed. *Der ostdeutsche Volksboden*. Breslau, 1926.

Wäber, Alexander. *Preussen und Polen*. München, 1907.

Wagner, Franz. *Der Friede und die von uns besetzten Länder*. Oldenburg, 1917.

———. *Heinrich von Tiedemann zu seinem 70. Geburtstage*. Posen, 1913.

———. *Was wird aus unserer Ostmark?* München, 1918.

———, and Vosbert, Fritz. *Polenspiegel*. Berlin, 1908.

Wagner, Georg. *Sudeten-SA in Polen*. Karlbad and Leipzig, 1940.

Wahl, General Ernest von. *Zwei Gegner im Osten*. Dortmund, 1939.

Warschauer, Adolf. *Dertsche Kulturarbeit in der Ostmark*. Berlin, 1926.

———. *Die deutsche Geschichtsschreibung in der Provinz Posen*. Posen, 1914.

———. *Geschichte der Provinz Posen in polnischer Zeit*. Posen, 1914.

———. *Heinrich Heine in Posen*. Posen, 1911.

Weber, Max. *Gesammelte politische Schriften*. München, 1921.

Wegener, Leo. *Der wirtschaftliche Kampf der Deutschen mit den Polen um die Provinz Posen*. Posen, 1903.

Wehler, Hans-Ulrich. *Sozialdemokratie und Nationalstaat*. Würzburg, 1962.

Weise, Erich. *Die Schwabensiedlungen im Posener Kammerdepartement 1799–1804*. Würzburg, 1961.

Weiss, Moritz. *Die Stellung des Deutschtums in Posen und Westpreussen*. Berlin, 1919.

Wendel, Hermann. *Die preussische Polenpolitik in ihren Ursachen und Wirkungen*. Berlin, 1908.

Wendorff, W. *Der Kampf der Deutschen und Polen inder Provinz Posen*. Posen, 1904.

Wendt, Hans. *Bismarck und die polnische Frage*. Halle, 1922.

"einer Westpreussen." In *Das gevierteilte Westpreussen und der Versailler Vertrag*. Stolp, 1926.

Widdern, Cardinal von. *Die Unterwerfung Oberschlesiens durch die Posener Polen*. Berlin, 1910.

———. *Polnische Eroberungszüge im heutigen Deutschland und deutsche Abwehr*. Lissa, 1913.

Wiegand, Berthold. *Die antideutsche Propaganda der Polen von 1890 bis 1914*. Danzig, 1940. [Dissertation.]

———. *Polnische Priester*. Danzig, 1940.

Wingendorf, Rolf. *Polen. Volk zwischen Ost und West*. Berlin, 1939.

Winterstein, Franz. *Polnische Auferstehung*. Lissa, 1907.

Wolfram, Hans-Egon. *Im polnischen Korridor an der Grenze und in Berlin*. Berlin, 1933.

Wunderlich, Erich, ed. *Handbuch von Polen (Kongress Polen)*. Berlin, 1918.

Zeissberg, Heinrich.*Die polnische Geschichtsschreibung des Mittelalters*. Leipzig, 1873.

Zipfel, Friedrich. Review of five books on German-Polish relations, including *Ostdeutschland 1960–61 in der polnischen Presse*. In *Jahrbuch für die Geschichte mittel-und Ostdeutschlands*, 13–14 (1965), 633–636.

Zivier, Ezechiel. *Neuere Geschichte Polens*. Gotha, 1915.

Zoch, Wilhelm. *Neuordnung im Osten*. Berlin, 1940.

3. Relevant Polish Works—A Brief Selection

Borowski, Stanislaw. *Rozwarstwienie wsi wielkopolskiej w latach 1807–1914*. Poznań, 1962.

Buzek, Józef. *Historya polityki narodowościowej rzadu pruskiego wobec*

Polaków. Od traktatów wiedeńskich do ustaw wyjątkowych r. 1908. Lwów, 1909.

Chodera, Jan. *Literatura niemiecka o Polsce w latach 1918–1939.* Katowice, 1969.

Feldman, Józef. *Bismarck a Polska.* Kraków, 1947.

———. *Problem polsko-niemiecki w dziejach.* Katowice, 1946.

Grot, Zdzisław. *Dzialalność posłow polskich w sejmie pruskim w latach 1848-1850.* Poznań, 1961.

Historia Polski. Warsaw, 1950s–1960s.

Jakóbczyk, Witold. *Bismarck.* Warsaw, 1971.

———. *Studia nad dziejami Wielkopolski w XIX w.* Poznań, 1951, 1959.

———. ed. *Dzieje wielkopolski,* vol. 2. Poznań, 1973.

Karwowski, Stanisław. *Historya Wielkiego Księstwa Poznańskiego.* Poznań, 1919, 1931.

Klafkowski, Alfons. *Granica polsko-niemiecka po II wojnie światowej.* Poznań. 1970.

Komierowski, Roman. *Koło Polskie w Berlinie 1875–1900.* Poznań, 1905.

Kraususki, Jerzy. *Kulturkampf.* Poznań, 1963.

———. *Stosunki polsko-niemieckie 1919–1925.* Poznań, 1962.

———. *Stosunki polsko-niemiecki 1926–1932.* Poznań, 1964.

Kubiak, Stanislaw. *Niemcy a Wielkopolska 1918–1919.* Poznań, 1969.

Labuda, Gerard, ed. *Wschodnia ekspansja Niemiec w Europie środkowej.* Poznań, 1963.

Luczak, Czesław. *Położenie ekonomiczne rzemiosła wielkopolskiego w okresie zaborów 1793–1918.* Poznań, 1962.

———. *Przemysł wielkopolski w latach 1871–1918.* Poznań, 1960.

———. *Życie gospodarczo-społeczne w Poznaniu 1815–1918.* Poznań, 1965.

Marchlewski, Julian. *Stosunki społeczno-ekonomiczne w ziemiech polskich zaboru pruskiego*. Lwów, 1903.

Pajewski, Janusz. *Niemcy w czasach nowożytnych (1517–1939)*. Poznań, 1947.

———, ed. *Problem polsko-niemiecki w Traktacie Wersalskim*. Poznań, 1963.

Popiolek, Kazimierz. *Historia śląska*. Katowice, 1972.

Rachocki, Janusz, ed. *Polska-NRF: Przeslanki i proces normalizacji stosunków*. Poznań, 1972.

Rusiński, Władysław, ed. *Dzieje wsi wielkopolskiej*. Poznań, 1959.

Sułek, Jerzy. *Stanowisko rządu NRF wobec granicy na Odrze i Nysie Łużyckiej 1949–1966*. Poznań, 1969.

Studia historica. Slavo-Germanica. Poznań, 1973.

Topolski, Jerzy. *Wielkopolska poprzes wieki*. Poznań, 1973.

Trzeciakowski, Lech. *Kulturkampf w zaborze pruskim*. Poznań, 1970.

———. *Pod pruskim zaborem 1850–1918*. Warszawa, 1973.

———. *Polityka polskich klas posiadajacych w Wielkopolsce w erze Capriviego 1890–1894*. Poznań, 1960.

———. *Walka o polskość miast poznańskiego na przełomie XIX i XX wieku*. Poznań, 1964.

Wojciechowski, Marian. *Stosunki polsko-niemieckie 1933–1938*. Poznań, 1965.

Wojciechowski, Zygmunt. *Poland's Place in Europe*. Poznań, 1947.

Zimmermann, Kazimierz. *Fryderyk Wielki i jego kolonizacja rolna na ziemiach polskich*. Poznań, 1915.

INDEX